A TIME
TO LEAD

D0029238

A TIME TO LEAD

~

FOR DUTY, HONOR AND COUNTRY

Wesley K. Clark

with

Tom Carhart

A TIME TO LEAD
Copyright © Wesley K. Clark, Tom Carhart, 2007.
All rights reserved. No part of this book may be used or reproduced in any manner
whatsoever without written permission except in the case of brief quotations
embodied in critical articles or reviews.

First published in 2007 by
PALGRAVE MACMILLAN™
175 Fifth Avenue, New York, N.Y. 10010 and
Houndmills, Basingstoke, Hampshire, England RG21 6XS.
Companies and representatives throughout the world.

PALGRAVE MACMILLAN is the global academic imprint of the Palgrave Macmillan
division of St. Martin's Press, LLC and of Palgrave Macmillan Ltd. Macmillan® is a
registered trademark in the United States, United Kingdom and other countries.
Palgrave is a registered trademark in the European Union and other countries.

ISBN–13: 978–1–4039–8474–6
ISBN–10: 1–4039–8474–3

Library of Congress Cataloging-in-Publication Data is available from the Library of
Congress.

Clark, Wesley K.
    A time to lead : for duty, honor, and country / Wesley K. Clark ; with Tom Carhart.
        p.   cm.
    Includes bibliographical references and index.
    ISBN 1–4039–8474–3 (alk. paper)
    1. Clark, Wesley K.   2. Generals—United States—Biography.   3. United States.
Army—Biography.   4. Presidential candidates—United States—Biography.   5.
North Atlantic Treaty Organization.   6. Yugoslav War, 1991–1995.   7. Kosovo
(Serbia)—History—Civil War, 1998–1999.   8. United States—History, Military—
20th century.   I. Carhart, Tom.   II. Title.
E840.5.C58A3   2007
355.0092—dc22
[B]
                                                                                            2007006832

A catalogue record of the book is available from the British Library.

Design by Letra Libre

First edition: October 2007

10   9   8   7   6   5   4   3   2   1

Printed in the United States of America.

CONTENTS

PREFACE

IN THE LINE OF FIRE

Something touched my foot, and I was instantly awake. I squirmed around to face a dark figure looming over me, the muzzle of my M–16 still directed down the trail a few yards away through the jungle. He projected his voice in a stage whisper:

"It's o-five thirty, sir."

I turned and sat up, my eyes blinking in the dark. My answer was also a whisper.

"Okay, thanks. Get the other platoons on the horn. Make sure everyone is okay."

Other men were stirring around me, and I slowly rose up to a crawling position, stretching my arms and legs as I did. We had been lying on the jungle floor for the past six hours, a platoon of about twenty American infantrymen, strung out some ten meters back in the bushes from the edge of a heavily used path that cut through the thick underbrush. I was a captain and the company commander, but we only had two lieutenants to command our three platoons so I was out with the platoon on this operation. We had arrived at this place just before midnight the night before and assumed an ambush position off the trail. Half the platoon had stayed awake while the others slept for two hours, then they reversed their roles. Fifty percent security was high, but we were in the heart of enemy territory, and maintaining that level of alert was literally a matter of life and death.

I was fully clothed and wearing my jungle boots, which were laced up and tied tight. That was another feature of sleeping in the field during Vietnam: No one unlaced his boots at night. It was okay to take off your helmet before you lay down. Then you just lay out flat, rifle at the ready, and tried to stay awake while staring at the dark and listening to the night. And if you weren't extremely tough on yourself—and everyone else—you fell asleep even when you thought you were awake. You were on the ground like any other large animal, save only that you had your rifle in your hands and ready for use. If I ever found someone with his boots off or web gear lying around somewhere—where he couldn't reach into his ammo pouch at his waist and pull out the next twenty-round magazine— I would have had to come down on him. But I'd found that personal fear was pretty good at keeping the discipline taut, and this morning the troops were a little anxious. I knew they all had their boots on.

We were out to find the enemy, to interrupt his movements, to cause him to rethink his attack plans, and to hinder the assembly of his forces that could threaten Saigon. As a mechanized infantry unit, we ordinarily rode around on armored personnel carriers, APCs as we called them. But here we were on the morning of February 19, 1970, hoping that the enemy would make the mistake of coming down that trail into the kill zone of our ambush.

The previous evening we had set up the ambush about a half hour before sunset: We just backed into the jungle off the trail and lay down. The flank security hadn't even set up its defenses when I heard the rattle of a machine gun from the left. Two long bursts, and twigs and vegetation began to fall around me like rain as the rounds cut well overhead. Then silence.

Apparently, an enemy patrol moving down the trail had seen movement as the flank security took up their positions, and they had opened fire to cover their retreat. But they didn't hit us, and we never saw them. We had returned no fire, and I was pleased that the troops had maintained their fire discipline. I passed the word to reorient so as to provide stronger all-around security. After darkness fell, I moved the platoon, because I didn't want that enemy force to double back and find us.

We moved a couple of thousand meters up the trail, pulled off, and set up a hasty ambush, waited, and moved again, around 10:30 P.M., to the overnight position. This was real, and the troops sensed it.

This time, after I was woken up, I glanced left and right and lay back down. We were at the crucial time, just like hunting: The game would be moving around dawn, and every man had to be ready. The sky was still jet-black, and I knew it wouldn't start to soften into gray for another ten or fifteen minutes, when the gray would fade to light fast. Then the sky would brighten above the jungle canopy as full dawn came, almost exactly at 0600 hours.

We waited another hour, to see if we would have any action. But by 0700, there had been no movement down the trail or in the jungle. Every man had been awake and ready to use his weapon for more than an hour, and it was time to move. I stood up, took a last sip from my canteen, chewed on a piece of date nut roll, and motioned to the men on my left and right, ready to move out.

We still had a few minutes, and I looked around. All the men were up, silently adjusting their loads. There would be no fires this morning, and no heat tablets would be lit to boil water for instant coffee. As my men drank from canteens or took their last bites from C rations, I went over our operations plan again in my head.

I was with dismounted elements of the 2nd Platoon of A Company, 1st Battalion, 16th Infantry (mechanized), from the 1st Infantry Division, about fifteen infantrymen, led by their platoon sergeant, carrying rifles, grenade launchers, and one of the two M–60 machine guns each platoon had. And I had my command group—my artillery forward observer and his radio telephone operator, and my two RTOs, one handling the company net and the other the battalion net, plus the company sniper team of two soldiers. We were not heavily armed, but we were very flexible, mobile, and, we hoped, able to move fast when needed. And on that early morning, as we restlessly girded up for combat deep in the enemy-controlled jungle, we wanted more than anything else to fall on a surprised enemy force, pin it in place, and hammer it.

In the winter of 1969–70, the 1st Infantry Division, commonly referred to as the Big Red One, was deployed as part of a defensive arc north of Saigon. It was expected that, over the next few weeks, large Viet Cong or North Vietnamese Army forces would try to make a major attack on Saigon from the north, just as they had done in February of 1968 and '69. If that was their plan, we suspected they would be staging the attack from an area of heavy jungle some twenty miles northeast of Saigon, a plot of ground about the size of Manhattan that had been a Communist stronghold for many years. It was known as War Zone D, and the rough, jungle-covered terrain was not crossed by any roads.

Our job now was to try to make contact with a major enemy force by running patrols through the more open jungle just south of War Zone D. Once engaged, we knew we could use our heavy artillery and air support to pulverize them. But this did not turn out to be as easy as it sounds, for making the contact that would pin the enemy in place was not a simple task.

As soon as we moved into the area to the east of Saigon, it became clear to me that the tracked and heavily armored (APCs in which our soldiers rode and fought might not be the right way to reach the enemy elements south of War Zone D. In some regions, of course, this was the best way to fight the war, and we ran a couple of mounted operations, with columns of APCs, usually accompanied by M–48 tanks, crashing and smashing through the jungle.

That's how we advanced most of the time. However, I often ended up having to put a dismounted jungle-clearing team out in front, their job being to partially clear our way forward with axes and chain saws. And while it seemed there was almost no jungle terrain that our armored beasts couldn't plough through, and no enemy force that could stand up to their fearsome firepower, the thick jungle often meant slow going.

But our vehicles were also loud. Very loud. The thunderous, roaring noise of their diesel engines, coupled with the crashing of the trees and jungle undergrowth they smashed through could literally be heard for miles.

Since our goal was to engage the enemy rather than scare them away, I thought we might better perform this specific task by conducting patrols on foot. I discussed the matter with our battalion commander, and with his approval, that was the way A Company began to operate.

In the early afternoon of the February 18, we launched this particular patrol after having dismounted from our APCs a few hundred meters from the main highway that ran through Long Thanh. These were left behind with drivers and gunners, along with the company command post vehicles, while I took the dismounted elements of the platoon and my command group and moved north into the jungle on foot.

This meant, of course, that we would be leaving behind both the heavy firepower provided by the machine guns mounted on the APCs and the protection offered by their armored sides. But it also meant that our movement would not be betrayed by the unmistakable noise our armored vehicles made.

In open country, a small infantry unit moves while spread out in a formation shaped like a roughly elongated circle, with plenty of firepower available front and rear as well as to the sides. But in the jungle this tactic usually wasn't practical and was seldom done unless enemy contact was imminent. If we had used such a formation, we would have had to move cross-country through the jungle, and that would have been not only slow, but also very difficult and noisy.

In order to move effectively, therefore, we had to walk staggered out single file on one of the many trails made by the woodcutters in the area. And that became our common formation on patrol. While moving through the jungle, we usually spread our column out so that there were about ten to fifteen feet between men, with more space added if the vegetation thinned out.

Normally we moved with a couple of men up front, the first being the point man, who walked "on point" and a backup to reinforce him, known as the slack man, who was supposed to "take up the point man's slack". After this point team came a few riflemen, followed by the platoon leader and his RTO. If I were along, I would be somewhere in the middle of the column, behind the platoon leader. But in this case, we had no platoon leader, so I moved close to the front, and I used my company sniper team as our point team to guide us through the jungle. They were the top soldiers in the company and they often traveled with me.

When we went on our first patrols on the trails of War Zone D, we were all tense, ever alert to any noise or movement that might seem unusual. But unfortunately for us, we didn't make much contact with the enemy. And although we walked on many trails that seemed to be heavily used, we had only fleeting contact with enemy soldiers: a sighting through the jungle, a burst of fire exchanged, and then nothing.

This was frustrating, to say the least, but we were doing better dismounted than mounted, so we decided to continue the dismounted effort. That was what we had done the previous day, and we had moved steadily northeast on a large trail for some three hours. But our movement had been rather slow, and I estimated we were only five kilometers north of our start point, information I relayed to battalion when we stopped for the ambush. Now we were another three kilometers north and ready to move again.

My company RTO carried the twenty-five-pound radio in addition to his other gear. It was always turned on, and he kept it tuned to a frequency used by our battalion back in the tactical operations center (TOC), a logistical nerve nodule where our battalion commander was positioned with his field headquarters and staff, and that would be the source of air and artillery support should I need either or both.

As the men swallowed their last hurried bites of their breakfast, we were ready to go, and I had to keep the TOC informed of our location so that they could keep artillery fires registered in front of us as we moved. I fumbled in my jungle fatigues for the CEOI—the communications-electronics operating instructions. I kept it tied on a lanyard attached to my uniform. It was classified—and under the new system, we changed call signs every twenty-four hours, aware that the enemy could monitor our nets. That day, my random call sign was something like H6A for the company, and as the commander I was 67. I held the handset up to my ear, pushed the broadcast button, and spoke softly into the microphone.

Battalion knew only our approximate location, but if we got in a jam and needed artillery support, the first round fired would be white phosphorous, whose bright flash could be more readily seen than those of high explosive rounds. While from beneath the jungle canopy we probably wouldn't be able to see the bright flash these rounds made, I had been in this situation before, and was confident that, just from their sound alone, I would be able to use the radio to adjust the impact of artillery fire until it hit on the enemy positions.

It was already a beautiful morning—bright blue sky, low humidity—Vietnam during the dry season. That was a strange feature of the weather in Vietnam: Near the equator, full daylight lasts almost exactly twelve hours each day, and there are only fifteen or twenty minutes of gray dawn or dusk before the sun comes up or after it goes down. That balance holds steady through the whole year, whether the season is rainy or dry. One of the few reliable truths we could depend on, I mused, that of the sun's regularity all year round. Of course, during rainy season, the bright sun was regularly obscured by everything from light clouds and mist to heavy thunderstorms

But we were in the dry season now, and as my men fell into their Indian file formation, ready to move down the trail, I felt good. We had made contact, we had moved, we were on to something in this area. The mission was, find the enemy.

We moved down a wide, hard-packed trail, sunlight splashing green all around us. I had told the point man to stay on a main trail headed generally to the north, and we passed intersections with other wide trails. Was it only woodcutting in this area, I wondered? I looked at the vegetation for signs of movement through it, and looked down for footprints. But the trails were smooth, and broad enough for four men to walk abreast. We moved patiently, slowly, everyone on high alert, stopping every few hundred meters to send riflemen off to either side and check for enemy presence in the jungle around us. But there was nothing.

Around 1130 we found a small clearing, large enough for a small helicopter to land, and I radioed in the location. That day I was to have lunch with the battalion commander at his operations center, get the update on the big picture from battalion, and review my plans in detail with him.

The flight out and lunch were uneventful. A couple of hours later, I rejoined the platoon and my command group in the clearing in the jungle, and we began to move again. I planned to move a few more kilometers and then call the M–113 armored personnel carriers that were the company's main transportation and weapons platform, to pick us up in late afternoon. That was the advantage of mechanized infantry, and I intended to use it—in and out, short foot patrols, and then back to the tracks. It kept everyone alert and avoided the kind of monotony that could lead to a fatal distraction. But by 1600 I was getting a little concerned; we still had more than three kilometers to go to the linkup point, and we had less than two hours of daylight.

I was the fourth or fifth in the column when we crossed a three-foot-wide bamboo footbridge over a beautiful little stream. Then the point man halted and turned back toward me, beckoning with his hand. I moved up the column, and was standing next to him as he turned and pointed forward.

"Sir, the trail just ends right there."

He was right. Suddenly, the big broad trail vanished. There was thick jungle all around us.

"It just ends right there, huh?"

"Yes, sir, looks that way."

"Hmm." I looked forward into the vegetation. Nothing. I looked down at the compass in my left hand. We hadn't drifted off azimuth. OK, I thought, we'd just stay on course. We were bound to pick up a trail somewhere up ahead if we kept moving in the same direction. I didn't want to backtrack, and the jungle floor was flat. It wasn't going to be hard to simply move forward.

I turned around toward my left to get the rest of the column moving, but as I turned, I sensed that I had dropped my rifle and suddenly became aware of a loud buzzing noise. I was confused. I never dropped my rifle. Not ever. Cardinal sin! And the buzzing must be hornets. Had I hit a nest? As I turned back to get my rifle, I saw something small and white on the back of my right hand, and glimpsed a dark stain on my jungle fatigue trousers right below the right knee. It was like my brain had been bypassed:.

"I've been shot!" I shouted, still in the act of reaching down for my rifle.

"Get down!" Specialist Mike McClintic shouted back as he bumped me off balance and kept me from going for my rifle.

Flat on my face I scrambled around and down the slight slope toward the bamboo footbridge. I was alive, all four limbs were moving, and I had no rifle. Bullets were zinging overhead and ricocheting off the hard-packed earth.

"Get the machine gun up. Set up a base of fire!" I was shouting out the commands, and, of course, attracting more fire.

Sergeant Bodine, the point man and head sniper, and Specialist Michael McClintic were with me there, McClintic a few feet in front and farther up the slope. They were returning the fire, and as I watched, a right-angle flap opened up on McClintic's jungle shirt, torn by a bullet as it grazed his back.

I scanned left and right, hoping the enemy wasn't maneuvering around us. I could tell something was wrong with my foot: It wasn't moving right, and now I could clearly see the broken bone sticking out of my hand. I wasn't in pain, but I really didn't want to be right here, right now—not like this. For an awful instant I remembered my three-month-old son at home, my son whom I hadn't even seen yet.

No, it wasn't going to end like this, and I suppressed the thought. Focus. Fight. Take charge.

"Get that gun going!" I shouted again, as I looked back under my left arm and saw the first troops come across the little footbridge. They were here. And they came running. Those peace-symbol-lovin', foul-mouthed, cussin', war-hatin', draftee American soldiers came, right into the firefight. They rushed right into the smack of the bullets, and the whine of the ricochets. They were called forward, and they came! God, I loved them!

The machine gun opened up, a long burst, sweeping the jungle, and men joined in with their rifles as the incoming fire continued to pour in. In the deafening roar of battle I hollered for the radio, and my RTO squirmed over to me, maneuvering his load and still trying to keep down. I called the battalion commander, reported our location, requested artillery fire, and asked him to help converge the other platoons on my location. Mass forces. Cut off the enemy's maneuver. We had them fixed. Now we had to finish them.

"Sir, stay still! You've got a sucking chest wound. Don't talk!" Suddenly there was a medic crouched over me, along with my RTO, both trying to hold me still as he wrestled a bandage around my chest. They could see the blood pouring out of my back, and just as they were trained, they were half risen up, risking their lives to try to keep me alive. But I knew it wasn't a sucking chest wound, as I wasn't having any trouble shouting. I pushed them off as they protested.

"Give me water! That's what I need." I gulped half a canteen. I wasn't thirsty, but I knew I was bleeding, and I didn't want to go into shock. This was my command, and I was in battle. The don't-want-to-be-here feeling was gone. I knew we could do this!

There was still no sign of any enemy movement on the right as the incoming fire began to drop off. We had fire superiority now, and the machine gun continued to roar a few feet to my left. I heard the first artillery spotting rounds fall a few hundred yards deep in the jungle, artillery fire that would have to be adjusted by us over the radio so that it fell on the enemy's positions. Then there was what seemed like a long pause in the incoming fire. This was our moment.

"Machine gun, shift fire to the left. You men on the right, on your feet, move forward and get them!"

And they did. They really did. They stood up, men from south Texas and the Bronx and Kansas and California, in a firefight in a jungle in Southeast Asia. Men who had been plucked out of their lives, threatened with jail if they refused, some who held master's degrees, others who hadn't finished the tenth grade, they were firing from the hip and shoulder, a dozen men, moving into the jungle to sweep what turned out to be a small enemy base camp. This was my company. These were my men. And I was still flat on my face, struggling to keep the medic off of me so I could direct the fighting.

Overhead I could hear the distant whine of the battalion commander's Loach coming in to take a look. He was on the radio, working to get the artillery and reinforcements into the area, while I was running the fight on the ground. This was how it was supposed to work.

I could hear the shooting and my men's shouts as they swept deeper into the jungle. Now some thirty meters or more to our front, they began to move to our left front as the enemy withdrew in that direction. After having walked into their surprise fire, we had now gained the upper hand and were driving the enemy before us. And though they were no longer even in sight, the adrenaline unleashed by this firefight was still coursing through my body. I was angry, happy, elated, determined, proud, embarrassed. But I knew I had to shut down the machine gun to avoid hitting our own men.

"Cease fire!"

And then the shooting stopped. It was over.

Soon enough, a medevac bird appeared on station. They let down a "jungle penetrator," basically no more than a strap on the end of a cable. My RTO and the medic roped me into it and the helicopter hauled me up.

As I rose, I looked down and saw the little piece of jungle we'd been fighting over. Didn't look like much. And I saw the men of my company for the last time as we lifted into the air.

A strange mixture of feelings flooded through me as they waved and our craft rose. I tried to wave back at them, and I felt awful about leaving them behind; they were my friends and family. They were American soldiers. They did what needed to be done, in spite of danger, in spite of fear, in spite of not wanting to be in the army at all. They had saved my life and overcome part of the enemy force. You had to have faith in us, in who we were, and what we could do. Faith against the odds, faith against the wiseass, too-cool attitudes that seemed to dominate in the enlisted ranks but quickly disappeared in combat. Faith. God, I loved those men, and I missed them already.

As the helicopter pulled around and surged back toward Saigon, a medic began to work over my wounds. I felt the ache and the throbbing, and I knew this could get uncomfortable. But I dared to think again about my family, about my young son, Wesley, and to thank the Good Lord for helping us that day. Even in the worst of circumstances, I mused groggily as the helicopter climbed ever higher, life can be very good indeed.

INTRODUCTION

In this book I want to tell you about leadership that works, leadership as I've seen it in the Armed Forces as well as in the civilian world, and the leadership America has provided for so much of the world. I've spent my life working for the U.S. Army and our country. I've been shot at and wounded, scolded and threatened, promoted and rewarded, in war and in peace through my thirty-eight years in uniform. Since then, I have continued to participate in public life as a businessman, author, TV commentator and presidential candidate.

I've seen successes and failures, good leaders and bad. But most of all, I've seen the critical importance of leadership—in war, in business, and in the nation. The right leadership can turn a group of fumblers into champions. Without it, All-American talents can be condemned to lose repeatedly or to engage relentlessly in efforts they can't possibly win.

Leadership is about performance. That's the bottom line. It's not how you look, dress or carry yourself. It's not whether you're short or tall, old or young, man or woman. Don't misunderstand—every attribute counts, of course, and everything matters. But in the final analysis, the distinguishing characteristic of good leadership is performance.

To lead, whether it's in sports, civic activities, business, or war, you have to be competent and you have to produce, so leadership is to some degree about knowledge and skills. In sports, perhaps you must know how to read defenses; in civic activities, how to work the tax system; in business, how to read an income statement, in the Army, how to read a map and then issue an order.

In the Army we talk about the "be-know-do" model of leadership, according to which a leader needs to have some particular character traits as well as specific knowledge and skills, and then act appropriately for the situation and circumstance to get the job done. And leadership also involves personal interaction: as General Eisenhower said, "Leadership is about persuading the other fellow to want to do what you want him to do," though I've found that sometimes you may have to be a little more directive in your approach.

Anyone can be a leader. I know; I started at age 14, as a camp counselor. Then, after my education at West Point and Oxford, I spent more than thirty years in uniform while serving in a wide variety of roles: combat leader, staff officer, college professor, Special Assistant to a Cabinet Officer, strategist, planner, and top level military commander, followed by my entry into the business and political worlds. And in every position I have filled, I have found that leadership ability is essential to success.

I want to share with you a selection of my experiences and some of the lessons I've learned—expertise and competence, self-control, establishing goals and setting standards, teamwork, and respect for others. You'll see some of the key concepts that worked for me, like "grip," "command energy," and being present at the decisive point.

But I'd be the first to say that these lessons were learned as a function of the situation or the context from which they were drawn. They reflect the America I've known, what it still stands for, and how we've changed. So this is a leadership story *about* America. I'm proud of our country and of our institutions, most of all of the people I've served with or met along the way. I'll be as objective as possible, and direct. But this isn't theoretical—it's personal, and it is as accurate as I can make it.

I'm going to tell you about successes I've had and some of the problems I've faced, and an array of issues that have troubled me. I hope you'll read it as a story of growth, in the sense that healthy people and sound nations change and develop. As my wife Gert used to say, if you're the same at forty as you were at twenty, then something's wrong. Everyone is changing—and hopefully changing for the better through growth and personal development—all the time.

Part of being a leader is being willing to stand up and speak out. In this book, I am doing just that. We need a deeper, more honest dialogue in America today, a dialogue about who we are, what we believe in, and how we ought to proceed in the world. Our nation is at war and our armed forces are fully committed. But we won't find a positive end to this war and win a lasting peace unless we really understand who we are. And even though we are "at war," the country is really being asked to give up very little. There have been no great tax levies, no mobilization of our youth, and no harnessing of our enormously productive and innovative potential, despite the public focus on Iraq.

We have been distracted politically from the public discussion of our future, including our challenges as well as our potential, and how we should move ahead. In consequence, we have neglected a whole range of concerns, like substandard public education, a woefully inaccessible health-care system, aging infrastructure, no national energy policy, and slackening environmental safeguards. And that's not the right way to face the future.

Today, the United States finds itself at a difficult juncture as the most powerful country in the world, embroiled in two simultaneous wars and a terrorist threat, and ever more deeply engaged in a dynamic global economy which will challenge America's economic preeminence, our long-term prosperity, and our own character and values. I'm appalled by the ineffective ways in which the Bush administration is trying to handle the problem of Iraq and the regional threat posed by Iran. I worry that America has lost much of its "legitimacy" in that part of the world, and I think about how we can recover it. And I'm most concerned that we find ways to keep the door open for ordinary Americans—people like me— so that they might have their chance to live the American dream.

But ultimately, winning peace and recovering our influence in the world may well come down to defining who we are as a nation and as a people. In order to succeed in our twenty-first century struggle to protect America, we must ask ourselves some tough questions: Who are we? What do we believe in? And how must we proceed?

This book is a journey through the main events of my life in which I hope to answer some of these questions. You will read about my youth growing up in segregated Little Rock, through West Point, Vietnam, Europe and my presidential campaign. These experiences, both difficult and rewarding, make up my history and inform my vision of America's future.

ONE

GETTING STARTED

My mother, Veneta, was my best friend when I was little, and everyone said she was beautiful. She could whistle, too, so all the other boys in the neighborhood were a little jealous. Her father was Robert Stetson Updegraff, born in 1878 to a family of Dutchmen who had come over with William Penn. His father and grandfather had worked timber across Ohio and Missouri, but his mother died when he was a boy, and he left home early, escaping an angry stepmother. When he ran away, he had been through only a few years of schooling. But he followed his father's line of work, which meant the mills and forests of south Arkansas.

Veneta's mother was a Reynolds, and she had blood ties through them to the Upshaws and Longs of Georgia. Thomas Wesley Reynolds, my great-grandfather, was the engineer who built the first bridge over the Arkansas River at Dardanelle, some eighty miles upstream from Little Rock. But it was said that the Reynoldses lost their money in the depression of 1893, and Veneta was pulled out of private school in the third grade.

Robert Stetson Updegraff eventually worked his way up to become a sawyer, a position of some authority in a sawmill, and he married my grandmother, Elsie Reynolds, when she was sixteen. My mother was born in the small village of Ava, Arkansas, on the eleventh of November 1906, the second of five children.

The Updegraff family never had much. They didn't own a home or even a car. Granddad's reading ability was quite limited, and he silently moved his lips as he traced his finger across the page below the print. But he did have the gift of being mechanically inclined, and he was a hard worker. And he and Grandmother made sure their daughter finished high school.

Mom graduated from Monticello High School, a hundred miles south of Little Rock, in 1923. Monticello was a county seat, and a number of wealthy families lived there in beautiful homes. Their daughters often went to finishing schools in the East, spent summers in Europe, and, if they chose, went on to college. The boys from Monticello High whose families could afford it went to the University of Arkansas or Tulane or Vanderbilt or to fine colleges on the East Coast. Mom married a young man from the wealthy Bogard family, and they settled in Little Rock. But the marriage quickly failed, and my mother soon found herself alone and adrift in Little Rock. She was young, divorced, and almost penniless. But she was not without spirit.

Like many other young women of her time, she decided to move to a big city where a capable young woman could get a job based on talent rather than family. She decided on Chicago, and she quickly found a job there as a secretary in a bank, rooming with her friend Lois in an apartment hotel on the south side of Chicago. She met a handsome man, a lawyer who worked as assistant corporation counsel for the city of Chicago, and they fell in love. Eventually, though they were of different faiths and he was almost ten years older, they were wed. They wanted children, but after seven years of marriage, they had pretty much given up on that dream. Then, as mom used to joke, she thought she had a tumor, but it was me.

In December 1948, I was not quite four years old, and I remember waking up in the middle of the night, then walking around in the apartment. There were a lot of adults standing there talking, but I didn't know what was going on. I wanted to go into my parents' bedroom, but the adults wouldn't let me. Just a few hours earlier, my daddy had laid down on the blue and green sofa and pulled me up alongside him to read to me. Now something was wrong.

My father was a big man, and he was warm and kind to me. I used to ride in his lap as he drove the car through the park, and he often bought me a present when we went out together. He took me out with him every Saturday morning to visit his friends, and he even took me to see the White Sox play baseball in Comiskey Park. Now I wanted to know why everyone was in our home in the middle of the night, why Mom was so upset, and why I couldn't go into the bedroom and see my daddy. I was looking up at them, but they were holding me back and trying to distract me.

I wasn't taken to the funeral. I later learned that when Benjamin Kanne died of a heart attack at age fifty-one, he left his good name, a diamond ring, a 1940 Buick, and about four hundred dollars in cash. But that was about it. There was no insurance, no trusts, and no other property. My dad had died and left my mom and me pretty much alone. At the age of forty-two, my mom was widow and had a four-year-old son to support. She got back her old job as a secretary in the bank, and I was shuttled off to a nursery school for eight hours a day. I'd never been around many kids, and now there were kids everywhere, and they didn't seem to mind the food or the discipline or to miss their homes, like I did.

After a few weeks, Mom realized this wasn't working, but she never gave up hope. Hope and spirit, that's what I remember about her. She gave up her job in the Chicago bank, packed our clothes into the Buick my father had left us, and drove down through Illinois, across Missouri, and back to Little Rock, her home. When we arrived, we moved in with her parents in a little rental house on West Thirteenth Street.

But Mom had kept her old resourcefulness. She could type and take dictation, so she soon got a job as secretary in the Commercial National Bank. She lied a little about her age to get the job, telling them she was just forty, and they paid her twenty-five dollars a week.

I was now a Yankee living in Dixie, and I had a strange name—Kanne—and no father. Granddad was still working off and on at age seventy-one, still looking for saws to sharpen and adjust at Mr. Dierks's lumber mills. Grandmother took care of me, but there were other grandchildren, too.

After a long summer, Mom arranged to buy a house using my father's eligibility for a loan under the Veterans Administration, a nice two-bedroom home on North Valentine Street in the Pulaski Heights area. It rained hard that October day we moved in, and I remember standing on the front porch and watching as someone brought a pot of coffee over for us.

The neighborhood was filled with kids, and I found playmates in nearly every house. But I missed my father. Other kids talked about fishing with their dads, or going to ball games, or even just playing catch. But I didn't have a father to take me fishing, or to baseball games, or anything else normal dads did. Mom was one of the only working mothers around, and because of that she didn't socialize much in the neighborhood.

We probably didn't have much money, although she never mentioned it. And there were other differences that I felt every day. They all thought I spoke strangely, and I had picked up a speech defect that further marked me as being "different." Even as I played and had fun, and ran with my friends through their yards and homes, I felt a strong urge to really belong.

But through all the confusion and occasional loneliness, my mom was my friend. She worked hard to provide for us, and we really didn't have much. But she made do. During the first year or so we were in Arkansas, when it was almost time for her to come home from work I would go up the hill to Kavanaugh Boulevard and wait for her at the bus stop.

I especially remember that, when I was four or five, I took a quarter from her purse, and she noticed it was gone right away. In 1949, that was probably her lunch money, and she asked me if I had taken it. I admitted that I had, and she told me to put it back and to never again take anything that didn't belong to me. I was so ashamed. She never spanked me, and I never tried to steal anything again.

The old Buick wasn't doing too well. So my mother saved her money, and in September 1950 she bought a new car for $600, a two-door maroon-colored Dodge. It was the year-end stripped-down model, with no radio and a standard three-on-the-column transmission, but we were proud of it.

It was about that time that Granddad got hit in the eye by a splinter as he was fixing saws for Mr. Dierks at the lumber mill. He lost the eye, and we visited him in the hospital, where they had put in a new glass eyeball. But after he came home, he gradually slipped into the unhappy state of being old, poor, and out of work, and he no longer seemed to get out much.

There was no kindergarten at the time, and when I was five, I started first grade at Pulaski Heights Elementary School. My mother took me to school that first day for registration, and when they asked after my father, she said, "He's deceased." I knew what she meant, and I choked up.My first-grade teacher, Mrs. Tolifero, took a broad view of her responsibilities, and we were expected to learn and to participate in class. And she made sure we knew about the world. This was during the first year of the Korean War, and there was a lot of concern about the action over there. When General of the Army Douglas MacArthur was relieved of his command and later addressed the U.S. Congress, we heard it live on radio in our classroom. His words were spooky and confusing, as he concluded, "Old soldiers never die; they just fade away." I wasn't sure what that meant, but the reference to death I clearly understood, and it was a formulation that nagged at me. It seemed a little frightening at the time but I finally understood that this was just his artful use of rhetoric.

Mom always made sure my clothes were clean and neat, but I was a lot of trouble. My feet were too wide, and they were flat, and so I had to have special shoes. They were the big, clunky kind that you bought at special stores, the places where you put your foot under a fluoroscope that showed the bones inside.

And I had a speech defect. I knew I couldn't say, "Stop, Spot" or "Run, Randy, run," and I called my neighborhood friend "Wibby Ann" instead of "Libby Ann."I guess people thought my speech defect would go away by itself, but it didn't. And in the second grade I was taken once or twice a week downtown to the old MacArthur house on Ninth Street, which had been converted for Special Education. There, a nice teacher had us read as she listened closely. Then she taught us how to form our lips, and we got prizes if we pronounced words correctly. And sure enough, after a few months, my speech defect was corrected.

Looking back on that later, I realized that I was a kid with special needs, but I was able to get the appropriate special education that made things right for me. Because I was involved in it, I now understand the particular benefit many youngsters receive from our public educational system, a special blessing about whose value many people know very little.

The kids in the neighborhood became lifelong friends, but I really missed having a father. I missed some of the activities other kids had with their dads, and there were tears at night. But it was the kid talk that really hurt. Kids in the neighborhood would talk and brag: "My dad did this . . ." "Well, my dad, he can . . ." And then, the inevitable "Well, my dad could beat up your dad." My mother would occasionally go out with a man at night, and I would later often ask, "Is he going to be my dad?" But nothing ever seemed to come of it.

Then one night, when I was seven, my mom let me fall asleep in her bed because she was going out. And I awoke from a dream in which I was holding a big hunting knife. Then I looked and in my left hand was the most beautiful hunting knife I'd ever seen. It was in a scabbard, with a long blade and a beautiful curved brown-and-white bone handle. And Mom introduced me to the man she'd been out with, who'd brought her back to the house and put the knife in my hand.

"Honey, this is Vic. Thank him for giving you the knife."

Gradually, Victor Clark grew into an important force in my life. He was a banker, in his early fifties, and he drove a big Mercury. He would take us both to the drive-in movies, and later on he taught me how to hold and shoot a pistol. He even took me fishing. He taught me how to bait a hook with minnows and worms, and how to cast a line. He had a tackle box filled with the most amazing lures: Lazy Ikes, road runners, jitterbugs, incredible rubber frogs with hooks sticking out of them, and popping bugs with whiskers and feathers.

Best of all, he told wonderful stories: how his uncle George had fought a mountain lion in her den, and how he'd caught big "Appaloosa" catfish weighing up to a hundred pounds with his bare hands. He also told me how, when he was young, he had played football and basketball, had boxed, and had been very good at swimming, diving, and gymnastics. He was five feet nine, and he told me, "Kid, I've got arms like a gorilla and hands like meat hooks."

And these weren't made-up stories, either. He had played semipro basketball and could palm a ball, dribble it low and fast with either hand, and do what I now know was a running dunk. He could walk around the room on his hands, swim like a fish, and sprint really fast. He was like a dream come true as a father. Would he be my father, I wondered?

"Can I call you Dad?" I asked one day. His eyes became moist with tears as he said yes.

But there were issues. He was married, but was estranged from his wife and son down in Texas. His job in Arkansas called for him to travel, and socialize, and win deposits from Arkansas banks for his big bank in Dallas. And he drank. A lot. Jim Beam was always around, on the fishing trips and in his apartment and wherever we went.

And there were emotional scenes, like when he told Mom that his wife, Mary, wouldn't give him a divorce, something that both enraged and frustrated him. He and my mom seemed to argue a lot, but they always made up. And he bought me model airplanes, and he took me outdoors with him. He was good to me, and I loved him.

In 1953, he entered a sanatorium in Missouri to dry out for a few months. Then he moved back to his parents' farm in Berryville and did manual labor there for another few months.

In the fall of 1954, he finally got his divorce. He'd long given up his big banking job, but at least the Jim Beam was gone. He married my mother in November, in Greenville, Mississippi, and he moved into our home. Grandmother and Granddad moved down to Monroe, Louisiana, to be with Mom's little brother, my uncle Ray. And at long last I had a father. I soon began to call myself Wesley Clark.

But there were problems. Dad always seemed to be upset, and it seemed that he didn't, or wouldn't, eat much. He had a job representing Investors Diversified Services, one of the first mutual funds. He drove all over the state trying to sell funds, but unfortunately, he just couldn't do that. He knew too many people, it seems, and they remembered him from when he was a heavy drinker. Even his old friends wouldn't buy from him.

Mom and Dad had no social life, and very little money. Dad wanted to go to northwest Arkansas, where he didn't have a reputation, and start all over. Dad described a place in the country where I could have a horse, and I was all for it. There would be fishing and hunting every day, just like the way he'd grown up. I was ten or eleven, and I got pretty excited about it. But Mom didn't trust his ability to earn a living, and she refused to move. She wouldn't give up her job and she wouldn't give up my education. There was a lot of Busch Bavarian beer drunk, and a lot of shouting and crying. Dad even slept in his car for a few nights. But we didn't move.

The truth was, Mom had gotten pretty invested in my education. Year after year, she'd encouraged me to study hard, and she made sure my A's were rewarded. She bragged about my studies to the girls at work, paraded me through the bank, and even clipped out the newspaper columns listing me on the honor roll. Mom was what in the South we call "sweet" or "nice," but she also knew her own mind. I came to understand that though she had to juggle everything, my welfare was going to remain the top priority. She didn't train me, or coach me, or even try to teach me skills. She just loved me, and I felt it very deeply.

What I really wanted to play was basketball. Dad put up a hoop for me above the garage door, and I practiced faithfully. Free throws, lay-ups, dribbling, and the two-handed jump shot. I was always after Dad to teach me, practice with me, play with me. I could beat some of the kids at H.O.R.S.E., and I could dribble, but I wasn't a star. And one day, when I was eleven or twelve, Dad broke the hard news to me: "Kid, you're never going to be a great basketball player. You just don't have what it takes. You need to find a sport you can be good in, something you like, like swimming."

And so the Clark family survived in Little Rock, Arkansas. There are a lot of families like this across America, certainly even more today than when I was growing up. And it takes strong parents, and especially strong mothers, to make it work. I still find myself wondering today, when I see the single moms, if they understand how much their kids depend on them, and what those bonds of love can do for a child's future. And I hope the moms understand that their kids can sense their expectations—and that a mother's expectation means so much.

Over the past several decades, women in America have won an enormous new freedom to reach their true God-given potential in many areas, often in fields that were simply closed to them during my youth: doctors, lawyers, firefighters, police officers, business leaders. They are no longer barred from those once male-dominated areas, and life has been opened to them in dramatic and important ways. Indeed, though I can never know the answer, I sometimes wonder how far my mother would have gone had she had access to the range of opportunities open to American women in the twenty-first century. I'm sure she would have been an outstanding business leader and enjoyed a more satisfying professional life—and would still have given me the love, friendship, and support I needed so desperately.

But I worry that not every single mother has the kind of family network my mom had. As a nation, we need to help single moms with child care, cooking, cleaning, the opportunity to advance their skills, and all the other support that's so easy to take for granted.

~

For me, the eighth grade was a watershed year, when a lot of lessons came together. Little Rock was in the national news because Central High School was going to be desegregated. The plan had been to start from the top down: high school first, and then junior high, and, eventually, the elementary schools. There was a large crowd of angry whites at the school, and only one black girl showed up, and she was chased away. It was on the evening news that night, in black and white.

Eighth grade was a time for growing up, all the more so because throughout the country the reputation of our town was damaged and tarnished. There was a picture in *Life* magazine of a man who'd been chased at bayonet point onto a porch near Central High. Somehow his arm had been cut open, and there was blood. And this picture was just the most egregious of a daily savaging by what today we'd call the mainstream media.

"We're not that kind of town," my parents said. "There are nice people here, but if you just go by what they're saying about us, you'd think we were the worst people in the world."

It was the anger of Southern whites, a refrain that dominated much of American politics over the following years. But these were good people, I believed, respectable, churchgoing (at least some of them), and here they were on the wrong end of all this publicity. It was true, there was a Supreme Court decision that schools had to be integrated. But white Southern community leaders and opinion makers would say that Little Rock wasn't the only place with problems. And anyway, I heard, we treat "ours" better in the South than they treat "theirs" up North. Here we like "them" as individuals, while "up there" they don't. And what about property values, if "they" start buying homes in our neighborhoods?

It was confusing to many of us in the eighth grade. The Arkansas National Guard was first called out to prevent blacks from going to school. Then some federal troops, the soldiers of the 101st Airborne Division, were sent in to bring them into the school, and the Guard was federalized and made to switch sides. There were huge reputations made, and people unknown became famous, like Daisy Bates and the NAACP, and Governor Orval Faubus.

Sure, the African American kids had a right to go to school, and the law was the law. But why was it being enforced here and nowhere else? Why was our community judged so harshly? And why did my parents and so many others seem to be opposed to what was happening? Was Faubus a hero or a villain? What was right, and what if my parents didn't agree?

Mom and Dad had never said anything bad about African Americans, except that Dad didn't like Elvis Presley on TV, wiggling his hips and making "their" kind of music. But I remembered he had introduced me to the African American barkeeper at the Arlington Hotel in Hot Springs one night when he was hosting a bankers' reception there a few years earlier, and the bartender and I had had a real conversation.

It seemed like almost everyone but us had an African American maid. They rode the bus up Kavanaugh Boulevard in the mornings, always in starched white uniforms, walked down the street, and stayed in my friends' homes all day.

Little Rock was steeply segregated. The swimming pools were just for whites, and in public places there were separate facilities, even separate drinking fountains. And of course the Pulaski Heights Baptist Church that I attended had no black families. The buses did carry both blacks and whites, of course, but the blacks were sent to the seats at the back, in a marked-off section.

This problem in Little Rock was a personal conundrum. I knew what my parents said and believed. And I loved Mom and Dad. But I also sensed that they were wrong, somehow. If it took all that much wriggling around to defend competing ideals, then maybe, just maybe, something wasn't right. We still played "Dixie" at football games as a school fight song, but it no longer felt right. Mom always said her favorite song was "The Battle Hymn of the Republic." I think she was trying to tell me something.

For years, I struggled to make sense of the conflict. I loved and respected my stepfather, but he was so wrong . . . he and so many others in my town. He was a good man, but good men can be wrong. Wrong, utterly wrong, despite their sincerity, their fervor, and their wisdom in other areas. It was simple prejudice against black people that they felt. There's just no other term for it.

I saw prejudice at an early age, and came to dislike it in all its forms. Maybe I was acutely sensitive to it since I'd come to Little Rock from Chicago. Over the years I've seen prejudice against blacks by whites, prejudice by Northerners against Southerners, and by Southerners against Yankees, by jocks against nerds, by the educated and snobby against the undereducated and poor, by liberal intellectuals against the military, by Irish against Italians in New York City, by Serbs against Muslims in the Balkans, by conservatives against liberals on talk radio and various TV news programs, by straights against gays, and every manner of religious prejudice.

Most of us carry some form of prejudice inside. Today, though, most Americans feel as I do—that everyone should be treated equally. Sometimes it's difficult for us to see our own prejudice because it's hidden in institutions, habits, traditions, or in language itself. But when it's pointed out, it's almost always corrected. Sometimes it takes a while for the corrections to come through, but they have, and I believe they will continue. And this is one of the greatest attributes of our country: We try to live by the very standard of equality that we professed two hundred and thirty years ago in the Declaration of Independence. But for many people such corrections come too late. I believe no one should be denied a crack at a team, a neighborhood, a school, or a job because of race, ethnic group, gender, religion, or any other unfair discriminator. Because of this, I am a strong believer in Affirmative Action.

❧

Despite the social unrest at Central High School on the other side of town, my junior high school life went on. Acting on Dad's advice, I had found a swimming team I could join, downtown at the Little Rock Boys Club. Most of the Boys Club's members were poor kids who lived downtown. Membership was $0.75 per year, gradually rising to $3 per year when you were sixteen. They had an indoor pool, and there were several other kids at Pulaski Heights Junior High on the team. And you could win a school letter!

After a few weeks, practices had begun to seem routine. It meant skipping supper, or eating alone, but it got me out of the house and away from the arguments and criticisms that passed between my parents. Even though my Dad was recovering from his drinking problems, there always seemed to be issues between my parents. And I wanted to be the best of the new swimmers. We were all twelve years old, and I had little to offer beyond hard work, but somehow I hung in there.

The big test for the team was to be part of the annual pilgrimage to swim against the freshman team at Northwest Louisiana Sate College at Natchitoches. It would be a full weekend trip: We would leave before dawn on Saturday for a four or five hour drive, swim Saturday afternoon, stay over in the college Saturday night, and make a long ride home Sunday. Everyone talked about how much fun they'd had last year on the same trip.

But our coach was a determined young man. Growing up poor in southern Arkansas, Jimmy Miller had had a hard youth. In World War II, he had fought as an army infantryman at Guadalcanal. After he got out of the service, he eventually put himself through college on the GI Bill while working as a coach at the Boys Club and starting his own family. And he wanted a winning team.

He gave each of us the times we had to meet to make the travel squad with the team. He read them out to us one evening at practice as we sat cold and huddled on the steps beside the bleachers at the pool. In the Boys Club at the time, you didn't wear a swimsuit in practice. There were no girls, and it both saved money and, they said, improved sanitation.

For the one-hundred-yard freestyle, I had to beat 1:12.4, while another boy on the team, Mike Stewart, had to go 1:12.5, so we knew what was expected. But that seemed unfair to me because Mike always beat me in practice. I thought maybe Coach Miller had gotten us mixed up. At the next practice I asked him why my time had to be faster than Mike's even though he was a better swimmer.

"Because you're stronger," he said.

On the night of the dreaded time trial, Miller called us up, two by two. I was paired with Mike Stewart. Mike had a sunny, confident disposition, and we all liked him. He always seemed to say the right thing.

Then Miller told us the rules: "You will all make your assigned times. If you don't, you won't go on the trip. And just to make sure, you're going to get one pop of the wet towel on your fanny for every tenth of a second you miss your time."

He cracked the thin, wet towel against the tile floor. It sounded like a rifle shot.

So we began, with the youngest going first. Most of the boys made their times, though one ten-year-old missed his by two-tenths. "All right," Coach Miller said to the unfortunate swimmer, "bend over, and grab your ankles." Crack, Crack! The boy came whining back to the steps to sit down, rubbing two red spots on his rear end.

By the time he called up Mike and me, I was concerned, and not at all confident. "Take your marks." Tweet, he blew the whistle and we dived in, two prepubescent boys engaged in a titanic struggle to make the trip to Natchitoches. We had to swim five lengths of the pool.

By the end of the fourth length, Mike was a body length ahead of me, his feet thrashing a steady beat. My arms felt like lead. I seemed to just sink in the water, and I was incredibly tired.

Mike finished well ahead of me, and Coach Miller looked up from his stopwatch, smiling. "Mike, well done. You made 1:12.5 on the nose. You're on the trip." Then he frowned down on me as I stood in the chest-deep water. I looked up, my eyes filled with disappointment and fear.

"Son, you didn't make it. You missed your time by a full second. Get out and walk down to the other end of the pool."

I was feeling so sorry for myself that his voice seemed to come from down a long tunnel. I got out of the water and moved to the indicated place.

"Now bend over and grab your ankles."

Ten pops. They stung. Tears came to my eyes. I had failed. And I was publicly humiliated. I turned around, head down, to go back to the steps and nurse my feelings. It was very quiet. But Coach Miller stopped me.

He asked me quietly "You know what your biggest problem is?"

"No, sir," I said.

"It's you," he replied. "You didn't believe you could do it. Now go sit down."

After a few more swimmers made their times, practice was done. There was excited chatter in the car going home, but not from me. I had a problem: I was going to be left out of the trip. Rejected. Different. Failing. Couldn't even make the swimming team. And my rear end still stung from the towel.

The trip was scheduled for the following week. At Wednesday night's practice, the last before we left, Coach Miller announced "I'm going to give a couple of you another chance."

He called me up by myself. Alone. I felt nothing as I stood at the edge of the pool. No fear. No worry. Just nothing. Numb.

But when I hit the water, I swam. I swam hard. I wasn't tired. My arms weren't heavy. I didn't sink. I just swam. I slapped the wall and looked up. I knew it was good. Miller smiled a little: "One eleven seven," he said. "So, you did it, just like I knew you could. You were the only one who didn't know it. Now you do. Now get back over there and sit down."

That was what I came to learn from Coach Miller, "Mind over matter." He forced you to change your mind, to change how you saw yourself. He forced you to believe that you could be more than you were. He did it by bullying, threatening, humiliating, and only occasionally explaining. Maybe he learned that in that draft army of 1942. Or maybe he learned it through the school of hard knocks. Or maybe it was just him, struggling with himself. But whatever it was, he had a kind of magic for me.

I've always been around young people, in the military, or teaching, or at the Boys and Girls Club or at the swimming pool, or applying for internships, or working in political campaigns. And I always wonder if anyone has ever taught them what real potential is inside each of them, and how much they can achieve if only they will ask it of themselves. I can't teach it with a wet towel, of course, and I wouldn't want to. But Jimmy Miller gave me a great gift, and in my own way I've always tried to pass it on.

~

That same year, the Soviet Union launched the first Sputnik, a small satellite that transmitted a single radio pulse as it orbited the earth. The launch sent a chill through America at the time, and for many of us, it became a significant marker in our lives. Of course, I'd been aware of the Soviet Union already. I had memories of the Korean War and Stalin; I remembered doing duck-and-cover drills at our desks, and the urgency of marking civil defense air raid shelters. I remembered vaguely the discussions about our needing to go to war with the Soviet Union before they could create an H-bomb like ours. I remembered, too, the vicious fighting and terrible reports of torture as the Soviets suppressed the Hungarian Revolution of 1956. Now they were surpassing us technologically. Was America lost?

But instead of panicking, America went to work. Yes, we lived with the fact that missiles were aimed at our cities, and that nuclear annihilation was possible. But we didn't give in to our fears. New legislation was passed promoting the study of science and technology, and American industry and our educational systems were updated to meet the challenge with research and development tax credits and the National Defense Education Act. And I was one of thousands and thousands of youngsters who did what we could to catch up by learning about rockets, some of us even trying to build our own in the backyard.

Soon, the United States did launch its own satellites. And America wasn't invaded. In fact, less than forty years later, the Soviet Union itself collapsed, without our ever firing a shot against them.

For so many of us who lived through that time, international challenges have to be answered, but with confidence that we can prevail. In the 1950s, America didn't take counsel of its fears and wage preventive war, even though some recommended it. And so, from an early age, I have believed in our country's resiliency and strength, and our ability to surmount any challenge by drawing on our courage and creativity and not giving in to fear. Our country's leaders owe it to us to make sure that the children we are raising today do not grow up with dread, but rather with hope and optimism for the future. Our children must not be raised in fear, whether of Osama Bin Laden or anyone else, nor be left without some opportunity to help our country.

TWO

HALL HIGH SCHOOL

In Little Rock in those days, the 9th grade wasn't actually high school—it was the last year of three-year Junior High. And in 1958 that was a very significant distinction, because in late August of that year, the Little Rock School Board voted to simply close the city's two High Schools—the famous Central High and the brand new Hall High, located on the western edge of town—rather than submit to mandatory school integration. Over two thousand high-school students were stranded by the decision, unable to attend classes.

In the 9th grade at Pulaski Heights Junior High School, my friends and I were totally unaffected. My Boys Club friends Ranny Treece and Danny Hirby were star halfbacks on the football team, with the popular Jerry Bass as end and place kicker. Si Dunn was the star runner in the quarter-mile—his :55 second 440 was one of the top times in the state. There were school dances, and Buddy Holly and the Big Bopper were still competing with Elvis Presley and The Platters. Many of the kids were "going steady." I'm sure that most of the rest of us had crushes that we kept largely to ourselves. And the most advanced were getting their learners permits at 14 and sneaking out with the family car on weekends.

For me it was mostly about swimming with the team at the Boys Club. We began training early in the fall to compete in the Phillips 66 meet in Bartlesville, Oklahoma. I was also editor of the school newspaper, *The Tip Top Times.* Our schoolwork was pretty standard—Algebra, Civics, English, first-year Latin, General Science, and Physical Education.

Most weekends Mom would drive us down to Stuttgart, about an hour and a half east of Little Rock, to join Dad in the bait shop (Clark's Worm and Cricket Ranch) that we had bought the year before with a few thousand dollars I'd received when my father's mother died. "Kid, can we use your money for this?" he'd asked.

Of course I said yes, and the money covered the down payment for the bank loan to buy the business. It had given Dad a sense of hope and purpose in his life, and we desperately wanted it to succeed. My job was to tend the crickets and the worm beds, and pack them for sale (25 to a $0.50 box). In this I worked with Joe, a young African-American who was a couple of years older than me and knew what he was doing. We had a lot of fun talking in the shed while sorting out the "red wrigglers" and "African nightcrawlers" that local fishermen liked. Occasionally, I would also help Dad wait on the customers.

But the separation was a further strain on my parents' marriage, and the business was totally dependent on weather. It had been a struggle from the very beginning, marked by rainy weekends, strange infections of the minnows, and some petty thievery by Dad's one full-time employee, Jim. I could overhear Mom and Dad's worried conversations at night, and knew the business wasn't living up to Dad's expectations.

Still, Mom always found money for Christmas. That year I was given a Remington .22 semiautomatic rifle with a four-power scope. As Dad said, every boy needs his own rifle, and he had gotten his first rifle at age 6. I was proud of the Remington, and occasionally used it to hunt rabbits and squirrels while Mom and Dad fished.

But beneath the surface, our homes were churning, as parents watched the older kids struggle to find a place with relatives out of town, or gain last minute attendance to private schools, including some just-opened makeshift schools in Little Rock. It appeared to many that there simply would be no more public high school in Little Rock for the foreseeable future, and some parents began to plan accordingly. Some of the kids were talking about Lawrenceville, Andover, or Sewanee.

My mother began to talk private school for me, out of the state, perhaps a military school. We had just enough money left in the small inheritance from my father's mother, Ida Kanne in Chicago, to pay for two years of private schooling. We sent away for the catalogs, and I studied them closely. Kemper, Columbia, Culver (too expensive) and Castle Heights. Ultimately, it would be Castle Heights, in Lebanon, Tennessee. I took an entrance exam, and we sent in a large deposit.

With friends on the swimming team there was always a lot of talk, and much of it was about America and the Soviet Union. There seemed to be an overwhelming sense of competition, and we were emotionally connected with it, even as 13 and 14 year olds. I found my way over to the University of Arkansas Medical School library, a mile away on Markham Street, where they were said to have textbooks with which I could try to learn Russian, and got serious about mathematics and science at school. Through the National Defense Education Act of 1958 money was already being disbursed to strengthen U.S. science instruction, even in Little Rock. I was invited to join the after-school "Federal Radiation Project," where along with a few other hand-picked ninth-graders, I could raise and irradiate fruit flies and learn about genetics and advanced biology.

The summer was glorious, with swimming meets almost every weekend. At the Boys Club camp Miller trained us three times a day in a 25-meter pool and at 14 I was at the top of my age group and doing well in meets around the state. And despite the three hours a day in the pool, for the first time, I was given real leadership responsibilities—14 boys in my cabin. I had to know about them, coach them, meet their parents, and make them successes at camp. From reveille at 6:00 A.M. until lights out at 9:00 P.M., they were my charges. Some I taught to hit a baseball or swim, others I taught to stand up against bullying. I looked after mosquito bites, poison ivy, and homesickness. And I was really proud of them when they won ribbons in the camp competition. Three terms of two weeks each; it was some of the best leadership experience I have ever had.

At home, Dad found an alternative to the bait shop in a job with the Arkansas civil service in the Revenue Department, and we managed to recover most of our losses there by selling it to a new owner. And then all too soon it was Labor Day weekend and a long, slow drive across Tennessee to Castle Heights.

Mom and Dad came with me into the main hall to register, and I inquired about my schedule—I had to be able to take calculus in the 12th grade. In the catalog, Castle Heights showed a calculus class, and not even the Little Rock schools taught calculus. I wanted that class. It was somehow connected in my mind to patriotism, and doing my part for the country. And to get calculus, I knew I would have to double-up on math as a sophomore, taking Plane Geometry and Algebra II the same year.

"No, that's not on your schedule," the woman said at the registration desk. Then they brought me in to see Colonel Bradley, the Dean, who explained that doubling up on these courses wasn't normal. Particularly for someone with my background and test scores, he wouldn't advise it. Mom and Dad were silent as we left his office.

Not five minutes later we ran into Jerry Bass, my junior high friend who was also attending Castle Heights, and in passing he mentioned that he was enrolled in both Algebra II and Plane Geometry. I was stunned, and I turned right around and went back to the Dean. With Mom and Dad standing there, I argued that I too should be allowed to take both math courses. At that point there wasn't much he could say, and I got the class schedule I had wanted.

As Mom and Dad drove off, I was instantly homesick. It was like an empty feeling in my stomach, a kind of an ache, and a longing that I fought to keep under control. It seemed to hit me the hardest as I walked up the long steps to the third floor room where I was assigned to stay. Fortunately, once the school year started there were lots of activities, good teachers, the swimming team, and my roommates, David Bixler and Joe Reed. We put up with a little harassment and hazing from the upperclassmen, and some tough, white-glove Saturday morning room inspections. But we were busy. In addition to class, I had swimming team trips all over Tennessee and Georgia, a good Baptist church to walk to downtown, and close friends both on the swimming team and with other Little Rock boys.

It was a military school. We wore uniforms, and shined shoes. I didn't particularly like the regimentation, though with the daily swimming practices and study in the evenings there was a purpose in the routine. But I did find the daily formation around the flag pole for retreat a somber and beautiful ceremony. What was it like, I would wonder, to actually be in the service, and to fight for that flag? I watched the real soldiers and sailors in uniform at the bus stations on my way back and forth to Little Rock. Mostly, they looked lonely and sad, just the way I would find myself late at night in those bus stations. And I wondered about the purpose in their lives, for I was discovering purpose in my studies, and in my leisure readings of Toynbee and Plato, about the rise and fall of civilizations, of leadership and government. Would America survive, I wondered? And what would it take to make a difference in her future? It was the faint sense of purpose that seeped out from beneath the questions that seemed to make the pain and loneliness go away.

Eventually, after a lot of political noise, the Little Rock high schools had opened that September. After another summer in Little Rock, then, I had to give serious thought about whether or not to return to Castle Heights for the 11th grade. I talked it over with Mom and Dad, and I went to visit the guidance counselor at Hall High. She promised me that they would have a calculus class for us when we seniors, so Jerry Bass and I agreed to attend Hall.

I was surprised by the exhilarating sense of freedom I found that fall. Somehow, I had more time to pursue my priorities. And I had no difficulty maintaining purpose, even in the seductive world of sock hops, Friday night football, and dates to the local drive-in.

Above all, it was the quality of the students that made the school. We had a little over 300 in our class, and I was proud to know almost every one of them. Even though the smartest boy from junior high, Johnny Bilheimer, had stayed at Andover, there were plenty of others who, like me, were interested in rockets and mathematics as well as in sports and girls. Together we made up the calculus class—and with a sympathetic teacher, we basically taught ourselves, through analytic geometry and into differential and integral calculus.

Members of that class were also the presidents of the student council and the senior class, and most of the extracurricular activities in school, as well as captains of three varsity teams and the king of the High School homecoming. Lifelong achievers all, they became my closest friends, tennis partners, and touch football teammates. And they were smart: that year, we learned that our class at Hall High School, proportional to its size, had the third highest number of National Merit

Scholarship semifinalists in the nation. Some of these friends went on to Harvard, MIT, Rice, Washington University, Columbia and Dartmouth. They were then—and still are—the group with which I was probably most closely bonded.

~

In June 1961, I watched carefully as the West Point cadet on the stage described the United States Military Academy on the Hudson River in far-off New York State. His distinctive gray uniform with white trousers fit him like a glove, and he looked sharp, confident, and in command, as his audience of a thousand Arkansas high school seniors at the American Legion Boys State convocation sat spellbound.

The cadet said he'd been here himself as a high school senior at the Arkansas Boys State only three years ago. In other words, he was one of us. But as we listened to him, he seemed to be miles above us. We sat there in our shorts, sneakers, and Boys State T-shirts, and he just radiated authority. He spoke of duty, of leadership, and of the purpose of the military. But the most important thing to me was that this sharp young man, demigod that he seemed, also wore glasses.

It seems to me now, thinking back, that I'd always wanted to be a pilot. I'd built model airplanes since I was five years old, and after Sputnik was launched in 1957, I worked hard to actually build functioning rockets. Mine were of modest proportions, of course, and they not only wouldn't go into orbit, but I worried about them even clearing the rooftops in our neighborhood. Still, I had the bug.

In my 9th grade civics paper, I had said that, when I grew up, I wanted to be an aeronautical engineer and that I hoped to win a scholarship to study aeronautical engineering. I'd looked longingly at the catalog for the beautiful new Air Force Academy in Colorado Springs—what a dream come true *that* would be!

Then the bottom fell out. During the eleventh grade, I discovered I needed glasses. Glasses. Imperfection. A failure. That disqualified me from military aeronautics. And I could never become an astronaut, either.

But now, at the Boys State Convention, here was this truly spectacular West Point cadet promoting his school to all of us. In glasses. Talking about leadership, about getting a great education, and in the face of the

Soviet threat, about public service. I was almost overwhelmed. I could wear glasses and still go to West Point.

That cadet speaking to us was all I needed. I walked outside with Jerry Bona and Bill Sims, two of my best friends, and exclaimed "I'm going to West Point!"

True, I'd already spent my tenth grade at Castle Heights Military Academy in Lebanon, Tennessee. I'd made good friends there, and good grades. But the inspections, the isolation, the regimentation, the time away from home—it just wasn't for me.

But, somehow, West Point sounded different. More mature, purposeful. A combination of Harvard in the social sciences and MIT in the sciences. I could get a good education. Fully paid, which meant no more dependence on Mom. And I could lead. Lead. Not sit around some office somewhere, but actually be out in the field. Outdoors. And I could do it in glasses. Maybe the fact that I'd made it through tenth grade at Castle Heights made it easier to think about West Point.

It was clear right away, however, that getting in would be tough. The classes were small, and only about eight hundred candidates entered after something like ten times that number applied each year. Student leaders, Varsity sports captains, Eagle Scouts, National Merit Scholars. The credentials of those accepted were intimidating. I knew kids like that, and I worried that I would not be good enough.

As I investigated the matter further, I learned that admission was strictly a political process. Each congressman and senator could nominate one cadet each year, with the remaining cadets selected from among eligible candidates who were either young soldiers themselves or the children of soldiers. Well, my father wasn't in the army, so it was going to have to be the political appointment route.

My family knew no one, which was a bit depressing. But I gathered my courage and wrote to one of our senators, J. William Fulbright. A few days later I got a postcard from his office: The appointments for the next year had already been committed, and no others would be available. My mother said she wasn't surprised, that she'd heard such appointments tended to be reserved for children of those who did favors for the senators.

I was undeterred. I wrote our other senator, John L. McClellan. I actually got a letter back, inviting me to come and meet the senator to discuss West Point.

It was an afternoon in early September when I took the elevator to Senator McClellan's Little Rock office in the city's tallest building, the 14-story Donaghey Building. As instructed, I knocked on his door.

"Come in," he said, looking me over as I stepped in front of his desk.

"So, you're the young man who wants to go to West Point, huh?"

"Yes, sir," I said, standing at attention to address him.

There was a pause.

"Boy, how old are you?" he asked pointedly.

"Sir, I am sixteen years old."

"And how much do you weigh?" he followed up.

"Sir, I weigh 137 pounds." I had weighed myself at swimming practice the night before, so I knew exactly.

"And I guess you make good grades, huh?"

He was obviously sorting me out: This is not the football player type, just a skinny little kid in glasses.

"Yes, sir," I replied enthusiastically, playing right into his hand.

"How good? All A's?" He asked questions with a hard edge, just as he had in the televised Senate Racket Committee hearings.

"Yes, sir, well, except I got a B in the first grading period in honors math last year, but it counts as an A they said, and . . ."

He let me dribble on, but clearly he wasn't impressed. Then he cut me off.

"Boy, you aren't old enough, you aren't big enough, and you aren't smart enough to go to West Point," he summed up. "But you can come back and see me next year if you're still interested."

I was disappointed, and his words weren't exactly a promise that I'd make it next year, either. As a junior in 1961 I had helped Hall High win the state high school swimming trophy over the summer, and I'd also worked managing and life-guarding at two pools. Coach Keopple, the track coach, had seen me run a 220-yard dash one afternoon and asked me to run track and cross-country with him. I had gotten one of the highest scores in the state on the National Merit Qualifying exam, and I had made the highest grade possible in the math portion of the Preliminary Scholastic Aptitude Test. Maybe Senator McClellan had decided against me, but I was not discouraged at all.

I had one more chance, our new congressman, Dale Alford. He told a friend of Dad's that he did have an appointment to West Point to give out; but that so many people had called to ask about it that he didn't know what to do. A couple of weeks later, I heard that he'd decided to have each applicant send his records to West Point and also take the U.S. Civil Service test, and whoever scored highest would get the appointment. That was my chance, so I took the test.

When the Harvard recruiter came by Hall High School in December, he asked to see several of us. "He wants to talk to you about a full scholarship to Harvard," explained Miss Mayhan, the guidance counselor. But I was committed to West Point. I wanted that challenge, the leadership, the outdoor life, the adventure, the chance to follow in the footsteps of men like MacArthur and Eisenhower.

"No, ma'am," I replied. "I really want to go to West Point, and nowhere else. You haven't heard anything from West Point about me, have you?"

The winter months were anxious for me, but I had confidence that somehow I would be accepted. I went to swim meets, began interscholastic debate as part of speech class, won the state debating championship with Bill Sims on the topic of federal aid to elementary and secondary education, found a girl to go steady with, and talked and dreamed about the future. And in April the telegram arrived. I had received the appointment. I would be required to report to West Point on the morning of July 2, 1962.

I was in! I was ecstatic but I was a little uneasy, too, because I knew it would be tough. The rest of the school year passed in a blur: the last swim meet, the "senior skip" day, the year book which my high school girlfriend helped edit, the last papers, the graduation ceremonies (a torrential thunderstorm soaked us all as we walked into the gymnasium), the all-night party afterward, and watching the sun come up over the Arkansas River.

In high school, you had to figure out where you fit in and find the opportunities to express yourself. It was all very judgmental, and some kids wore better clothes, drove better cars, and had more money to spend. But at the same time, it was quite open and supportive, with supportive teachers and coaches working and mentoring, constantly encouraging you to do better and be more. To me, it truly was like a "preparatory" school. We would each go our own ways, but when we parted that spring, we knew we would somehow always be bound together.

The month of June flew past. I read up on West Point, dabbled at memorizing the useless "plebe knowledge" I had been warned about, and worried a bit. I learned about another young man from Arkansas who was also going to West Point whose father was in the Air Force. We met at the airport on a Friday morning. My mother walked me out to the big Lockheed Electra—you could do that in those days—and I climbed up the steps and looked back at her standing there. Tears were running down her cheeks as she dabbed at her eyes.

Public schools are the crucible of the nation. Training and testing grounds where standards are set and norms established, they are crucially important in shaping and solidifying the personalities and character traits of the young people who pass through them. Sadly, most young people today don't claim the experiences that I found at Hall, or in junior high, and fixing this is one of America's most urgent problems.

In Little Rock our schools were the pride of the community, not just for athletic achievement but for the quality of the school graduates overall. Businessmen and civic leaders were deeply engaged in the school board—sometimes, as in the 1957 uproar over integration, with tragic results.

By the time I graduated, a handful of African Americans were driven to Hall High every morning, and picked up every afternoon. They were mostly ignored by the white students, and I feel a terrible shame about that now. We could have done so much better, and today my classmates and I often speak of this with regret, wishing we could somehow make up for the coldness which these kids from the other side of town must have felt.

But to attend smallish, neighborhood schools, with close and continuing bonds between teachers and parents, is a great privilege. The civic pride that keeps schools clean, in good repair and updated, and the resulting community pride in their students, were gifts to me. But they should be the norm, and I hope to see every child in America enjoy a great educational experience in public schools, just like I did.

THREE

THE PROFESSION OF ARMS

Mike Mayhew and I traveled together to his uncle's house on Long Island, were taken to New York City to see *My Fair Lady* and then dropped off at West Point, to spend the night of July 1 in the Hotel Thayer, just inside the gates. The academy itself was still a mile away, and there were many of us there that night, young men holding appointments. But there was little we could say beyond nervous chatter. The first nine weeks of training we would undergo as "New Cadets," known informally as "Beast Barracks," were renowned for their ardor. And we were scared.

We had been told to report between 9:00 A.M. and noon that day, and we were all up early. Some said we should wait, as that would mean a few less hours of the hellacious hazing we knew awaited us. But I was anxious by 9:30 A.M., and I finally decided to just get it over with.

I was directed through a sally port that led into the Area of Barracks, and even as I approached it, the yelling from within was a continuous roar. It was simply terrifying. What are they doing, I thought, torturing people? I was soon to find out.

I walked through the sally port and into Central Area, as it was called, a square of cement that seemed more like an empty parking lot than anything else. It looked to be about a hundred meters on a side, and it was surrounded by four floors of barracks that had been built in the nineteenth century. I was carrying a suitcase in one hand that contained clothing and toilet gear, and a cadet in white pants and gray hat and tunic approached me almost viciously, snarling and yelling at me as if I had just killed his mother.

I dropped my bag on his command and immediately learned how to "brace," which meant to pull my chin as far as possible back into my neck, a truly painful experience at first. I was told that I would maintain that position at all times while I was inside the Area of Barracks—the area enclosed by the walls of the barracks–and in the mess hall during meals. Then I was sent, at a run, to various stations where elements on a list tied to my belt would be completed and checked off.

When asked anything by an upperclassman, we were allowed to make only three responses, all in a very loud voice: "*Yes, sir!*" "*No, sir!*" or "*No excuse, sir!*" The pressure was constant, with men in gray hounding us, hectoring us, yelling at us as we went from place to place.

"*Let's see some wrinkles there, smackhead!*"

"*Grind your chin in, mister!*"

"*What are you looking at, dumbjohn? Eyes to the front!*"

The errands included picking up cadet clothing, getting measured by a tailor for the clothing that would follow, getting shots, being fitted for shoes, getting my hair cut short . . . the list went on and on, and everything quickly became a blur as I struggled to survive. I turned in all my civilian gear, was assigned to a room on the second floor in an area known as Old South, and dressed in my first cadet uniform. Then, in late afternoon, having acquired only the bare rudiments of marching, all 807 of us New Cadets were marched out to Trophy Point, where we were sworn in. But that was just the start.

And it was even harder than I had expected. Much harder. In fact, I had never been through anything this rigorous in my life, or even imagined there could be such a place. The yelling from the detail of upperclassmen was constant; the criticism of everything we did was incessant. Run here, carry this, straighten out that.

"This is the way to finish off the toes of your shoes, Ducrot. No, no. *This* way! Can't you see how I am using my finger through the cloth?"

I tried to do everything they told me to do, and to do it the way they told me to. But that, I later learned, was intentionally quite simply impossible. Still, I did the best I could. The daily routine was getting yelled at in ranks, marching, learning how to fieldstrip and clean our M–1 rifles, harassment, more marching, polishing gear, more marching, attending a class on field hygiene, more marching. Then, at night, when we were supposed to be polishing our shoes and brass for the next day, we had to go through these maddening clothing formations, which meant running up and down stairs and changing in and out of certain uniforms within two minutes. And heaven help the New Cadet who was late into ranks. All of which was followed by a so-called shower formation, which meant bracing in our thin cotton bathrobes until we had sweated through them. Only then were we allowed into the showers.

"Two minutes in the showers, wash hard! . . . Okay, hot water off, cold water on! Thirty seconds left . . . Water off. Everybody out of the showers!"

And then to bed, only to be up six hours later at reveille, followed in five minutes by formation and inspection in ranks. It was beyond belief.

During the first few days, the confusion and the pressure were almost overwhelming.

"Mister Clark! What are you standing there doing nothing while your classmates are sweating? IRP?"

When an upperclassman yelled, "IRP?" in your ear, pronounced like Wyatt's last name, that was short for "Immediate Response, Please!" And I also soon learned that meant sound off with something—even if it was *"No excuse, sir!"*—in response or die.

Eating was a privilege you had to earn, and you had to do it sitting at attention and straining physically to pull your chin as far back into your neck as possible. We were told that our bites would be half the size of a pea, and the two upperclassmen at each table with eight plebes were unrelenting in their torment. You had to keep your eyes on your plate, and whenever either of them spoke to any of us, we had to put down our utensils and sit at a rigid position of attention. And when things were going too smoothly for us, all they had to say was "Sit up!" either to one plebe or to the whole table and everyone froze.

And then it was "Pass out your plates," which meant no more food. Our rooms were checked and our mail searched for contraband: No extra food was permitted.

I lost fifteen pounds during the first ten days of Beast Barracks. The yelling was constant, the tasks incessant, and down to the smallest detail we had to get it right. No, it was more than that: We had to get it perfect. And even when we did, we got yelled at:

"Mister Clark, you're indifferent, aren't you? You're not trying, are you? Answer me, smackhead!"

The barracks at West Point, viewed from above, comprise several large squares of stone barracks surrounding concreted areas. The two main such squares are Central Area, the largest, with its adjacent Old South and North Area. These lie on either side of the enormous vaulted-ceiling mess hall, known as Washington Hall, where all cadets eat all their meals at the same time. Washington Hall forms the corner of a right angle, with the outside row of barracks of Central Area and North Area forming two sides of a resulting square.

Enclosed on two sides by those large stone buildings, is a huge grassy area known as the Plain. A road borders the other two sides of this perfectly maintained level area, on which, several afternoons each week during the nine-month academic year, cadets march in parade. During Beast Barracks, formations of new cadets were led through the rudiments of squad formation on the Plain. And after the third week, they were also put through the physically demanding paces of bayonet drill.

During the first week, we had been issued M–1 rifles and long chrome bayonets that were attached to their muzzles for parade. The sun flashing off these bayonets added color to the impressive formation of uniformed cadets marching on the Plain for the Great American Public that chose to attend. But the purpose of the bayonet, we learned in that third week, is far more than to dazzle spectators who might have come up from New York City.

The purpose of the bayonet is to kill.

We learned that loud and clear at our first bayonet drill. Having dressed in the required uniform of fatigues, combat boots, and helmets, we carried our bayoneted rifles on our shoulders as we had learned to do for any normal squad drill on the Plain. But this time, we were formed into a company square in front of a small wooden platform some four or five feet above ground level. On that platform stood an upperclass cadet. He faced us, his feet shoulder-width apart, his back straight, chest out, and holding his own bayoneted rifle in his well-muscled arms. He wore a yellow T-shirt, across the chest of which were bold, black letters that read:

BAYONET

When we had stopped before him, he grasped his rifle by the middle of the stock in his right hand and thrust it up in the air toward us as he yelled a question:

"What is the spirit of the bayonet?"

Before coming out here, our squad leaders had told us the correct answer, but nothing more. And our response was not overpowering:

"To kill!"

The man on the stand was hot.

"*I CAN'T HEAR YOU!*"

More of us shouted the response:

"*To kill!*"

"*I still can't hear you!*"

Now we all yelled from the depth of our bellies:

"*TO KILL!*"

"*That's more like it! Now, assume the stand I am in! This is called 'On guard.' Let me hear you growl!*"

"*AARRRRGH!*"

"*Louder!*"

"*AARRRGH!*"

"*That's better! What is the spirit of the bayonet?*"

"TO KILL!"

"I will now demonstrate the short thrust series from the 'On Guard' position. You will take one short step forward with your left foot, at the same time . . ."

What followed was our repeating the exercises he demonstrated for us: short thrust, long thrust, vertical butt stroke. Our squad leaders were moving through the formation, correcting our postures or the ways in which we held our rifles. But the exercises went on, in all of which we practiced using our bayoneted rifles as instruments of brutal death for our adversary. And we were constantly urged to growl louder as we lunged, driving forward with our rifles and seeking to plunge our bayonets into the belly of an imagined foe standing in front of us, or to strike a downed adversary in the head with a butt stroke as we stepped over him.

Periodically, the man on the stand who was demonstrating the correct way to use these newfound weapons would again ask us:

"What is the spirit of the bayonet?"

And again, our answers had to ring out before he would allow us to return to our regimented practice:

"TO KILL!"

As we grew tired, of course, our voices weakened, which only seemed to infuriate the man on the platform even more. And as he yelled, we yelled back in our own raging fury. But it didn't take long before that fourteen-pound bayoneted rifle seemed to have grown to weigh a hundred pounds.

Bayonet drill was hard work, with a heavy weapon. And as we began to sweat, our emotions also began to flow. Soon enough, we got swept up in an emotional tide, and we really did want to kill someone, to drive that bayonet into his belly and crack him in the skull with our rifle butt as we stepped over him.

After an hour that seemed like a century, bayonet drill ended. We would go through the same drill three times each week for the rest of Beast Barracks. But that first time, after we had returned to our barracks rooms and started to shine equipment before the next formation, I began to think about what we had just gone through.

This wasn't like high school calculus class, and I certainly hadn't joined the Peace Corps. No, the business of this profession really was to kill enemy soldiers. But only at that moment did the full truth begin to dawn on me.

The spirit of the bayonet is to kill! And the bayonet was the symbol of the profession I was entering. But was that what I really wanted? Could I actually kill someone? I knew, of course, that in war people were killed. But could I kill someone?

As I quickly reassessed my presence at West Point, I began to realize that this single theme underlay all the handsome uniforms and the impressive demeanor of the cadets I had seen back home in Arkansas. I had voluntarily sought to emulate those cadets, to follow in their footsteps to West Point. But the underlying theme of West Point, so often and easily unrecognized by outsiders, is killing enemy soldiers. Was that really what I wanted?

Upon reflection, no. But would I do it? Yes. Yes, and they would do it to me. I could picture the scene in my mind, the quick thrust and parry, the desperate struggle from which only one would emerge alive.

Yes, I would accept this, not because I sought it, or would revel in it, but because it might become necessary. It was what defending the country might ultimately come down to, and I was determined that a democracy like ours that was often threatened by nondemocratic societies, had to be defended. In accepting an appointment to West Point, I had chosen that path. Dealing death to enemy soldiers really was the solemn truth that underlay my every moment at West Point, and that of every other cadet as well. It was a solemn realization, but one that was seldom acknowledged, except when I thought back to the Spirit of the Bayonet.

In the last few days of Beast Barracks, we set out on the Plebe Hike. Dressed in fatigues and field gear, we marched far out into the woods somewhere on the vast West Point military reservation for three days of field training. We set up our pup tents and then were inspected and harassed, something we had almost taken for granted. But this time, we really would be acting like soldiers in the field.

Elements of the 101st Airborne Division had been brought to West Point from Fort Campbell, Kentucky, to train the class ahead of us, the men who had just completed their own plebe year and were then undergoing more intensive military training out at Camp Buckner. But some of these paratroopers spent a few days with us, teaching us the rudiments of infantry squad drill. Finally, I thought, we are getting to act like soldiers. And after two months of constant harassment in Beast Barracks, I was actually thrilled by the change, as was the case for most of the other New Cadets.

We were trained at different stations in various rudimentary military techniques, like setting up ambushes, rifle platoon and squad maneuvers, all the basic stuff that was completely new to most of us. As we moved from station to station, we marched or ran in formation, and we usually sang as we moved.

The songs were filled with tales of the sort of bawdy behavior soldiers always sing about: "Ain't no use in cryin' alone, Jody's got your girl and gone," or "I know a girl who lives on a hill . . ." or even "There once were three gay caballeros." These songs were laced with the sort of obscenity common to soldier talk and as such inspired a sense of manliness, bravery and rebellion.

The men who trained us at these different stations were themselves young enlisted soldiers, privates or specialists, and they were often not much older than we were. It was clear they had been told to treat us roughly, so there was always a certain amount of yelling over trivialities to be expected when we got to each new station. But even though we were raw New Cadets, once we got out of the barracks and were actually out in the woods learning to be soldiers, we were still full of joy and even exuberance.

That was probably the first moment when we began to coalesce as a class, to feel that we were a team, and that we could stand up to the world, if need be, and never back down. It was mostly our movements in formation through the summer forest that gave rise to these feelings, raw energy ready to burst through our chests as life burned our cheeks and those gay, bawdy ballads spilled in loud chorus from our lips, throats, and lungs. Even though we knew we were going back to finish a hellacious Beast Barracks and be dumped into the unknown Corps of Cadets within only a few days, it was good then to be alive and laughing and singing, truly a band of brothers as we loped though the sun-splashed forest of upstate New York!

Then more harassment was at hand. After being awakened in the pitch dark one morning, we were told that our base camp was being attacked by the enemy, and we had to make a forced march of fifteen miles to rescue our rear element. This was the setup for the well-known Plebe Hike we had all been warned to dread. However, my squad leader had told us that, although it would be tough, he expected all of us to make it.

And we did.

The march was led by an old sergeant who carried no load other than a walking stick, and he walked fast, but at a steady pace. There was no drum or other regular marching step used for this movement; everyone went at his own pace. The men of our class strung out behind this sergeant in a column of twos, New Cadet company after New Cadet company, all of us carrying packs loaded with tents and blankets and other camping paraphernalia, and web gear from which hung canteens and folding shovels.

The result was a long, accordion-like movement. And the pressure was incessant from squad leaders walking along the side of our formation and hectoring us as we moved along as well as from other upperclassmen of the Beast Barracks cadre, none of whom carried any field gear. "Hurry up! Move it up! Close up the ranks! Don't let the man in front of you get away! Catch up, Mister!"

We found ourselves constantly running to catch up to the man in front of us, then trying to catch our breath for a few steps before the gap widened and, once again, we had to run. The pressure was unbearable. But we also were helping each other, particularly the weaker men who started to fall out of formation. And I found myself somehow stronger than I had expected as we all reached out a hand to pull a fading classmate along.

"Come on, John. You can make it!"

"No, I can't, I think I'm . . . I can't breathe! I've got to stop."

"No, you don't! Here, grab the strap of my pack and let me pull you along."

Then another classmate would take the weaker man's rifle, or shout encouragement to him. We were in this together, and no one would fall out if we could help it. This was more training in what we had been learning all along during Beast: You sink or swim as a class, and if one of you is weaker, it is your job—it is your *duty*—to help him along. And it was probably when the going got tough on our Plebe Hike that we realized the depth of that class bond, and classmates began to become closer than brothers.

Then, after three or four hours of torture, we were moving in the North Gate and on to the academy grounds. The pace slowed dramatically, and we all began to catch our collective breaths and close ranks. Stragglers caught up, and the last guys were closing ranks as we rounded the curve and the broad expanse of the Plain came into view.

Then, up front, a drum could be heard, and we all automatically fell into step. Around the long corner we came, dirt from the field staining our soaked fatigues, sweat streaming down our grime-caked faces. We had made it! And we were happy.

No, more than happy. We were proud.

Trophy Point and the Hudson were off to our left, the superintendent's house on our right, Washington Hall and the barracks of Central Area in front of us as we stepped onto the Plain, and then marched past the superintendent and his staff. I know we were a sight, but then again, we were soldiers coming in from the field, and spit and polish was not in order. Performance of our duty was. And we had done just that, having survived the notoriously difficult Plebe Hike.

At that moment, passing in review, we were a proud, bonded class.

We had finally come to the end of Beast Barracks, and before we broke ranks and returned to our rooms that day, we were told that we had earned the right to be accepted into the Corps of Cadets. From then on, we would no longer be called New Cadets. Rather, we were now full-fledged plebes. But our Beast company commander didn't want us to forget our place, and he asked his loud question of the hundred men in our company:

"And what do plebes outrank, smackheads?"

By this time, we knew how to sound off, and we even knew the correct answer:

"Sir, we outrank the waiters in the mess hall, the superintendent's dog, the commandant's cat, and all the admirals in the whole damned navy!"

"That's right, and don't you forget it. Dismissed!"

During Beast Barracks, all new cadets had been quartered in the barracks around Central Area. When the upperclassmen came back on the very next day, we were all assigned in groups of about thirty each to one of the twenty-four lettered companies in the two regiments that made up the Corps of Cadets. As such, we reported in to our new companies and moved to our new quarters. Some of these were found in Central Area, but they were also in Old North Area, New North Area, Old South Area, New South Area, and East Barracks, and the Lost Fifties. Assigned to Company E–2, I moved into Central Area.

And when the rest of the Corps returned, the biggest change, I suppose, was that the numbers changed. It was no longer a case of one upperclassman for every four or five new cadets. No, now, even though we were officially plebes, there were three upperclassmen for each of us. And although by now used to bracing, plebe year was hard.

Very hard.

≈

It was challenging on a psychological level as well, and many of our number realized that they had bitten off more than they could chew. By the end of plebe year, nearly one-quarter of my classmates had backed out and walked away. Most of those who quit headed home for a more "normal" college education. I, too, considered it once, but never very seriously, for I had achieved my greatest wish. Now, I was a West Point cadet. I was in. To me, that meant that no matter how much they harassed me, I wasn't going to let them run me out. And, by God, I wasn't going to quit!

During plebe year, we learned that West Point was all about self-discipline. You only felt the regimentation if you lacked the self-discipline to do what had to be done on your own initiative. Set goals and work hard to meet them. Get up early, focus on the daily math test, scan the assignments just before class. Focus, memorize, concentrate, perform. Again and again.

West Point was also about teamwork. "Cooperate and graduate!" was the first motto we learned. You taught each other, coached each other, helped each other. There were no individual stars. No one stood out from his classmates. The mission came first, then the team, then everyone else, and finally you. If someone couldn't keep up on a run, you helped them along. If they couldn't carry their gear on a hike, you carried it for them. If they couldn't march, you carried them. If they didn't understand the math, you tutored them. You did everything possible to help others: you left no one behind.

But West Point was also very competitive. Varsity athletes ate better and escaped the harassment of having to eat at "company tables" (this was a very important consideration to plebes, because if you were on an academy Corps Squad team, you ate at special Corps Squad tables, where plebes did not have to brace). Off-post privileges for upperclassmen were handed out on the basis of achievement. In most subjects, tests and examinations were given daily, or very frequently, and academic grades were publicly posted in the sally ports every week. We were even seated in the classrooms on the basis of academic standing. Awards were given, and, of course, there was "cadet rank," bestowed on the "firsties"—cade sergeants, lieutenants, and captains—on the basis of peer evaluations and tactical officer ratings. Cadets who underperformed, or were rated at the bottom of their peer group, were separated. They were sent home, dismissed as failures, which was not a happy lot for anyone. West Point was an achievement-training factory, full of pressure and stress. You were trained to succeed in the toughest environment.

By the end of that first year, I'd made strong friendships, qualified as expert with a rifle, learned boxing and wrestling, seen Greenwich Village a couple of times, and broken up with my high school girlfriend. I'd earned my freshman numerals in swimming and stood at the top of the class in academics. Analytic geometry, linear programming and matrices, calculus, Russian, geography, engineering drawing—they just came easily to me. And best of all, I truly admired other cadets I'd come to know who were members of different classes. Barry McCaffrey and John Pickler, both of whom went on to long Army service and many stars; Buddy Bucha, a swimmer who later won a Congressional Medal of Honor in Vietnam; and Mike Kilroy, our varsity swim team captain who was later killed in Vietnam, these were all men whose example had a powerful effect on me.

Early June 1963 was glorious. The weather finally warmed up, the trees burst into bloom, and plebe year was finally over. In a ceremony after the Graduation Parade, all the upperclassmen in my company of about one hundred cadets had shaken hands with the members of my class individually. Now we were no longer fourth classmen, or plebes; now we were third classmen, or yearlings. Now we could call the men who had been upperclassmen to us before by their first names, for we were upperclassmen ourselves. And no more bracing! It was an unbelievably joyful feeling for all of us. In my rosy glow, I walked a couple of dates around the academy, laughing and flirting. But no real spark hit me. And in a couple of days, I'd be heading back home for the first time in a year.

After a month of vacation, we came back to West Point in early July for seven weeks of field training at Camp Buckner, a clump of open barracks nestled on Lake Popolopen, a dozen miles out in the wild mountains on the western side of the West Point reservation. Patrolling, land navigation, communications, artillery and mortar fire direction, armor training, a helicopter-borne assault, and hand-to-hand combat training in a big pit of sawdust, that was the diet of our days. We had some pretty good runs every morning, and as we ran, our almost-carefree singing echoed through the forested hills.

Every weekend, girls came up from New York City, some fifty miles away. We had movies, a private beach with rowboats and canoes, and a dance Saturday evenings in screened-in Barth Hall on the edge of the lake. There was no alcohol, of course, but the social situation wasn't bad at all, even if you had to depend on a blind date with a complete stranger arranged by the Cadet Hostess, Mrs. Holland. We called that "going through the Holland Tunnel:" sometimes you struck out, but other times, you might hit one out of the park.

Through our plebe year, upperclassmen told us that our summer at Camp Buckner would be the best time we'd ever have at West Point. And it was. The camp itself was quite delightful, particularly on weekends, but I also discovered something very important about myself there: it was at Buckner that I found a real aptitude for soldiering. You had to be physically fit and able to quickly pick up new skills and think on your feet. Truly, I enjoyed it more than anything else I had ever done.

At the end of the summer I was selected as best cadet in First Company (there were six companies), and was sent up to the colonel in command to be interviewed for Best Third-Classman at Camp Buckner.

"Where are you from?" he asked, "What did you like best at Camp Buckner? How did you find your classmates?"

All seemed to be going well.

"And what could be done to improve the training here, Mr. Clark?" the colonel asked. He was a graduate himself, with over twenty years in the service.

To me, Camp Buckner was about focus and purpose, so I told him what I felt.

"Well, sir, I think you should get rid of the parades on Saturday mornings. They're a waste of time and effort. We could do more out in the field instead."

I saw a sudden cold pallor come over his face. Wrong answer!

"Thank you, Mr. Clark. That'll be all."

A couple of years later I found out that instituting those parades was his special contribution that summer, and he'd overridden several recommendations to the contrary. But, he had asked, and I told him what I thought.

Shortly after academics began, Jon Persson, Charlie Moore, Jack LeCuyer and I were called in by a group of instructors in the Department of Social Sciences. These men were the Army and Air Force captains and majors on the faculty who had been Rhodes scholars. "You men can become Rhodes scholars," they said, "you have all shown that you have what it takes, and you should try to do it. But you'll have to work for it."

These men became our mentors, along with some other thoughtful officers. Men you could look up to, who you might openly question and debate, and whose opinions could be trusted and respected. They seemed to know a great deal about the Army, our government, and much of the world. They even invited us into their homes to meet their families. These men pulled us into their orbit.

We each added intercollegiate debate to our schedules. It was the twenty-second of November that we were en route to our first debate tournament in Burlington, Vermont, flying in a military aircraft, when for some unknown reason, we turned away. Word came back to the passengers, but with no explanation. Not only that, but the pilots told us they couldn't find out why we were refused either.

We circled over Lake Champlain for an hour. When we finally landed, they told us all air traffic had been held in place because President John F, Kennedy had been shot and killed in Dallas. That was a blow to all of us, and the significance of the debate shrank rapidly in our minds.

But we tried to pull ourselves together, and we somehow made it through the debate tournament on Friday and Saturday. The leaves were gone from the trees, and there was maple sugar candy, a novelty I'd never seen growing up in the South. This was my first debate trip, really my first escape into a more normal university setting since I'd arrived at West Point sixteen months before. We slouched through a couple of parties that weekend at the university, once sitting in a basement room, sipping beer with some ROTC cadets. But there was no joy. We were stunned, cadets and college students alike. Kennedy was our beacon, our hope, our idealized father. And now he was gone.

Back at the academy, we learned that one of the plebes had said in formation something to the effect that Kennedy had deserved it. That was a jolt to most of us when we heard it, but I think we all understood that Kennedy had won a close election, and that not everyone liked him. But the cold-blooded murder of the president who was a true hero to so many—this was truly frightening.

Kennedy was more than just our president; he was the commander in chief of all cadets, and we loved him. And this was America. Presidents shouldn't get assassinated, we all felt, even with the deep divides in our society over racial issues and in spite of the supposed presence of Communists in our midst. Now, all of a sudden, in the wake of Kennedy's assassination, our secure world suddenly seemed less certain, and the future seemed somehow darkly threatening

∿

Over the next three years, we traveled to dozens of different campuses, often missing classes on Friday and then returning before the mandatory Sunday evening meal in the dining hall. We broke out of West Point's isolation, making friends and meeting peers at top schools across the country. And we had long conversations with the officer coaches who took us to the tournaments. Eventually I decided to drop swimming so as to keep up with the debate team. But it was this experience, perhaps as much as anything at West Point, that bonded me to the military and enabled me to take a long view of my potential service—to see beyond my first duty assignment as a lieutenant—and to ask critical questions about the academy and the Army.

∿

"Do you think I look like James Bond?" my roommate asked, admiring his strong jaw in the mirror as he slapped on his Aqua Velva before heading out for a date. John T. McKnight, my roommate that year, was from Georgia, from a military family. He was a diver on the swimming team with me, but he was also a fiercely competitive boxer. Every year, he was always in heated contention for the light-heavyweight title in the much celebrated winter Brigade Open Championships.

That competition was open to all cadets. All you had to do was sign up, get assigned to a weight class, and fight your way up through the preliminary matches. And in many ways, these fights represented the bare essence of West Point: two men the same size inside a ring, each trying to batter the other's brains out. Losing such a match was a downer, of course. But winning meant elation beyond reason.

The competition in the Brigade Opens was nothing short of ferocious. If you entered, of course, everyone knew that you had to be sure to have worked out in preparation. That was because, when you stepped into the ring, you could be sure you would face some wild tiger who was just your weight and size. Heaven help the man who had signed up on a lark.

As the competition moved through preliminaries, stories about individual cadets in the ring coursed through the Corps of Cadets. Then, when the Brigade Championship Finals were held on a Saturday night in the main gym, they drew a larger crowd than any other sports competition save only football games. And that year, John McKnight actually won the Brigade Opens at 175 pounds. To us, that one big win marked him as a true stud, and it was psychic glory enough for any cadet.

When John asked me if he looked like James Bond, of course, he meant Sean Connery in the movies. It was 1964, and his movie exploits as Agent 007 had captivated many of us. In truth, there was a fair resemblance between the two. And I figured that if any of us were likely to come close, it would be John.

"Yes," I told him, "you look like James Bond."

On Armed Forces Day, that May, all 2,400 cadets marched down Fifth Avenue in Manhattan, after which we were given a few hours of liberty in the city. It only seemed natural that John McKnight had found a naval midshipman's dance at the Commodore Hotel, that we could all, well, crash.

We arrived in early evening, drenched with perspiration from marching on a surprisingly warm May afternoon in New York. Several midshipmen and their dates were already there, and the bar was bustling. I was thirsty, and I knew just who to ask for barroom sophistication.

"John, how do I order one of those tall drinks that looks like lemonade and has the cherry and orange slice?" I asked. The drinking age was eighteen in New York State at the time, but back home in Arkansas, no alcohol was served in restaurants. I'd had a few beers, but I had never ordered a mixed drink.

"Just ask for a Manhattan," James Bond answered.

That's what I did, and just as I got my drink I noticed a very attractive young woman who had just walked in. I went over to her, and to strike up a conversation, I asked, "Can I get you a drink?"

"Sure," she said, "but what's the matter? You haven't touched your drink."

"Well, it isn't what I wanted," I explained. "I ordered a Manhattan, but they gave me this."

I looked down at it: short glass, brown liquor, no ice. There was a pause, and I looked up at her face and smiled. She smiled back, then introduced me to reality in New York City.

"That *is* a Manhattan," she said.

"Oh." The country boy comes to New York City. I flustered a bit, then just asked her what I should have ordered. "A Tom Collins," she answered. She was very cool, and not impressed. This wasn't Hall High School, either, I sensed. But then she said "I'll have a rye and soda."

I learned her name was Gertrude Kingston, or Gert for short. We talked and danced, and as she was leaving I invited her to come up to the swimming team picnic the next weekend at West Point. She said, "Maybe." But she also gave me her telephone number. It was a beginning, and it has lasted forty-three years.

That summer, I was assigned to Army Orientation Training with a real U.S. Army unit in Germany. For a month I served as a platoon leader, just as if I were already a second lieutenant. I learned about talking to troops, fixing broken-down tanks, and a little more about maneuver and gunnery. The leadership part felt familiar, for it was what I had wanted: it was like being a camp counselor again, but with more challenges and a very direct and immediate purpose.

A ten day vacation trip to Russia followed, complete with confrontations with KGB watchers and conversations with Russian soldiers as well as with dogmatic guides and museum curators. But those experiences only served to focus my commitment even more. That August, the Gulf of Tonkin incident made headlines worldwide. We learned the news in the Metropole Hotel in Leningrad, only to see the Soviet propaganda guns turned on America.

When I returned to West Point, I changed my academic focus. I would no longer strive to become a theoretical physicist. Instead, I would work to master strategy and international relations. War and Peace.

In the fall of 1965, I competed for a Rhodes scholarship. There was an essay to write, letters of recommendation and transcripts to be sent in, and an interview in Little Rock. That was followed by a tougher interview in New Orleans, on a warm, rainy Saturday just before Christmas.

Only thirty-two Rhodes scholarships were given to Americans each year (by geographical region, not by school), and in my regional competition, there were twelve of us in the running for four of them. I was up against several Harvard guys, some from other good schools, and a Naval Academy midshipman named Steve Abbot. He was captain of the squash team and stood seventh in his class.

We were interviewed and several of us were reinterviewed. What about Vietnam? Why fight there when you have Communists ninety miles offshore in Cuba? Tell us about your trip to Russia, and the people you met?

In late afternoon, one of the men came out of the interview room and read off the names of those selected. Three Harvard men and me. I swooned a little when the results were announced. For me, it was a life-changing opportunity. It was the end of the beginning, in a way, and the rest of that year fell into place with all the magic of a clearing sky after days of rain. Everywhere I looked I saw rainbows, from the papers I was still writing in my courses to lifelong friendships to my deepened sense of commitment to public service through what we quaintly called "the profession of arms."

My nearly four years at the U.S. Military Academy had begun to come into some meaningful focus. From the outside, West Point was all about the color, the ceremony, the shining brass, the flashing bayonets affixed to rifles as cadets passed in parade; truly, for visitors, it could look like the stuff of fairy tales. Or a regimented nightmare. But from the inside, it was much, much more.

For me, West Point had been a time of preparation, of learning, of stoic endurance while I sharpened my own sense of purpose. I made strong, lasting friendships there with men I truly admired, men with whom I had shared the most harrowing and rigorous experiences, men I knew I could always rely on and trust in a later time and place. Yes, at graduation we would all become second lieutenants and full-fledged members of that Long Gray Line. And the men that I was being mentored by—the members of the Social Sciences Department—were captains and majors, all on fast tracks to influential positions, and they would be called upon to be soldiers and scholars, soldiers and statesmen, soldiers and diplomats. They knew history and art and music; they could discuss philosophy and foreign cultures. They encouraged us to think in decades, not in months, and to discuss campaigns, not just firefights.

The mission of the academy then was to prepare its graduates for a lifetime of service, not just to produce capable lieutenants. And they delivered on that mission. But I never lost sight of the Spirit of the Bayonet: it was always clear that we had to be soldiers first.

This reality was brought somewhat brusquely to the attention of our class one evening in February 1966. At supper that night, all first classmen were told to report to South Auditorium at 1930 hours for a special lecture.

When we filed into the auditorium, on the stage before us we were somewhat surprised to see Jack Price, a man who had graduated from West Point in 1964, a man many of us had known when he was a cadet. On this evening, he was wearing his Army green uniform, but he had his coat draped over his left shoulder, for his left arm and shoulder were heavily bandaged.

On the left shoulder of that uniform, he wore a blue patch with a white wing holding a red sword, topped by a tab that read AIRBORNE. This badge was that of the vaunted 173rd Airborne Brigade, a few thousand paratroopers who were all then serving in Vietnam. Over his left breast, he wore the prestigious silver musket on a blue background, all wreathed in silver: the Combat Infantryman Badge, which meant, reasonably enough, that he had served in combat as an infantryman. He also wore a few medals, but we couldn't help noticing that among his decorations was a Purple Heart. The Purple Heart is awarded for wounds suffered in combat.

When we were all seated, a major approached the microphone in the center of the stage and introduced our guest. As we all knew by then, he told us that Lieutenant Price had graduated from West Point in the class of 1964, and about a month earlier, he and his platoon had been caught up in a major firefight in Vietnam, a firefight in which he had been seriously wounded. He had come up from Walter Reed Army Hospital in Washington, D.C., that day, with the specific purpose of sharing his experiences with us.

The auditorium was hushed as Lieutenant Price approached the microphone, but he spoke to us as his contemporaries, in an almost conversational voice. Before getting into the specifics of combat he had experienced, he gave us a direct and perhaps chilling warning: When you get to Vietnam and are about to enter combat, he said, don't try to be a hero right away. There will be plenty of opportunities for you to be a hero down the line, moments when you will *need* to be a hero. But that moment won't come right away, and it would be tragic for any of you to get killed out of eagerness before you even know what's going on.

As he went into the details of how his unit was brought under fire while crossing an open space and how he and his men had returned fire and reacted, his warning resonated deep inside me. This was what it was all about. As I waited to graduate and be commissioned, I could only see that this was a man who had become a blooded warrior. And we all knew that, soon enough, many of us would walk that same path.

As we sat there, he told us in almost casual terms about the blood-and-guts scenes in which he had been involved, the cold fear he had felt and suppressed, the life-and-death decisions he had made—had been forced to make—in split seconds. This was beyond real, and his words simply grabbed us all by the throat and squeezed hard.

I remember vividly when he said, "So I just put my weapon on rock 'n' roll . . ." He was talking about the M–16 rifle with which all our troops in Vietnam were armed, and he obviously meant that he had put the selector switch on automatic fire. But this was a weapon we had not even held as yet, and we were simply stunned by his words, by glimpses of the bone-chilling terror that must come with being personally under fire, by thoughts of the raw power that gorges your body and floods your senses as you spray bullets at an enemy.

After he had answered a few questions from the audience and accepted our applause, we put our overcoats and hats back on and slowly filtered out into the driving snow, making our way back to the barracks. I remember stopping in the empty street and talking with classmates about what we had just heard. One of them was my roommate, Art Parker. This is what it's all about, we said as we looked at each other. Almost four years after the anxiety of entering West Point, this would be our next challenge. Lieutenant Price's talk had been sobering, but we had confidence now that we would be up to the task.

Art would be killed in Vietnam two years later.

Thirty-one members of our Class of 1966 were to be killed in that war, and many more grievously wounded. That night we all had our first sense of what the short-term future really held in store. That night, as we left the auditorium, some of us silently and some of us openly reaffirmed our commitments to each other and to our country. From that moment on we were the Long Gray Line. And I was very proud to be part of it.

So, this was West Point. Take several hundred talented, inspired young people. Find out first who's got the motivation and guts to stick with something that proves to be very difficult. Break down some of their ego, so that they're able to learn more about themselves, about just how much more they can accomplish under pressure than they thought possible. Let them learn about each other when they have been forced to drop their normal social masks and other defenses. Help them find larger purposes in life. Let them experience military reality from the bottom, learning first how to take orders and sense the difference between good leadership and bad. Give them the broadest possible academic education in science and mathematics, so they'll be able to keep up with a lifetime of booming growth in technology. Teach them enough in the fields of history, literature, and social sciences so that they will see life from a broader perspective. And above all, imbue them with the bedrock principles of Duty, Honor, Country.

The "Country" was pretty straightforward. It meant patriotism, selfless service to our nation, especially service in uniform while protecting our people from the ravages of war or the numbing fear or overwhelming intimidation that could destroy the independence, values, rights, and freedoms that are distinctively American.

The "Honor" was more difficult, even a little tricky. It wasn't about morality *per se,* nor was it about military glory. Rather, it was a code of trust, of speaking straight and not tolerating the kind of lying, cheating, or stealing that might undercut your unit or even the Army as an institution. It applied to the big things, but also to the smaller issues in life. You didn't cheat a waitress on your bill at a restaurant, you didn't steal a dollar from your roommate's wallet, you didn't steal a tool from a motor pool. You didn't evade a proper question—did you shine your shoes this morning? And you didn't break an Army regulation you had promised to obey. On the other hand, there was nothing about "Honor" that said you couldn't speed on the Palisades Parkway, sneak a beer or a girl into the barracks, or tell your hostess you loved the brussels sprouts even if you didn't. This was the "Honor" we learned at West Point.

But the real gut-grabbing word that stuck with us was "Duty." Responsibility. Obligation. You did your duty, no matter how inconvenient, no mater how difficult, no matter how dangerous. Duty before self. Duty—your mission—even before the welfare or very lives of the men and women serving under you. And you took the larger view of "Duty". It wasn't just a specific set of instructions—it was service loyal to the purposes of the unit, of the US Army, of the nation. And that might mean taking the initiative in that service. We learned that in the "5th General Order" we memorized as plebes learning interior guard duty: "to take charge of this post and all government property in view." You learned it in the hand-to-hand combat training at Camp Buckner, when it was your *duty* to step forward and attack. You learned it in class and after-hour discussions and while reading military history And if West Point and the other service academies do their jobs, they'll imbue their cadets and midshipmen with that strong sense of duty that has animated so many of us.

It was this idea of Duty that drove the Honor and Country. It was purpose—a sense of mission larger than oneself that would animate us throughout our lives. It was a gift, really, to be able to work beyond the personal, for the benefit of others, including those of future generations. And, in some ways, it was a curse as well. One Army wife called us "military monks," meaning, I suppose, that we were willing, despite the hardships it often meant for our families, to make great sacrifices and endure unreasonable hardships in pursuit of a supposedly higher calling.

Devotion to "Duty, Honor, Country" resulted in a kind of cult with its own code of behavior, though it was nondenominational and profoundly secular. You put your trust and your very life in the hands of others. Religious faith could help us deal with the stresses and anxieties—and I sought the Almighty's help many times. But there was nothing in the code that made any of us distinctly Christian or anything else. This wasn't the Ten Commandments, after all. Rather, it was about building those who would le ad our armed forces into the future, in times of peace as well as of war. And it was a terribly powerful force in our hearts.

Today, West Point and the other service academies continue to educate and train outstanding young men and women for a career of service in the armed forces. And just as we did then, young men and women are reading the newspapers, being mentored by the faculties, hearing the war stories from recent graduates, and steeling themselves for the challenges that lie ahead. They hear the fractious arguments about Iraq, as we heard the arguments about Vietnam. But they understand that they will implement the policies of the commander-in-chief when they wear the uniform, not dispute them publicly. And they understand that the essence of American government is civilian control over the armed forces.

In the meantime, they do their best to juggle academic work, sports, extracurricular activities, and just plain growing up. As we identified with President Kennedy in my day, many of the young academy students and the recent graduates probably identify with the current commander in chief as he battles a skeptical news media and delivers a message that sounds like resolve and determination to many.

Years later, if the education and mentoring have the effect they should have, these same young people will come to reflect back on what they've been engaged in from an informed position. They'll always be proud of their units, but they may have much more nuanced positions on the larger strategy and policy. And it's that growth that we hope will provide the wisdom and judgment needed in America's armed forces in the future. Every general and admiral who will help protect our country ten, twenty, or thirty years in the future is already in uniform, or preparing to join, somewhere across America. And we want to bring the best into our nation's military.

FOUR

STANDING UP
FOR AMERICA

After graduation, I was commissioned a second lieutenant in the U.S. Army, along with the rest of my class. But they would go off to army careers, while my own would be delayed for two years while I attended Oxford University under my Rhodes scholarship. I had a few months free before sailing to England on the *Queen Elizabeth II,* and my mother, of course, wanted me to come home. But I had other plans.

By this time, Gert and I were quite close, and her father was an official with the Catholic Relief Services. Through him, I learned about "Summer in the City," a Neighborhood Youth Corps Program sponsored by the Catholic Archdiocese of New York.

I won't deny that I was young and in love and looking for some excuse to stay in New York City and spend more time with Gert. Luckily, her father had helped me find just the vehicle I needed: I became a "Summer in the City" leader in the South Bronx, with about a hundred teenagers to supervise in the area of Tremont and Third Avenues.

It was a transitional area, formerly Italian and Jewish, becoming African American and Hispanic. I spent several weeks organizing trips to

Orchard Beach, playing stickball, and refereeing local quarrels and concerns. It was a matter of treating everyone with respect and demanding the same respect in turn.

When the local toughs with the rolled-up T-shirt sleeves catcalled from their cars, we asked them to join us. When they joined us, we asked them to demonstrate their competence in sports. And when they engaged, they found they had a lot in common with everyone else. And of course they lost their intimidation factor, too, when it became clear that some of us could hit a stickball farther than any of them.

After returning home and getting a very short haircut, I drove to Fort Benning, Georgia, for Airborne School. Many of my West Point classmates were there, and we compared notes on our graduation leaves while sharing the excitement of being brand-new second lieutenants. On our rare trips off post to grab fast food, we saw the groups of lonely wives and young children left behind when the 1st Cavalry Division deployed to Vietnam. I found it disturbing that the army, somehow, wasn't taking better care of them. They were required to leave the quarters on post where many of them had lived, and although their husbands were going off to war, their families got no special treatment. It was almost as if they had simply been abandoned by the army when the unit deployed, and that didn't reflect the army ethic that we had learned at West Point.

Three weeks later, I had just crossed the Arkansas River bridge headed back to Little Rock, jump school successfully completed, when I pulled into a filling station. In those days here was no self-service, and shortly the screen door swung open and a local fellow walked out. He caught a look at the New York license plates on my car, halted, and without a word went back inside.

"Uh, excuse me, could I get some gas?" I asked, my shaved head glistening in the afternoon sun.

"Not serving any Yankees" he said, and turned his back on me. My protests that I was from Little Rock didn't move him. I drove to another station, thinking about how some things apparently never change and how much I had learned from those teenagers in South Bronx.

With the other Rhodes scholars, I sailed the five-day voyage from New York to Southampton and we were bussed up to Oxford. It was a beautiful day in early October, the skies clear and the air crisp. The streets were bustling with traffic and the excitement of a new term was in the air. I found my way to Magdalen College, was shown the austere rooms in the eighteenth-century dormitory where I would live, and began to meet the other students, mostly British, with a sprinkling of South Africans and Rhodesians and a couple of other Americans.

Oxford consists of some thirty-nine independent colleges, each of which might be compared with one of the small liberal arts colleges across America. Oxford University was founded some time in the early twelve century—the exact timing remains a lively issue of debate for some—and has long been renowned as one of the great learning centers in the world.

There were about 16,000 students at Oxford University when I went there, spread across town in the colleges that provide their students with tutors, lodging, meals, libraries, sports and social facilities and play a sort of pastoral oversight role. My field of study was philosophy, politics and economics, known as PPE.

Every subject was taught at university lectures, but by far the most effective segment of my time at Oxford was spent with tutors one on one. You carried two subjects per eight-week term, and were assigned a series of books and a paper to write each week in each subject. You didn't buy books; you just went to the libraries and studied them there. And since the libraries weren't open very late at night, or on Sundays, there was plenty of time for other activities. I tried boxing and crew but went back to the sport I liked best, swimming, and along with my friends sampled the range of other activities. It was the exact opposite of West Point: pure freedom.

But I also missed Gert, who was working in New York, and I brought the ring home from England after my first term at Oxford. We went out to a fancy Italian restaurant in Manhattan, had a great time, and then as we were leaving, I remembered I had the ring with me. So I proposed in the backseat of a New York cab on the way back to her parent's apartment in Brooklyn. First Gert laughed at me, knowing that I had momentarily forgotten the reason I had planned that whole evening, and then she said yes.

Gertrude Kingston. She was beautiful, full of life, smart, and great with people. And she was especially great with me, for I had never before been so bedazzled by any other woman. We set the date for June, after I finished my first year at Oxford. We agreed that she'd give up her job as a secretary on Wall Street, fly to Oxford in time for the six-week break around Easter, and stay with my West Point friend and fellow Rhodes scholar Capt. Alex Hottell, and his wife, Linda. Under the terms of the Rhodes scholarship, I was required to live in the dorms for the remainder of my first year, and I wasn't allowed to marry.

Gert arrived a few weeks before the Easter break. We saw London together, drove the English countryside, crawled Oxford's pubs, visited palaces and museums. Then we took off for the Continent, first to visit army friends in Germany, and then to explore Italy. I bought road atlases and Italian dictionaries, and Gert laughed at my artless Italian.

"You have to use your hands more," she explained. "I can do better than you, and I don't have to say a word."

She was right.

On the advice of a friend, I had bought an inexpensive British sports car, a Morgan Plus–4 Drop-Head Coupe, a few weeks after I arrived in Oxford. It was not particularly fast, and not very practical, but it had been made by hand, and had all sorts of exotic features, such as the windscreen held in place by a sturdy ash wood frame, rather than the metal used in all American cars. I thought it was cool, and so did Gert, but I'd never been a car person.

Gert and I were wedged tight in the car as we bounced along the highways in Germany, the expansion joints in the old concrete autobahns jolting the car's stiff suspension to the point that the body threatened to break apart. We skidded through snow and slush in Switzerland, drove over some perilous heights with spectacular views of the Alps, then down through the Brenner Pass and into Italy the week before Easter.

It was a nice holiday. We drove down the Mediterranean coast, lazing along the beachfront and stopping wherever it fit our fancy. We stayed a few days at the Isle of Capri, where I saw the bluest, clearest, most beautiful water I'd ever seen. Then we came back to Rome and crowded into St. Peter's Square to see the pope and receive his blessing. Before we left, we made sure to take in some of the city's other dazzling sights, like the Colosseum, the catacombs, the Trevi Fountain, and we even made it to the Appian Way. At every stop, friendly Italians would come out to look at our odd little British car.

To save money, we drove back through the Brenner Pass at night and soon made it back to our army friends in Germany. A day later, we left in the morning for the long drive to Ostend, Belgium, there to catch the ferry back to England.

For both of us, it was the first time we'd ever felt totally free, away from our families, obligations, and, really, any concerns. Americans were well-loved in Europe, Vietnam was a long way away, and my lieutenant's pay of $222.30 per month, plus a little more for housing and food, seemed like a fortune.

We got to Ostend late at night and found we had missed the last ferry. Our youthful frolic would not be slowed even by this, and we decided to drive on, west along the channel, then catch a ferry from a French port very early the next morning.

As we started down the coastal road, the light sprinkle we were in grew into an unexpected blizzard of blowing snow, sleet, and rain. But that didn't matter to us: We were in love, and this was an exciting adventure together. As I was bragging to Gert about the car's nice little heater that kept us snug and dry in a growing storm, the engine began to cough and sputter. It was about 2:00 A.M. Then, as we held our breaths, the little engine just died. Right there on the coast, with sand and ocean spray howling across the road.

And we were all alone, the road dark and deserted.

But I was not going to give up. Okay, things didn't look too good. But, after all, this was just the sort of thing West Point had prepared me for, wasn't it? An unforeseeable crisis hits you at an unexpected time, and you alone must devise a way out of trouble. It wasn't really like it was going to be what I would call fun, but I could almost feel my spirit rising to the challenge.

I quickly reviewed my options. There were no lights anywhere, no sign of life, and we had no idea how far down the road we might have to go to get help. The last town behind us was at least a half hour's drive away, but leaving Gert was out of the question, so I decided we would keep going in the same direction. I would get out and push the car to get it rolling down the road, then trot alongside it while Gert steered. Maybe it wasn't the final answer, but at least it would be a start. And hopefully, another car would soon come along to our rescue.

Having decided on a plan, I told Gert that I would get out and push the car, and that as soon as I left my seat, she should slide over behind the wheel and steer. I opened the door and stood up into a hard, wet wind, a howler that just took my breath away. But before I could close the door, Gert grabbed my hand. She had to yell to make herself heard, to remind me that she was a true New York City girl:

"But, Wes, I don't know how to drive!"

I had to yell back as I reassured her:

"That's okay, honey. You can handle this. Those two pedals on the floor are the clutch and the brake, but the car is in neutral, so leave them alone. Just hold on to the wheel and try to keep us going straight! "

She smiled up at me, looking a bit unsure of herself. But I waved my hand and nodded, confident that she would be all right. All she had to do was steer; what could go wrong?

Then I closed the door, and suddenly, Gert and I were in two different worlds: hers was warm and dry, mine was cold and wet. I was wearing an English trench coat over a new woolen suit I had bought from a tailor on Savile Row, one of the few extravagances I spent money on for myself during my first year at Oxford. Despite the wind and water, the trench coat seemed to be keeping me dry at first, but I had no hat, and my head and hair were quickly soaked. I walked to the back of the car, planted my palms squarely on the trunk and gave a good push. The car didn't even move, and I lost my balance, slipping in the mud and falling to my knees.

I slowly stood back up, red-faced I am sure, and rubbed my palms off on my trench coat. So much for that new Savile Row suit, I thought. I put my hands back on the trunk, took a deep breath, and really leaned into the car. But again, nothing happened.

I paused to reassess things in my mind: Why isn't it moving? I'm no giant, but I'm certainly strong enough to get this light little English car rolling. Without my realizing it, an issue of pride was involved, of me being able to show Gert that I had the strength to get things going and at least play some kind of manly role in our rescue.

I spread my feet a little more, planted my feet firmly in gravel, lowered my hips so that I could push up as well as forward, and then gave it every bit of strength I had in my body. But again, the car didn't budge.

I stood up again, now embarrassed as I realized I was going to have to tell Gert that I just wasn't strong enough to get the car moving. I was thinking of how to say that when she rolled down the driver's window and looked back at me. Her shout was clear:

"Do you want me to keep pushing on the brake?"

After she had moved her foot, I was able to roll the car down the road. But there were still no lights, no buildings, nothing. And the trench coat I was wearing was made of tightly woven cotton, not plastic, so it really wasn't waterproof at all. All too soon, the trench coat and suit were soaked through in places, and I forgot about everything but staying at my task. Truly lashed to the wheel, I somehow just kept us poking along.

Another car finally came out of the storm. Fortunately, he stopped. It must have been obvious to him that I either desperately needed help or was a raving lunatic. We were lucky enough that he had a chain, which he hooked to our bumper, then towed us into a village just a few miles away. Nothing was open, of course. That meant that, pulled up in front of a local garage, we sat in the car for several hours as we waited for it to open in the morning.

I was exhausted from my night's work, but sleep eluded us both, as did small talk. I was madly in love, but I was also as miserable as I have ever been in my life. We sat there silently as I shivered, watching the black sky gradually soften to gray. Dear God, please let this garage open soon!

At 6:00 A.M., a man showed up, and he was able to give us the mechanical help we needed. It only took him a few minutes of work on the carburetors, and our Morgan started right up. We caught the morning ferry, and by early afternoon we were back in England, driving down the M–2 motorway past Canterbury, looking forward to getting back to Alex and Linda's place. It had never stopped raining, of course, but that didn't seem the slightest bit unusual; after all, we were back in England.

What started as a wonderful, blissful trip had ended somewhat unpleasantly on the Continent, but now we were almost home. We were driving along at the speed limit of seventy miles an hour and there were two big tractor trailer rigs ahead of us in the outside lane, moving slowly. I started to pass on the inside when, with no warning, the trailing truck swung out right in front of me. I jerked the wheel to go around him, but

I couldn't, we had gotten too close and things seemed to be moving at light speed. I managed to hit the brakes, but it was too late, and then we hit the right rear tire on his cab with our left rear tire.

That was all our light little Morgan needed, and it flipped like a kite. *"This can't be happening!"* flashed through my mind as I gripped the steering wheel. With no contact left between car and pavement, our whole world was whirling. We literally turned over, first taking out a solid signpost in the median with a front tire, then sliding upside down along a grassy strip at the side of the road.

The car finally stopped, then everything was silent. I was still upside down, hanging to the wheel for dear life, but at first didn't know where I was. And I could think only of what might have happened to the love of my life:

"Gert! Gert!"

"I'm right here, Wes. I'm okay, I just got a cut on my ankle."

I was surprised that her voice was so soft and calm. She was right side up, twisted around and lying on what was left of the shredded convertible top. There was wet soil inside the car, and I scrambled as I tried to get my feet under me so I could get out and try to push the car off of us.

But I also felt someone else lifting the car with me. I crawled out, breathless, and pulled Gert out. Then I turned to face a middle-aged man wearing a blue suit.

"I saw you flip over onto the center strip, and I stopped to help," he said. "What happened to you?"

The truck hadn't stopped, and apparently no one else had even seen it. It was our great luck that the Morgan's ash frame on the windshield had acted like a roll bar, literally saving our lives. But the little sports car was totally destroyed.

Gert spent the night in a Rochester hospital, and the next morning we rented a car and completed our drive. When we finally got to their house, Alex and Linda were still away on vacation, though we had a key. Gert's ankle was more than cut: She was now in a cast up to her knee and couldn't put weight on that foot. And I was sick from that night of exposure on the French coast.

Next morning, in an apparent attempt to add to our misery, the bobbies came around to threaten me with arrest for not having returned the rental car that day. We had already discovered that there was no food in the house, and after I had turned the car in, we had no means of transportation. And to just top things off, we had no cash.

It was a rough few days. The bathroom was upstairs, the kitchen was downstairs, and I carried Gert back and forth in a dizzying fever. Finally, she looked up at me as I was carrying her and said:

"If we can make it through this, honey, we can make it through anything."

And she was right: We've been together for forty years now, and we're still going strong.

We married in June, honeymooned in Puerto Rico for a week, and then spent the rest of the summer idling in a little house on the lake in Hot Springs, Arkansas. I puttered at reading British history and economics, but mostly we water-skied, fished, watched TV, and generally loafed. Friends came by to visit. The water was warm, and we idly drifted around the dock on floats reading paperbacks.

Every day seemed to laze by, the sun slowly dropping and the shadows growing across the lawn down to the dock while we cuddled and cooed on the porch. There was absolutely nothing wrong and nothing to worry about: not about parents, children, house, exams, money, or profession. Nothing. It was just us, and our spell was broken only when my parents and my grandmother came by on weekends. But that summer, we cared for no one and no thing in the outside world. That time was really all about nothing more than the two of us being together, in love, as the long days went by.

Then, like everything else in life, those six idyllic weeks were gone. When we got back to Europe, we bought a new car: a cute, practical, and even less expensive Opel Kadett. We picked it up at the factory in Germany, then took it on a quick trip to visit friends in Switzerland. From there, it was back to England on the ferry, then a very cautious drive up the M–2 highway. When we finally got to Oxford, we moved into a little house I'd rented there. It was my second year, same routine with the tutorials and the sports, but now Gert was alongside me.

That autumn we were visited by Maj. Powell Hutton, a West Point graduate from the Class of 1959. He was one of five Rhodes scholars the Military Academy had produced that year, and he had returned briefly to Oxford to help dedicate a music room at one of the colleges to Jim Ray, his best friend and a fellow West Point Rhodes scholar recently killed in Vietnam.

Powell took us to a nice restaurant near Oxford, and over roast beef and Yorkshire pudding, we talked about Oxford, West Point, the army, and Vietnam. He had already served there himself, and Jim Ray had died there. He was reflective and nostalgic, but was also very much the mentor as he looked over at Gert and me. He paused for a moment, then smiled at us:

"You know, you two are starting life with the dessert course."

That was something we had already begun to suspect. For all its reputation, study at Oxford wasn't too difficult, not after West Point. At least, it wasn't too difficult academically. But it was terribly difficult emotionally. Each week we'd scan the casualty lists printed in the *Army Times* newspaper, and too often find the names of classmates and friends. And at the same time, the Oxford environment was strongly antiwar and increasingly anti-American. Even my fellow Rhodes scholars had turned against our policy in Vietnam—and against our soldiers who were carrying it out.

But there were a few of us who stuck together and maintained our conviction that opposing the expansion of Communism was right and necessary. We also maintained our belief that somehow the Vietnam effort could be made to work out. Even so, I tried to keep friendships as best I could across the growing intellectual and emotional divide. It was a little like what I had already experienced over racial issues while growing up in Little Rock: Good people could profoundly disagree, and sincerity was no assurance of virtue.

And I carried the dialogue a step farther as a participant in the American embassy's speaker program, I was invited to speak at foreign policy debates across Britain. It was an interesting way to see the country, but not always without conflict.

In November 1967, Gert and I drove the little blue Opel to Hull, on England's eastern coast, for a teach-in sponsored by the Quakers. I was paired with an assistant from South Vietnam's embassy and spoke against the local member of Parliament, a Communist labor leader, a Pakistani Oxford-educated student leader, an American draft dodger, and several university faculty members.

It was one of those gloomy early winter days in England, the cold air damp and heavy with the sweet smell of burning coal, a thick cover of clouds, the streets slick with moisture, and people's cheeks bright with the chill. We began the teach-in at around two, with my wife Gert seated alone in the front row, some four hundred bundled-up spectators packed in behind, and a few bobbies standing in the back.

As the Quaker chairman moved to the podium, a group of Maoists began chanting, "Bobbies out! Bobbies out!" After a few minutes delay, the police quietly filed out the door. The chairman then indicated firmly that he was against this war, and against the Americans, and encouraged the audience to make their views known, too. I could see Gert shiver a little in the front row, but I knew I had at least one strong supporter.

The opposition began with the local Labour MP making a rousing fifteen-minute attack on America and South Vietnam. The audience applauded vigorously. I took the podium in rebuttal, to a respectful smattering of applause. The South Vietnamese official spoke briefly, admitted his wife thought he was crazy to defend his government's policies, and then announced he was leaving early, so I would be left on my own to rebut the next five speakers.

Interestingly, one of the key issues concerned the legitimacy of the South Vietnamese government. The government's opponents triumphantly quoted an alleged 1955 statement from then-president Eisenhower that North Vietnamese leader Ho Chi Minh would probably win any election.

But whether that was true or not, I countered, it was irrelevant. The country had been legally divided, and the South had its own president and elected leaders. There was no legal basis to justify the North's invasion. Still, it was a signal warning: If your policy takes you against the most powerful and popular leaders of a country—even a divided country—maybe you ought to be looking at who you're aligned with, and why. Or at least find another place to make a stand.

The program continued without pause until almost 8:00 P.M. when we finally adjourned. I had spoken five or six times, and been treated with respect by the audience, though it was clear they weren't agreeing with me. The Communist Party leader of northeast England graciously invited us over to his house for a light dinner, and we accepted, as we were expected to do.

A few minutes later we were in the party leader's comfortable home. As the "novelty" guest, we were fawned over and proselytized by our host. Seated in front of a cheery coal fireplace, he was explaining to Gert how women were much better treated under Communism. I was relaxed, enjoying the repartee and a pint of bitters, when I heard a commotion behind me.

"I'm going to kill you!" someone hissed.

I looked around. Was this some kind of a joke? There was a ruddy-faced fellow leaning in my direction, grimacing with threat— toward me!

"You're killing my comrades in Vietnam, and I'm going to kill you!"

I could see that this was no joke, at least not for him. All conversation suddenly stopped. I saw his naked hostility and felt my ears start to burn as I rose to my feet. There was a sofa between us, and I was judging angles and distance when the host also stood up and gave an order:

"Get him out of here! Lieutenant Clark is our guest."

But the evening was over. We left shortly thereafter, departing with a British couple who had volunteered to put us up for the night. But once we got back to their home, they showed little sympathy.

"You must understand," they said. "People over here are very angry."

Sure, I thought, but I won't accept this. We left early the next morning to drive back to Oxford, and I was more determined than ever to stand up for what I believed. Our troops in Vietnam were doing their duty, fighting against cross-border aggression aided and abetted by the Soviet Union and China. Standing up against that aggression was an American obligation, and this was where we determined to make the stand.

I respected our army, its soldiers and its leaders. They were as noble and high-minded a group of American warriors as had ever stood in harm's way. They weren't in it for spoils or adventure; it was a cause, the cause of protecting America and securing our freedoms. They were my classmates and faculty from West Point. They were good men. And they and our cause should be respected, not attacked.

I talked about the experience with my friend Alex Hottel one night. We agreed that what was worth living for was worth fighting and dying for. We would fight in Vietnam, and, yes there were personal risks. But we would accept them.

~

One day the next summer, a few weeks before we were due to leave Oxford for good, Gert told me that I had gotten a phone call from someone named Molly Friedman, a woman who claimed to be my cousin. Then she asked me if I had ever heard of any Jewish roots in my family. I was completely surprised by this, but I didn't really know much about my biological father's background, so I told her that it might be possible. Then I returned Molly's call.

We soon met Molly and her husband, Lester, and I learned about my father's side of the family. My father, Benjamin Kanne, was the son of Russian Jewish immigrants. Just before the turn of the century, his father Jacob had emigrated from Minsk, along with his brother, his fiancée, and her little sister, and had settled in Chicago. There were three brothers, and they had nineteen children of that generation. My father was the oldest.

A week later, another cousin called, and we had dinner with him and his family, too. He was my first cousin, Dick Cardozo, who hadn't seen me since I was four years old, and he filled in more of the story. Both families were passing through London on the way home from visits to Jerusalem, which had been captured by the Israelis in the Six-Day War the previous summer.

I was Jewish!

Well, not really, they explained. because to be Jewish by descent your mother has to be Jewish. But still . . .

I rolled the idea around in my mind, and it was stunning. I had a family with a past, at last. And a family to be proud of, a family that had courage and determination, a family that had made its way in a new land.

I was proud of them. And I was proud of my ethnic heritage, too, as I thought about the gallant soldiers of the Israeli Defense Force, and how they consistently fought and won, outnumbered and outgunned by hostile neighbors. I thought about the ethic of the kibbutz, and what I knew of Israel, of the West Pointer Mickey Marcus, who had supported the emerging state in the days after World War II.

Yes, it felt right to me. I felt complete, somehow, in a way I hadn't felt before. I was aching to go back to Chicago now and reconnect with the rest of my family, my father's five sisters, their children, and a younger brother and his family who lived in Arizona. I could hardly wait to tell Mom.

~

I came away from Oxford with an education. I had lived in another culture, where Englishmen could say and mean it, "What are laws for except to be obeyed?" It was a culture where Alex Hottell was once attacked by an elderly woman with an umbrella for trying to cut into a queue at a bus stop; a culture with a rigid class system, where excessive taxes drove the wealthy to spend lavishly on parties and gifts lest the money be taken by the government anyway, and to discriminate against those who lacked the proper accent; a country still struggling to recover its emotional bearings after winning a war and losing an empire. Yet it was also a country of enormous charm and wonderful people. And the fact that we didn't agree on everything stood as no bar to friendship. I learned once again that friendship is about mutual respect and common interests, not about identical perspectives.

I learned about my country, too. In Great Britain at the time, the United States was resented, misunderstood, and often maligned. You had to talk through the issues and help people see what was behind the headlines. But when you did, and if you spoke in a respectful and open manner, rather than defensively, you could often win their support.

But some things just weren't easily explained. That spring of 1968 Robert F. Kennedy and Martin Luther King Jr. were assassinated. Like many others, I was stunned: how could this have happened in our country? The image abroad was that America was out of control, and as the passion against the Vietnam War intensified, I felt less and less able to identify with emotions at home.

The public image of young Americans as angry and rebellious was far removed from my own personal experiences. I could feel my generation ripping itself apart. It was an extension of all the tensions I had understood about civil rights and justice, but now associated with countervailing passions and personal rebellion I had not experienced. The rampant anger was a world apart from me and most of my West Point classmates, from ideas of duty and protecting our country. It was time for me to head home, put on a uniform, and take up my army duties.

FIVE

VIETNAM

We had started hearing about Vietnam back in the early sixties at West Point, and a few of the faculty members had already been there. We read about the deepening war in the newspapers; we discussed it occasionally in class and often in the barracks at night. And by 1965, with the commitment of U.S. ground troops, we all knew, and kind of half-hoped, that we'd be going there. Yes, we'd heard all the scary talk about the Korean War: "The average life expectancy of a second lieutenant in combat is eleven seconds!" But personal combat was still out there for us, a sort of Holy Grail, and it beckoned. We were young warriors, and many of us wanted nothing more than to be tested in the heat of combat. It may sound strange now, but for many of us, there was a certain amount of adventure, even a thrill involved in the anticipation. In the words of President John F. Kennedy, we would "pay any price, bear any burden, meet any hardship, support any friend, oppose any foe, in order to assure the survival and the success of liberty." And in Vietnam, I was proud to be standing up for what I believed in.

But by the spring of 1968, this war was no longer abstract to me. My friends from West Point were in Vietnam, or had already returned home, or, while I was studying at Oxford, had already been killed there. Billy

Flynn, a toughened soldier when he came to the academy, died in a fierce fire fight only six months after graduation. My former roommate and close friend, Art Parker, who loved playing the Rolling Stones loud on his stereo and who, with his fiancée, Connie, double-dated with me and Gert to the Old Union Hotel for dinner and cigars in the soft May evenings before our graduation—Art was killed when he was hit by a helicopter blade while trying to save the life of a Vietnamese soldier. Rich Hood was killed by gunfire in the battle of Dak To. Skip McKibbin was killed by the " splash" from a rocket propelled grenade that hit his tank while he was standing in the commander's hatch and firing its machine gun. Dave Crocker, whose best man I'd been when he wed Ruthie in June of 1966. Jack Fera, who had roomed across the hall for a year and was the first to tell me about a new English group with funny haircuts, the Beatles. Chuck Johnson, from South Carolina, one of my two roommates from Beast Barracks that first summer at West Point, with whom I had illicitly whispered back and forth at night about our friends and loved ones back home. The list went on and on. Altogether, 31 of the 579 who graduated with my class at West Point were killed in the Vietnam War.

They had done their part, and I would, too. I felt a certain amount of guilt for having gone to Oxford for two years while my classmates were at war. I felt a need to make up for lost time and a longing to return to my classmates and take up my duty. We had become members of the Long Gray Line, now fully sharing in the traditions and histories we'd been taught. It was a culture of service and sacrifice, of battlefield struggle, and long, boring years in between; of men like Eisenhower and Patton, of Grant and Lee, and thousands of others who answered their country's call and put duty before self or family.

I was three years out of West Point, including two years of study at Oxford, a few weeks at Airborne School, nine weeks in Ranger School, six weeks in basic Armor Officer School learning about tanks, communications, and basic company procedures at Fort Knox, and then five months of commanding a tank company of ninety-one troops at Fort Riley, Kansas in the winter and spring of 1969.

When we finally got to Little Rock after Oxford, I asked Mom why she hadn't told me the truth about my family's background. I meant it as a casual question, not an accusation, but she took it that way. She began to cry, and through her tears simply said, " You were a little boy with no father, growing up in a strange place. You didn't need one more problem. I did it to protect you."

I know now that she wasn't just crying for me, as those were hard times for both of us. And given the latent prejudice she knew awaited us in Little Rock in the late 1940s, my father's ethnic identity was a secret she had chosen to keep. The tragedy that the loss of her husband must have been for her could only have been made worse for both of us if it were known that he was the son of Russian Jewish immigrants.

Gert was four months pregnant when I left for Vietnam in July 1969, and we were able to set her up to live with another waiting wife. I would leave behind Gert as well as my mother and stepfather, and I could imagine what they felt. But I tried not to think about that too much, I just kissed Gert goodbye at JFK airport and walked away. I wrote, and I called, and I loved her, but Vietnam was what I wanted to do. It was time to go.

In July 1969, I stepped off the chartered Boeing 707 and into the bright sunshine of Vietnam, carrying the mixed baggage of homesickness, hard determination, and a lot of suppressed excitement. This was it. I had arrived, one of more than 500,000 American soldiers and Marines inside Vietnam that day, one of the more than two million who would serve on the ground in that war.

My first impressions were of the noise and confusion. Everything and everybody seemed to be in motion. And the heat seemed unbearable. At first, I didn't know how anyone could live in this environment. But I gradually learned that you accepted it and adapted; there simply was no other choice.

I filed off onto the tarmac of Bien Hoa airfield in Vietnam, loaded my duffel bags on the designated truck, and got on the bus that was taking us over to the Replacement Depot at Long Binh. The lush green vegetation, slashed here and there with the red scars of clay on which new buildings were going up, the rising columns of diesel smoke in the clear morning sky, the flimsy wood construction of the billets, the ever-repeating songs from the musical *Hair* blaring from portable radios—"This is the daw-ning of the Age of Aquarius"—and overhead the occasional thump-thump of helicopters, the roar of fighter jets taking off from Bien Hoa Air Field.

After I had settled into the transient barracks at the replacement depot, I learned exactly what those columns of diesel smoke represented, and where that sickly sweet smell that wafted across the camp came from: the contents of the metal barrel halves in which the product of open latrines was collected and burned off every morning by some poor soldier who had somehow angered a first sergeant somewhere.

After a couple of days I got word that I would be assigned to the 1st Infantry Division. The Big Red One, whose main base camp was at Di An, a few miles north of Saigon. It took less than an hour to get there, and as soon as I had disposed of my duffel bags, I reported in to the headquarters.

I was hoping, of course, to be given command of a company in combat, though I didn't know what my chances of getting such an assignment were. But they had long known I was coming, and my duties had already been decided for me.

The next day, other new arrivals and I were given a class and taken out on patrol. (" This is how we do it here," they said, " and this is how you will do it.") It was about infantry patrol movement, and flank security, and setting up claymore mines, and making sure everyone had enough water. But we had live ammo, and we might, theoretically, have to fight. However, there were no tracks, no indicators, and no enemy. As it turned out, this training patrol was just a long walk through waist-high grass and the occasional cluster of palms. And, in the rainy season, it was about standing around in a drenching tropical downpour that went on for two hours.

Early the next morning, I got the summons: "Captain Clark, get your gear. You're leaving early."

But instead of heading into combat to lead an infantry company, I was being sent to the division headquarters, another thirty miles north at Lai Khe. I was going to be placed on the division staff, as one of a couple of hundred officers associated with the headquarters. It was rear-area duty. No patrols. No air assaults. No leadership.

What a disappointment! But that's the Army, I figured. You don't always get the job you want. You just have to do well the job they give you.

I spent six months in Lai Khe, interrupted by the occasional helicopter ride or jeep trip out. For the first month I helped out the division's assistant chief of staff, Lt. Col. Tim Murchison. Then I was sent to work for the division operations officer, or G–3, Lt. Col. Ric Brown. He had been one of my mentors at West Point, and when he learned I had arrived in Vietnam, he managed to get me assigned to the division headquarters, out of the normal rotation cycle, in order to beef up his staff. I headed up a small team that helped analyze operations and plan future efforts, and, in addition, I became the division's briefing officer. Every afternoon at 5:00 P.M. I had to succinctly summarize that day's operations for the commanding general and other members of the division staff.

The job was challenging and interesting. I could go anywhere, ask just about anything, and report back in with information. It was a great education in how a 17,000-man division operated in combat. I watched the division commander chew out a battalion commander for driving his vehicles across a rice paddy and ruining the crop. I heard the concern in commanders' voices as they sought air and artillery support in battle or offered battle analyses and suggested new operations. I became more aware every day of the anxieties that burden high-level commanders in war. But mostly I had to prepare the daily command briefing. And this was more difficult than it might appear.

The main problem was that the information that came in was often incomplete or inaccurate or both. Was it two rifles or two machine guns captured? By which company of the 1st Battalion, 2nd Infantry? And what had they done with the captured enemy soldier? Wasn't that where they found a weapons cache last month? And what was that Vietnamese army unit doing in the area, anyway? It was ten minutes of briefing followed by ten minutes of " gotcha," if you weren't careful.

"Sir, for the last three days, the first of the sixteenth has been conducting a sweep from northwest to southeast in search of VC main force units thought to be operating in the Ben Suc area, in this general region."

Maps were all-important aspects of these briefings. About eight feet tall and attached to wall panels, they were slid back and forth on rails to face the seated men drinking in the information. Before each briefing, friendly forces were shown by symbols of various colors scotch-taped to the acetate-covered maps, while suspected enemy locations were shown similarly, but always in red. These acetates were updated whenever new intelligence came in, but the locations of units and their use—on both sides—could be very tricky. I used a pointer to illustrate my briefing by indicating on the map either specific or general locations I was discussing, marking each event with a blue or red acetate number. But my audience was seldom passive, and my interaction with those being briefed was almost constant.

"Sir, at location one, our intelligence indicates that, four or five days ago, one VC patrol came into the Tan Uyen area over here, to join a platoon already in place in order to—"

"Captain Clark, you just said one platoon was already in place in the Tan Uyen area, but that's news to me! How long has it been there?"

"Sir, I'm not sure, and the intelligence is mixed. Some of our sources have been reporting its presence for some time, but most of those early accounts were deemed unreliable and ignored."

"Well, that's pretty important information. Our intelligence yesterday said there was no VC main force unit there, now which is it?"

"Sir, right now I can't tell you."

"Well, find out! I want you to get together with the G–2 on this, and work it out between you, and then get back to me right away."

"Yes, sir, I will meet with the G–2 and the G–3 after this briefing."

"Okay, continue."

You always took responsibility first, then sorted it out later, for that was the military ethic.

I went in with shined boots and freshly pressed jungle fatigues, and I was lucky if I came out in one piece, since the division's senior officers had been out flying around all day, visiting units, checking activities, and getting a sense for what was happening, knowing that at every moment their men's lives were on the line. Occasionally an enemy rocket would land in the headquarters area, which meant we weren't exactly safe. And I habitually slept with a loaded M–16 in my bunk on the base's perimeter. Still, it was definitely rear-area duty.

The one saving grace of the assignment was a few free evenings that I used to meet with an army chaplain so I could convert to Catholicism. I had grown up a Baptist, but as I went to mass with Gert at Oxford, I had become especially impressed with Father Michael Hollings, a former infantry officer in the British Coldstream Guards, a regiment that had fought in World War II at the Battle of El Alamein. We talked about God, life, the Catholic Church, and war. The Protestant ministers I met seemed to take a shortsighted view of Christian duty during wartime, and I often heard our soldiers condemned for their service, as though these ministers could deny us access to God. Never from Father Michael. He understood the terrible dilemma of duty. Through him, my appreciation for the structure and strength of the Catholic Church grew stronger. I only needed the time and relative stability of the base camp in Vietnam to convert.

My staff job at division headquarters was still interesting, for I had access to most of the same information as the division commander, and I was seeing the war from his perspective. But I desperately wanted the chance to command a company in the field. It didn't matter which company I commanded. I just wanted to engage, to start actually fighting this war instead of watching and analyzing as it happened around me. I knew that command of a company in combat could be an all-important part of learning leadership in the army.

I often thought back to West Point. In our military history class we had been studying Napoleon, and one morning I encountered my company tactical officer, then Capt. Ward LeHardy, West Point Class of 1956, as I was walking out of the classroom.

"Well, Mr. Clark," he asked, " how's your study of Napoleon coming?"

That particular morning we'd just finished discussing Napoleon's great victory at the Battle of Marengo, where he demonstrated his developing skill at maneuver while commanding an army of some thirty thousand troops. For me, it had been one of those revealing moments, and I was leaving the classroom pretty fired up.

"Sir, we've just been going over the Battle of Marengo, and now I think I know how he did it, and how to direct an army!"

"That's fine, Mr. Clark," he answered, " but don't ever forget that you have to know how to lead a company before you can lead an army."

No, I had not forgotten

Meanwhile, the weeks passed. Rainy season was almost over. An effort to move the division to a different area had been nixed by higher headquarters, and the division soon was told that it would be sent home, the first full combat unit to depart Vietnam under President Richard Nixon's Vietnamization program.

I began to wonder if I'd ever get a company command assignment outside the headquarters. I knew it was natural for them to keep me there, since I had earned their trust, and the time was almost too short to train someone else to handle the assignment. Still, I couldn't forget Ward LeHardy's advice to learn how to command a company.

On the other side of the base camp, my friend and West Point classmate Capt. Dave Arthur was departing after his year's tour. He had done it the normal way, beginning as a company commander and then, after six months, moving up to become the assistant operations officer for 3rd Brigade. I went by to say goodbye and wish him well.

"Wes," he said, " be careful when you get out there. Stay alert, and don't get ahead of yourself. I had a close call. A guy popped up out of a spider hole as we were going through a base camp. Right in front of me. He looked up and saw me and tried to raise his rifle, but I nailed him. Face to face."

"You never got hit, did you? I asked.

"Nope," he said. " I was lucky."

But he was also good, I thought. Dave was one of the most capable and competent leaders in our class. He was a real soldier, a fighter, and a man any soldier would follow.

I spoke to Colonel Brown and asked for his help in getting out to the field, and the division chief of staff, Col. Al Hume, was sympathetic. He understood the torture of being sidelined, and may have felt it a little himself in the division headquarters, despite his critical position there.

At last, there was an opening, not in an armor or armored cavalry outfit—which I was best qualified for—but in a mechanized infantry battalion, which had armored vehicles, occasionally worked with tanks, and was often commanded by armor officers.

In early January 1970, I was given the command of A Company, 1st Battalion, 16th Infantry (Mechanized).

For the first few days, we simply continued the standard operating procedure, which was to conduct mounted patrols through areas designated by the battalion commander. Sometimes we were assigned to reconnoiter a specific objective, which we normally did while mounted in our armored personnel carriers. Sometimes we were accompanied by tanks and their heavy fire support, but usually we were not. The major danger here was from mines, and since the APCs were loaded with ammunition and explosives, most of us rode on top for our own safety. If there was a firefight, we could either dismount or jump down inside, and if we hit a mine, the theory went, we'd simply be blown off the top of the vehicle. However accurate that may have been, it was standard operating procedure.

When we arrived in an area in late afternoon, we set up an R.O.N. (remain overnight) position. We chopped down trees or removed brush in order to clear landing zones for the medical evacuation helicopters we called dustoffs—angelic miracles that would arrive on call after less than half an hour and could usually carry their wounded cargo to an American hospital within even less time than that. Little did I know how important this near-miraculous medical rescue capability would soon enough be to me personally. We formed our APCs in a rough circle, with me and my command vehicle in the center. I usually slept on a cot pitched right beside my vehicle, but I slept little because I would get up every couple of hours to walk the perimeter. Each morning, just before sunrise, we had a stand-to, which meant everyone was up and at their weapon, ready to fire, and radio checks were made with higher and lower headquarters. Then we began that day's operation

At night and in the afternoons, I would talk with the soldiers, always assessing, probing, or motivating. I always watched as we moved, looking for techniques we might improve on, or mistakes we could correct. If we weren't fighting, we had to be training, not just riding along while waiting for the next day.

Our intelligence said that the enemy had begun to break his forces down into small units, and so the hard part was to find him and make contact, after which we could mass our firepower against him. So I began to more frequently break the company down and have my three platoons go out independently on foot patrols, Each day I would try to join one of the platoons, and that's where I was on February 19, 1970, when I almost bought the farm.

The lessons of leadership I learned in Vietnam would last a lifetime: working with a diverse team to impart skills, to motivate and inspire; innovating and adapting; taking the initiative; above all, making an honest appraisal, and taking honest feedback, including the kind of veiled criticism you can pick up if you're tuned to it, in order to make a better outfit.

It was leadership, plain and simple. What people look like on the outside isn't always who they are on the inside; and what they say often isn't what they mean. You read their body language while maintaining distance and composure, but you take a personal interest in their families and problems. You listen more than you speak. When you make a decision, you explain it, and then hang tough. And when people, especially leaders, fail, you face up to it and take action. Leadership is about experience, not books—and people, not theories.

The company commander had to set the standard, and he had to live it himself, not just enforce it. You had to be personally competent and " squared away" . You were always on display, and every word, act, or expression was judged. Just like at West Point, you were " graded every day." You had to teach others who weren't as good. And in this army of conscripts, you had to motivate your soldiers. You did that with humor and personal interest if you could, and while an occasional sharp word might be needed, you never made or allowed a personal attack. For anything negative that involved your men, you used the chain of command—lieutenants and sergeants normally handled and resolved such issues before they reached the " Old Man" at the top.

The company commander always had to have a plan. He had to know where he was and what he was doing. No uncertainty, and no waffling or wavering on decisions. Mostly, these weren't life and death matters, and many of them were insignificant. But you had to build the kind of informal authority that bonded men to you and would command their respect, obedience, and support when the issue *was* one of life and death.

Years later, one writer called this the " mask of command" . But it wasn't a mask—it had to be authentic and deep, because when you're living with men day in and day out, there is no privacy, and any such " mask" would quickly be exposed. Phonies couldn't make it, and you had to really lead, not pretend.

One day early in my command, I had watched as one of my platoons moved past on mounted patrol about a hundred meters away. Each of the " tracks" carried five or six men, and I observed them closely: a driver, a vehicle commander crouched behind the 50 caliber machine gun, and three or four other riflemen sitting or lying on top. Some of them were eating from C-ration cans, some were reading magazines or books, while most of them just looked groggy in the unrelentingly hot sun. This was my " baseline" assessment. We could and would do better: more alert, more disciplined, more effective. So I worked steadily to make the men more alert and the unit more effective. But there were limits to what we, a bunch of young Americans, could be or become. We weren't social workers, or linguists, or experts in economic and political development. And it wasn't our country, either.

But experiences in the field, some flawed more deeply than others, provided food for thought. Were our tactics right, or might we have done better with smaller groups of more highly skilled soldiers, able to live in the jungle and fight the enemy on his own terms? Was our approach to the Vietnamese culture correct, or should we have been more in touch with the local Vietnamese, the people we were supposed to be protecting but whom we never got to know, at least in the 1st Infantry Division, with whom I served? From what I saw, we were trying hard to follow the counterinsurgency guidelines of winning the hearts and minds of the people. At least, I heard a lot of talk to that effect from our senior officers. But were we really able to do that? And was our strategy right, with the continuing withdrawals of U.S. forces after about 1969, the on-and-off negotiations with the North, and the Vietnamization program? I sensed I was too close to the issues to have good answers then—but I was open to the questions.

Today, there are many young men and women serving in Iraq and Afghanistan who believe in each other, and in America. They are doing their best with the mission our country gave them. Some of them probably wouldn't change a thing; others are asking questions, and some would probably want us to bring our forces there home right away. I just want them to take care of each other while following their orders and adhering to their guidelines. It's up to the political leadership and the top brass to think through the political issues and the strategy. But so far, they haven't lived up to their obligations to the troops—or to our country.

SIX

IN THE WAKE OF WAR

It was around 5:00 P.M. on the nineteenth of February 1970 when the helicopter landed me at the 93rd Evacuation Hospital outside Saigon. The medics on board had looked at my wounds and taken me to the hospital for the less seriously injured. The really bad cases, the men with the sucking chest wounds and guts ripped open, the ones who might not make it and would require extensive time before they could be moved again, were sent to the 24th Evac.

I was pretty much out of it by this time, just trying to avoid thinking and feeling pain. The next thing I remember was a doctor looking down at me after X-ray. "You've got the million-dollar wound," he said.

I tried to talk without showing the panic I felt, for I thought that phrase had something to do with the ability to father more children.

"Relax," he said. "You've taken four rounds—shoulder, leg, hand, and butt—and not a major blood vessel, bone, or nerve has been damaged. You're a very lucky guy, and you'll be headed back to the States soon."

I was getting very groggy as I was taken into another room and moved from the gurney to an operating table. As I lay back, I again felt a needle pricking my arm. Then the lights went out.

After surgery, I slept for quite a while. When I woke up, I found I was in a bed in a ward with perhaps a dozen other wounded. Some of the officers from the division came to see me, including Lt. Col. David Martin, my battalion commander. Two of my soldiers had also been wounded in the action, though not as seriously as I was. We had overrun the base camp and found some enemy blood trails where they had pulled away their dead or wounded. The other platoons had eventually arrived on the scene after I had been evacuated, and the area had then been cleared of enemy presence.

I watched a few minutes later as an injured soldier, a young African American man who had lost his arm above the elbow, smoked and talked with his friends.

"How's Big Dog? What happened to Smitty? Stay in touch, you hear?" He was still connected, engaged, and missing his unit, and I knew exactly how he felt. But I looked at the stump of his arm, and wondered what life would bring to him, whether he would be able to maintain that positive spirit when reality hit him a few months from now. And I prayed that he would, for I knew that many of us were headed home with wounds that would never really heal.

A few days later they hooked me up to a portable IV, then put me on a stretcher and loaded me on a bus with eight or ten other stretcher-borne, homeward-bound casualties. The bus lurched across rough ground to the airfield, stretchers swaying in their slings, men moaning from the heat and the rough ride. But the driver had a portable radio turned way up loud, and the latest hit that poured through the bus was a not-so-strangely-soothing number by Peter, Paul, and Mary, with the mellow, haunting words "Leaving, on a jet plane . . ." In ways beyond verbal description, that song, wherever and whenever I hear it, still touches my soul.

~

There were two great joys awaiting me when I got home: Gert and our four-month-old son, Wes. Gert met me in the hospital at Valley Forge, Pennsylvania. We sneaked out, with me in pajamas and casts on my leg and hand, to have dinner somewhere, and she was so excited she drove over a curb and into a ditch. It was raining lightly, and there I was again, three years later, outside the car and pushing.

But that didn't matter. Nothing mattered, really, for I was finally home.

A week later, I was given convalescent leave to go to Brooklyn, where we would stay with her parents. As soon as we got there, with my right arm in a cast and my hand formed around a steel hook, I held my son.

"Don't drop him," Gert said as she put him carefully across my right arm. It was one of the greatest days of my life.

I spent a few more weeks healing in the hospital, but as soon as the wounds closed and I could remove the casts, I was on my way to my next job at Fort Knox, Kentucky, where I became a company commander in the 194th Armored Brigade, a school support unit. I was given command of a tank company that was authorized ninety-one men but only had about seventy assigned, and our job was to fix tanks that were used in the school cycles for training new lieutenants. Most of my men were early returnees from Vietnam, some of whom had been wounded, while others had various personal problems. But the majority of them were just waiting to complete their enlistments and get out.

It was the draft army of the late 1960s, and we had soldiers of every background and motivation. Some were drafted after finishing college or graduate school, when their student deferments ran out. These men were smart. They could have gone on to Officer Candidate School, but had chosen to ride out their two years of service "in the ranks." Sometimes all that education made them the kind of informal leaders that everyone listened to, regardless of how many stripes they had. On the other hand, some were pretty unhappy about serving.

Some were drafted after high school graduation, the more gifted of whom went to an additional army school and became sergeants. They were a little inexperienced compared to most of the other sergeants, but they were usually well motivated. And with casualties in Vietnam a constant drain, they were sorely needed.

All of these men were draftees, and our job was not pleasant: to fix broken-down M–60 tanks so that new lieutenants could train on them. Needless to say, morale was pretty low when I took over. We would get a standard mission to deliver twelve tanks to range such and such at 0400 hours, all with operating infrared sights, and so on. Then we would pick them up at 0100 hours the next day and get them ready for the next cycle of lieutenants. So this became a sort of around-the-clock school support mission, in which we would go straight-out for weeks, and even months, at a time. In fact, that summer, we worked more than eighty straight days and nights, weekends included. When you add the command maintenance management inspections, or CMMIs, that we had to undergo, there was quite a bit of pressure on us.

That summer was a crazy time in the army, with the Vietnam War at its peak. Experienced noncommissioned officers were refusing to reenlist, and serious discipline problems were frequent. One night a soldier from another unit lobbed a Molotov cocktail at the military police station, and another night two soldiers fought a duel with .22-caliber pistols. Absent without leave (AWOL) offenses as well as drug abuse incidents were rampant. And the army had just been directed to transition to an all-volunteer force.

In Vietnam, meanwhile, the fighting continued. My friend from Oxford, Alex Hottell, had extended his tour for another six months. He'd had a rough go already as an infantry company commander in a very high risk area, and had earned a reputation as a tough, savvy, and coolheaded leader in combat. Because of the high risk, Alex advised his men to write a letter home "just in case." When there was a break in action, he wrote a letter to Linda, from which the following passages are excerpted:

> I loved the Army: it reared me, it nurtured me, and it gave me the most satisfying years of my life. Thanks to it I have lived an entire lifetime in 26 years. It is only fitting that I should die in its service. We all have but one death to spend, and insofar as it can have any meaning, it finds it in the service of comrades in arms.
>
> And yet, I deny that I died FOR anything—not my country, not my Army, not my fellow man, none of these things. I LIVED for these things, and the manner in which I chose to do it involved the very real chance that I would die in the execution of my duties. I knew this, and accepted it, but my love for West Point and the Army was great enough—and the promise that I would some day be able to serve all the ideals that meant anything to me through it was great enough—for me to accept this possibility as a part of a price which must be paid for all things of great value. If there is nothing worth dying for—in this sense—there is nothing worth living for.

As a fighting infantry company commander, Alex saw a lot of combat, and he earned two Silver Stars for valor. Then he was reassigned, and as an aide to the division commander, a major general, he no longer had any reason to think that he might die a violent death in Vietnam.

No one ever did.

On July 17, 1970, Alex Hottell was killed in a helicopter crash.

But he got it precisely right: our country, our army, our fellow men and women.

Something to live for.

~

At Fort Knox, leadership was a matter of caring: putting in the hours, working alongside the troops, and, above all, standing up for them. I was still convalescing from my wounds and soon discovered that I couldn't run, do the monkey bars, or shoot a pistol. But I was there, walking through the barracks at night, getting soldiers released from jail for minor offenses off post, helping change track in the mud on Saturday afternoon, inspecting maintenance records on Sunday morning, leading tank columns around at 3:00 A.M. on the tank trails at Fort Knox, and, above all, pep-talking the troops, often one by one.

This command had a profound effect on me. These men performed out of pride in themselves and duty to their country, many of them still gimped from wounds, others champing at the bit to start over on the outside. But they pulled together. We were a "sacrifice" outfit, as we saw it, and we were brothers. With them, I had family, real family.

I commanded that company from May through September 1970. Then I went to the Armor Advanced Course for a nine-month course that was designed to bring us into the inner sanctums of tactics, logistics, and leadership. This was done mostly through lectures, memorization, and monthly examinations. Here I would have time to regain the strength in my wounded hand and learn to run again on a leg that was missing a lot of muscle. Here, too, more of the army's Vietnam-era problems were on display. We were a special group, a bunch of infantry and armor captains, all Vietnam veterans, whose assignments had somehow gotten out of sequence, so we were thrown together in what might have been an "overflow" course.

Many of us had deep problems, some with their wounds, some with their marriages, others with the army and the guilt and frustration over the war. Some were now affected by the anger on the "outside" directed against us; they wore their hair a little long, and slouched a little, and brought some of that "cool" into our group. There were the predictable quarrels among us, but, above all, we shared a deep anxiety about the war, the army, and the country.

Gen. George S. Patton III, the son of the famous World War II commander, was sparkling in his fancy mess blue uniform at the dining-in for the hundred-odd captains and majors in the Armor Officer Advanced Course Class 501–71. It was late April of 1971, and Brigadier General Patton had recently arrived at Fort Knox, where he was assigned as assistant commandant of the U.S. Army Armor School. And he was determined to impart his fire-breathing, hard-charging style of combat leadership to the Vietnam-veteran captains listening intently to his analysis of Vietnam and leadership, for he, too, knew we were having real leadership problems across the army.

In the news that week, a U.S. infantry battalion had failed under battle stress along the Laotian border, with an infantry company having refused to advance toward the border, despite the best efforts of the company commander. He had been replaced, and another commander also failed to get the unit to move.

The army was failing under fire. It was unforgivable.

"If I'd been there," said Patton, "I'd have simply moved out myself. Walked on forward. Led them on foot, personally. These are American soldiers. They'll follow brave leaders! They wouldn't let me go into battle alone! Do any of you doubt that? Well, do you?"

I looked around at my fellow officers—at the rows of Purple Hearts and Bronze Stars. You could fairly see the skepticism boiling over. We knew it wasn't that easy. I'd worked hard the year before, and my men had come forward under fire, but would every unit respond the same way, and to someone they didn't know?

We challenged him, forced him to defend his assumptions and recognize the doubts that so many had about the reliability of a draft army fighting the sixth year of a bitterly unpopular war. The old respect for authority was disappearing. In its place were doubt, cynicism, alienation, isolation, and hostility. A good leader could still motivate troops, but it took a good leader, not just a set of captain's bars on a collar.

General Patton was one of those leaders; he didn't bark us down when he was challenged. Instead he listened and engaged with us. He knew, too, that the army was in trouble, and he was doing his best to help.

Much of the army had simply been used up. Good officers and non-commissioned officers were being killed, wounded, or retired. The individual replacement system in combat was producing units of strangers who, without extraordinary leadership, simply didn't bond. And the troops themselves, who increasingly felt discriminated against and picked on by a society that forced them to fight a war that it largely opposed, were simply not reenlisting.

Some armies can be defeated on the field of battle. Ours was not. But we who lived through the trauma of Vietnam can never forget the sense of an army that had lost its edge, and was rapidly losing its capabilities.

The summer of 1971, I was sent to the Pentagon for three months to help work the transition of the army to the all-volunteer force. When that assignment was over, I was off to West Point, to repay the support and mentoring I had received by giving back to others as an assistant professor in the Department of Social Sciences. I wouldn't be back with troops for five years.

West Point felt like home. I would be one of perhaps a thousand officers on the faculty and staff, and one of fifty-odd in the Department of Social Sciences, all of us focused primarily on developing the cadets.

I taught economics for part of a semester and then moved over to teach an elective seminar in political philosophy, from Plato to Herbert Marcuse. It was a time of civil disobedience, of popular questions about the Vietnam War and the legitimacy of government, so the course was in high demand among cadets.

In addition to teaching, I was able to coach the debate team and serve as one of the assistant coaches for the swim team. With Gert's family close and Wes a toddler, it was a busy, family-oriented three years. After the first year, we were able to move into a wonderful old apartment within walking distance of Thayer Hall, where my office was. There were tailgate parties for football games, a walk a few hundred yards to the hockey rink, and easy access to many friends.

But much of the action at West Point was out of sight of the cadets, for West Point at the time was all about Vietnam. Our superintendent, Lt. Gen. Bill Knowlton, had served as an assistant division commander in Vietnam with the 9th Infantry Division in the Mekong River Delta, and almost everyone on the faculty had served a tour somewhere in Southeast Asia.

By this time, of course, the war was deeply unpopular in the civilian world. Most of the officers on the faculty had been exposed to a healthy dose of academic skepticism or even criticism when they attended civilian graduate schools in preparation for returning to teach at West Point. But especially for those of us too young to have served in Korea in the early 1950s, Vietnam was the centerpiece of our army experiences, and it weighed heavily on us.

At the same time, as the 1971 army was being ripped by tides of racial unrest and deep soldier unhappiness, draftees were still coming in, bringing with them all the frictions and tensions in the larger society.

Writing a review of David Halberstam's *The Best and the Brightest* for an academic journal, I was forced to confront and think through my views on Vietnam. It wasn't easy, and I finally produced a rather complicated analysis, full of hypotheticals and conditionals, and the editor rightly asked for clarifications. As I did so, I worked through some of the issues with a military colleague and former social sciences instructor who was then serving in the White House under President Nixon. My questions and hypotheticals must have hit a raw nerve: "If you have to ask questions like this, you aren't on the team!" he wrote back on my marked-up draft.

It was chilling. This wasn't the army I was part of. Or was it just the proximity to the Nixon administration that fueled the response?

I sensed that much of the army outside West Point was "hunkered down," repaying civilian hostility with an enforced loyalty that served the extremes in both cultures. But that loyalty only worked to further isolate the military from the society it was formed to protect.

I stayed firmly fixed on the bridge between the two perspectives. I was an army officer, and we weren't "baby killers." And I loved and respected the men and women I served with. On the other hand, it was hard to believe that no mistakes had been made in Vietnam. Similarly, it was sometimes hard to defend every previous civilian policymaker who took action to contain Communism at its periphery and enforce international legal decisions which decreed South Vietnam a separate and independent state. There were good people—and well-intentioned people—on both sides of this painful debate.

Once again I was reminded of the disputes over desegregation in Little Rock years before. People argued superficially about facts, but the real disagreements were about principles. Each side mustered many of them. To make headway in any discussion, you had to work on small, specific areas of discussion where some agreement might be found. And in the process, you risked being misunderstood or even attacked by both sides.

By early 1973, the Nixon administration had concluded its negotiations with the North Vietnamese to gain the freedom of our captured American pilots. The price was assent to a North Vietnamese army encamped in the center of South Vietnam. *The New York Times* sent a reporter to interview several of us. Will it work, we were asked?

It was a flawed agreement, I explained. It may have been the best we could get, given the American public's determination to end our involvement there. But by leaving a North Vietnamese force inside South Vietnam, we were guaranteeing that the conflict would resume, and the outcome would probably be bad.

I had a sinking feeling as I criticized the agreement. Our country had been working almost five years to achieve this, and I respected the hard negotiations and tough choices that had been made. No doubt it was the best that could have been done. Here I was, a captain on active duty, publicly criticizing the commander-in-chief. I was uneasy about being critical, but, largely, I was conscious of the need to judge, the weight of the assessment and the risk of being wrong, and being wrong publicly. I felt a heavy sense of responsibility and weighed my words carefully. This, of course, is precisely how we learn to make high-quality judgments, and it is always serious and anxiety-ridden. The key is to have foresight and to be accurate in what is foreseen.

During the summer of 1973, I was given a three-month position on the army staff in the Pentagon, with a charter to investigate three issues: Was there an energy crisis? (Yes, but artificially created.). Would it impact Department of Defense operational readiness? (Not really.). Would there be any role for U.S. military power in dealing with the situation in the Persian Gulf? (Yes, but not immediately and not necessarily in open warfare.)

But in recommending that military forces might become part of a U.S. response, I had crossed another red line: Political leaders wanted no further mention of possible military missions. One of the wise lieutenant colonels on the army staff delivered the warning unforgettably:

"Young Captain, you put that recommendation in your report, and that Senator Fulbright is going to call all of us in front of him for an explanation, and it won't be pretty."

So, savvy officers watched what they said, and what they wrote. They heeded the political overtones, didn't address issues above their pay grades, and stayed away from policy—and the politics associated with it—if at all possible. After all, this was not the Social Sciences Department.

Among its other virtues, this approach assured that the military could enthusiastically support whatever policies were adopted by their civilian superiors, without awkwardly having to retract their earlier views. General MacArthur had clearly spelled it out to us in his June 1962 farewell address at West Point:

"Others will debate the controversial issues, national and international, which divide men's minds. But serene, calm, aloof, you stand as the Nation's war guardians."

I was in a bit of a quandary. I was working on policy, and everything I'd been taught told me to speak up—not publicly, but privately—and give my bosses my best, unvarnished judgment. I had gone to Oxford precisely to gain better understanding of the civilian society in order to help the military serve it better. This was about integrity, not gamesmanship. I didn't feel undue concern or fear when I talked about these issues. I just looked at the facts and reasoned it out. Wasn't this what was needed?

Ultimately, I did brief the leadership and laid out my prediction. The three-star nodded and remarked, "You may be right."

The autumn of 1973, I returned to West Point for my final year of teaching. Capt. Dan Christman and I wrote an article for *Military Review* suggesting that because of the energy crisis, the Middle East had taken on new significance and that U.S. forces might be required to stabilize the region.

Of course, we had to submit the draft article to the Pentagon for clearance. Four and a half years later, it was published. I wasn't called up in front of the Senate, but neither had the savvy lieutenant colonel been wrong, exactly, as I learned repeatedly over the years. There can be a high price to be paid for addressing policy matters, even if you're later proven right. For that reason, policymakers too often go uninformed by the kind of military reasoning they say they want but don't always receive. Leaders brave in battle sometimes need encouragement in the conference room.

In the spring of 1974, Gert and I took four cadets to an academic symposium on civil-military relations at Brown University. It would be a long weekend away, and a useful effort, I thought.

The symposium crowd was friendly enough. Issues pass quickly on college campuses, and with the draft a historical relic, students quickly forgot the anger generated by the war. But the speakers didn't.

Gazing down from the stage at the four cadets and me, all of us in uniform and seated near the front, Congressman Les Aspin pointed us out, and said,

"Those cadets and that officer there—they'll never again see the time when American troops are deployed overseas to combat!"

It was a bold statement, and issuing from the lips of a Rhodes scholar, a member of the House Armed Services Committee, and one of the up-and-coming stars of the dominant Democratic party, it was authoritative as well.

His statement also struck me in an odd personal way: Why would I want to stay in the military (I had just turned twenty-nine) if we would never again be called on to defend the country? But the flip side was equally troubling: If there was to be a big war in Europe with the Soviets, why would anyone want to be in the middle of that?

The cadets enjoyed rubbing elbows with their civilian contemporaries, but I carried the disturbing questions away with me: What was the usefulness of the army? Would we ever be needed again? And what were the right lessons to take from Vietnam? No one seemed to have any answers.

All too soon, we were packing to leave the academy. Young Wes was four years old, and I was to be a student at the army's Command and General Staff College, at Fort Leavenworth, Kansas.

West Point had been good to us. I had lots of time there with
Gert and Wes, with close friends, and with family nearby, and I liked
both the teaching as well as my colleagues in the Social Sciences Department. If this wasn't quite the dessert course, like Oxford, it was
pretty close. I was eager to get back to soldiering with the troops, but
I also realized that, when I left the faculty at West Point, the future
was unknown. To me, much had been given, and I'd spent a wonderful three years giving back. Now, I believed, I could get on with the
real army.

～

They called it the Big Bedroom, an auditorium that held the whole
Leavenworth class of some 1,200 officers. But nobody was asleep that
early summer morning in 1974 when we assembled for the welcoming
ceremony at which we would be briefed by the commandant of the U.S.
Army Command and General Staff College.

We stood around spotting friends from other assignments, former
bosses, or classmates from previous schools. Most had earned medals in
two tours in Vietnam: Bronze Stars, Vietnamese Cross of Gallantry, Air
Medal, Army Commendation Medal with V device, Purple Hearts, Silver Stars, and more.

We saw the foreign officers in our midst—German, Peruvian,
British, Israeli, Jordanian, Ethiopian, South Vietnamese, Cambo-
dian—all in all, more than one hundred officers from dozens of different countries.

Then we took our seats, stood, sat, stood again, and welcomed our
commandant, Lt. Gen. John B "Jack" Cushman, former commander of
the 101st Airborne Division, the "Screaming Eagles". He stood before
us, ramrod straight, broad-shouldered, and with a full head of dark hair.
He had a reputation for shaking things up, and he'd already made a mark
in just a few months with the previous class. But we were to be the first
class he would have for a full year.

As General Cushman explained it, we would have to learn to think
and reason tactically. Rote memorization of some of the basic facts
would still be required—the range of a Soviet antitank missile, say—but
the curriculum would feature more electives, including advanced tactics

at the highest levels of command. And that meant more responsibility for the students.

What we didn't talk about was Vietnam. And you couldn't talk about your Vietnam experiences, simply because that topic just wasn't tolerated. We'd all had some heady times over there, but the war was over and it was time to move on. Occasionally, someone would start a thought with, "When I was in 'Nam . . ." only to be met by a low hiss of disapproval and people turning away. There were no good war stories from Vietnam. Not anymore. Instead, we were busy studying the new Soviet equipment and their threat to Europe, and reflecting on the 1973 Yom Kippur War, where the Syrians and Egyptians had used Soviet tactics and equipment to nearly defeat Israel in the early days.

But for me, the questions raised by Congressman Aspin were still nagging. I mulled over how to wrestle with the challenge—does the Army really have a future?—and stumbled into a method: I would do some real individual research on the use of force. I volunteered to skip a couple of electives in order to write a thesis and gain a newly accredited postgraduate degree, master of military art and science, that the college was now empowered to award. The subject would be contingency operations since World War II.

I started with the German philosopher of war, Carl von Clausewitz, and his magisterial work, *On War.* For him, it was the connection between war and political ends that was the key. For in Clausewitz's time, war was used to attain a short-term political end. In his day, when there were no nuclear weapons and international conflict didn't threaten all of civilization, war was just another set of activities that, properly understood and used, would lead to the desired political outcome.

Within this framework, it would be possible to ask whether various military actions met the higher aims of political leaders, and if so, to determine the characteristics of these successful operations.

In the course of the inquiry, I was unable to avoid reopening the issues of Vietnam. I'd seen most of the literature before, but now was the time to go back through it—the Pentagon Papers, Frances Fitzgerald's *Fire in the Lake,* Thomas Schelling on his theory of compellence, news articles, policy pronouncements, and other materials. What were we thinking at the time? And how could it have gone so wrong with the public?

Gradually, I teased out the major pieces of a modern military and foreign affairs policy appropriate for our nation: having a clear goal, knowing your enemy's character and aims, going in with overwhelming power, maintaining a psychological and physical dominance if the level of fighting intensified, beating the enemy on the battlefield in order to beat him in the negotiations. It was diplomatic in purpose, military in means. Coercive diplomacy was what some of us called it. I spent time at the kitchen table every night, with a box of three-by-five note cards, the references, and my old portable typewriter from West Point, pecking out my ideas.

Then in late March, General Cushman assembled the class again in the Big Bedroom. "Men," he began, "today Saigon has fallen to the enemy . . ." He went on for a few minutes to speak the requiem to America's long and costly war in Southeast Asia.

This was no war story. And nobody hissed. There was a stunned silence. We looked at each other, a few eyes glistening as we thought about all the friends we'd lost, the blood we'd spilled, the months and years of our lives we'd given to that cause. Until that moment, it had been easy to push it off the front burner, though it continued to simmer slowly in the back of all our minds.

But now, Vietnam was front and center once again, and it simply couldn't be avoided. The fall of South Vietnam to Communism was pure raw pain: pain for the loss, pain for the wasted effort, and pain for the humiliation of our country.

We were never the same class again. The Cambodians left immediately to fly home. The Vietnamese officers—eighteen of them—left promptly to take any cash-paying job in Kansas City, where a couple ended up as waiters in restaurants. At least they had their families with them, because they weren't going home again, not for a long time. As for the rest of us, we found ourselves approaching our studies with a new purpose and a new resolve. This wasn't going to happen again, not to our country. We wouldn't let it. We would win. We would speak out, demand what we needed, and refuse to be misled or buffaloed by the politicians at the top. That was a resolve many of us shared.

As I looked back on Vietnam it became ever clearer what had gone wrong. If the struggle could have been won militarily, it would have taken greater and earlier pressure on North Vietnam, more direct action to cut the Ho Chi Minh trail in Laos, far greater risks in dealing with the problem of Soviet and Chinese assistance to the North, and a greater emphasis on population-centered protection efforts far earlier in the war. We had committed a lot of American power, but we hadn't fought smart at the strategic and geostrategic levels. The generals had been hesitant to ask for what they really needed, and the politicians had been reluctant to take the risks we needed to take in order to win. If there was a single lesson, it was this: no half measures; don't commit American forces unless you commit enough to win.

I would carry those lessons with me. Repackaged in the introduction for Project 14, General Wickham's transition report, they became the basis for the Powell Doctrine. In the mid-1990s I drew on the same set of ideas when organizing the military annex to the Dayton peace agreement. And once again, as a fifty-four-year-old general serving in General Eisenhower's old command as Supreme Allied Commander, Europe, waging war against the forces of Serb dictator Slobodan Milosevic, I found myself drawing on the lessons I'd pulled out of those few months at Fort Leavenworth, as a thirty-year-old captain trying to understand Vietnam. They are the lessons of modern warfare, and they are equally applicable today in Iraq, where political leaders intervened in a far-off land, committed a force too small, and failed to deal effectively with Iraq's neighbors who fed the conflict.

No two strategic problems, of course, are identical. But just as the Johnson administration avoided applying full power against North Vietnam for fear of Soviet and Chinese reactions, so, too, has the Bush administration failed to reckon with the interests of Iraq's neighbors. Some of them, despite their denials, have worked steadily against the American effort in Iraq in order to protect their own quite different interests. Instead of threatening these states, the Bush administration needed to find a way to make them part of the solution in the region. That, however, would have required diplomatic engagement and sustained dialogue, key governmental tools that the Bush people avoid like plague.

I had made a lot of good friends at Fort Leavenworth, friends Gert and I would try to keep up with in the years ahead. I knew I was about to be promoted to major, and in every way that matters, I felt I was a very lucky man. But I also felt a strong resolve to pursue my military career, and I was hoping to play a part in building a new American army.

After the course at Leavenworth, I had been lucky enough to have been selected for what is known as a White House Fellowship. This is a competitive program for rising young American leaders interested in public service, under which they spend a year working as special assistants to cabinet secretaries or other high-ranking members of the executive branch. It gives participants a wonderful exposure to the governmental processes from the very top, and while both Gert and I were pleased that I had been selected, even at that level there were ups and downs.

When I arrived, I found that I would not fill a military position, nor would I be required to perform any military duties. Instead, my actual work assignment would be as a special assistant to James T. Lynn, the Director of the Office of Management and Budget. There, I would work on a wide array of programs—Social Security, food stamps, welfare, education, Medicare and Medicaid, transportation, as well as national defense issues to which Jim Lynn might direct my efforts. The staff here were reputed to be of the highest quality in government service. And from this office, virtually every government program would be visible.

"I want all the White House fellows out. Leave the room."

It was an impersonal announcement, and I looked around the Cabinet Room. I was seated against the wall, waiting for President Gerald R. Ford to come in, and so far as I could tell, I was the only White House fellow among the dozen or so backbenchers. I got up and walked out. This was Donald Rumsfeld's White House decorum.

With Rumsfeld as White House chief of staff and Dick Cheney as his deputy, the White House could be a rough place: secret memos, winks, nods, and a conspiratorial air seemed to perpetuate all the worst reported tendencies of the Nixon White House. As one senior staffer told me, "Wes, the West Wing of the White House is the only place on the world where, if you were about to fall on your face, everyone around would back up and give you room so you'd hit very hard!"

You wouldn't have known it from that meeting, but I'd been given a privileged place there. Only a few weeks after I'd started the fellowship, I'd been given the opportunity to move next door for six weeks and work as a special assistant to former Virginia congressman Jack O. Marsh, counselor to the president. He was running the administration group that backstopped the Senate and House committees as they ripped the intelligence community apart, and I was recruited to help him work the group as the executive secretary of the interagency committee.

The committee would include Henry Kissinger, secretary of state; James F. Schlesinger, secretary of defense; William Colby, director of Central Intelligence; William Levy, attorney general; and Philip Buchen, counsel to the president. Jack Marsh would chair. Brent Scowcroft, Kissinger's deputy at the National Security Counsel, and Bill Hyslop, another Kissinger deputy, were also involved.

I was thrilled, for to work around these experienced and able leaders was like a dream come true. The group would respond to the congressional queries, deciding what information could be withheld, who could testify, and what they would say. It would meet in the White House situation room, and I'd be seated along the wall next to Mr. Marsh, taking notes and doing follow-up for him. So, I thought, I was finally going to be getting into the national security policy world.

The day I reported in to the West Wing, Jack handed me a stack of yellow phone slips.

"Tell me whose calls I should return, and in which priority," he said. "I'll be back soon. Oh, and let me introduce you to Michael Raoul Duvall, who was on the advance team in '72. He'll be joining you as executive secretary."

Then they walked off to have lunch, leaving me with the dozens of phone messages: "Jim called—urgent," "Call Tom on the Hill," and so on. I had no idea who the people were or what the issues were.

It was a beginning.

Two nights later, I was at a White House fellows reception when, from across the room, our host said

"Wes Clark—the White House is calling for you."

Everyone froze, conversation ceased. Three months ago we'd been applicants; three weeks ago we'd joined our agencies. Suddenly, I was so essential to the nation that the White House would call me on a Friday night? I moved to take the phone.

It was the operator, with Mr. Marsh on. "Wes, yesterday I gave you a special document and asked you to hold it for me and then get it back to me. I don't have it back. Do you still have it?"

So, it wasn't an attack on the United States or a riot or anything. Well, yes, I had it, and it was locked in the safe in the office. I should have asked when he needed it back and returned it. But I also learned that being on the inside isn't always glamorous, and that sometimes it is better not to have your name singled out! Once more, I was learning competence, attention to detail, following before you lead. I left the reception to find the document and take it over to Mr. Marsh.

Over the next six weeks I toiled over the classified documents, sat through precise but contentious legal discussions, and watched the interplay of personalities and issues, trying to help where I could. Within a week or two, I'd caught onto the rhythm of the work, and by the end of my time as a fellow I actually wrote and signed a memorandum to the president.

But I was very happy when Jim Lynn had insisted that I return to OMB, for I really loved working for him. He was open, active, engaged, and he had a kind of infectious enthusiasm that carried the whole team with him. My job was to work through the budget reviews and write or edit issue papers that described key decisions or elements of the president's budget.

And there were critical decisions to be made, especially in the "Great Society" social programs, where OMB was working feverishly to rationalize and prioritize a hodge-podge of congressionally mandated assistance programs with overlapping purposes, mandates, and targets. We would then publish and distribute these, along with the budget. Afterward, I continued to work several of the issues and ended up accompanying Jim and Don Ogilvie on a diplomatic trip, the purpose of which was an examination of U.S. foreign assistance requirements in Israel, Syria, Jordan, and Egypt.

But I was still an army officer, and that's where my heart was. In Jordan, we were met by Crown Prince Hassan and flown in three Alouette helicopters up the Jordan River Valley, then up the Yarmouk River to the Damascus-Amman highway and down to Amman. The land below us was dry and dusty, but two thousand years earlier it had been rich in soil, and had served as Rome's granary. Hassan slung a submachine gun over his shoulder as he left the helicopter. This was the Middle East in 1976.

Given Jim's important position, we were well received everywhere. In Jerusalem, Prime Minister Itzhak Rabin had us to a private dinner with his closest colleagues, Defense Minister Shimon Peres, Foreign Minister Yigal Allon, and Finance Minister Yeshua Rabinovitz. As the seven of us sat around the table, the talk turned to military matters, and I had an important question to ask:

"Prime Minister, what would you say is the most important military lesson that you could pass on to a young officer?"

Rabin never even hesitated. He related his experience as a brigade commander in Jerusalem in 1948, when subordinate commanders in his unit wanted to pull out, and how he had refused to do so, and how that determination eventually won the battle.

"Persistence," he said, "that is the most important quality any military leader can have."

The White House fellowship had been a real learning experience in seeing from the top how our government operates. But I'd learned about America, too. On a trip to Boston we'd seen the intellectual groundings of local and state government. It was a common perception that public servants on the government payroll are lazy bureaucrats, but that's not what I saw. Instead, I saw well-educated, innovative, and highly principled local leaders engaged in political struggles with rights, property, taxes, and education, issues that are every bit as engaging as my own profession's concern with the Soviet threat and how to deal with it.

A White House fellows trip to Africa reinforced my own sense of national privilege. In the rubble of Kinshasa, Congo, you could see the failure of decolonialization, and the difficulty of transporting legal systems and the cultural outlook and political attitudes upon which they rest from one country to another stood out in stark relief. We fight our many problems in America, certainly, but we have various rings in which we can slug them out, and some pretty sizable and soft boxing gloves. Unlike that well-understood political structure, however, for much of the world the fight was becoming no-holds-barred, bare-fisted or with weapons, and inside no ring.

As the end of my year approached, Gert and I were happy with a pending assignment in Germany, it was time for me to return to the army.

We landed in Frankfurt, Germany late one night in August 1976 and ultimately got to our new assignment in Bamberg, Germany. I was the new S–3 (operations officer)—the number-three ranking officer— in a tank battalion of 550 soldiers. But when I got there, I might as well have been back at Fort Knox, only this was six years later. There were some terrible stories running through the military community in Germany, stories of prejudice, drug abuse, criminal activity, and even murder.

Some young officers were having a very difficult time coping with these conditions, while older officers were wary. It was an army struggling to face a new threat from the Soviets, but not at all recovered from the tragedy of Vietnam, or from the fallout that came out of an inequitable draft. And fixing it would be a work of decades, not just a couple of years.

After eighteen months in Bamberg, we were transferred to Belgium, where I was assigned to be the assistant executive officer and speechwriter for Gen. Alexander M. Haig Jr., the Supreme Allied Commander, Europe. He was, in his own words, "a force," and I watched in admiration as he worked the diplomatic and military channels in NATO and with the Pentagon, arguing for a strong defense and working to help shape an effective security policy.

Over the year and a half in which I worked for him, he brought me gradually into his world, allowing me to see his perspectives on national strategy, the Middle East, the American political scene, and work with our NATO Allies. I bounced my ideas in those areas off him, slowly firming up my own views and beliefs in the process.

His war stories would hold my rapt attention, stories about MacArthur, in whose orbit he had been as a young officer, about Nixon and Ford, Vietnam and China, the Soviet Union and NATO, Israel and the Middle East. And these stories gave me critical grist for my own ideas. Indeed, many years later, I found myself reflecting on what I had learned from him. That commanders must have authority, and should demand it in time of war; that Presidents must have the courage to educate, and even, occasionally, buck popular opinion; that the U.S. must live up to its obligations, especially to allies in wartime; that the U.S. must support its friends and allies, but must also consult and listen, particularly in Europe and in the Middle East; and that public quarrels and name-calling with actual or potential adversaries are to be avoided as much as possible.

I was growing personally, too. Looking in the mirror on the morning of February 19, 1978, I reflected again on my near death in Vietnam and finally admitted to myself my own sense of failure for having been shot, and also for not even having seen, let alone killed, the man who shot me. It was as though I could finally exhale the suppressed and frightening anger. I let it go.

It had been nine years of teaching, study, reflection, and hard work at army posts in the United States and Europe, and within the executive branch in Washington, D.C. All this was partly a reflection of a military institution increasingly integrated with civilian policy. The old distinction between war or peace had broken down in practice, for the United States was under continual threat, and the responses to that threat had to draw upon military expertise and close military participation in the formulation of policy, whether in the intelligence community, or in the great questions of national strategy. This required military officers who had not only thought about their profession, but also understood its role within the broader array of U.S. aims and means.

Today, the army struggles to maintain its competence and character in the midst of a drawn-out war. And, if anything, the military is more closely bound with civilian policy than ever, when threats to the homeland, and the so-called long war against the terrorists are considered. This kind of war doesn't require just generals and colonels who will follow orders. The opposite is the case, for without their active participation in the process, the orders are likely to be ineffective or worse. We can't have an army of yes-men who shy away from the nuances of policy discussions on matters such as U.S. law and America's image abroad.

And always, there is another army, an army of those who have served, but serve in uniform no longer: our veterans. We released them by the hundreds of thousands after their service in the late '60s and early 70s, many wounded and emotionally scarred by the war. And we chopped away at the officer corps, too, screening officers and then releasing large numbers involuntarily. Some reverted to the noncommissioned officer ranks to maintain their pensions, while others sought duty with the National Guard or Reserve Forces. But it was altogether a painful process for everyone involved. Service was regularly disrespected, real medical needs were sometimes ignored, and long term damage was often done to veterans and their families.

The active duty Army usually doesn't know them, as the disabled, sick, or emotionally infirm are just washed out and disappear from sight.

We were all healthy or recovering, and it was the rare case that a permanently handicapped officer (like my good friend and West Point classmate, Bill Rennagel, who had lost his arm below the elbow, but with a steel hook played baseball, golf, and passed physical fitness tests) could remain on active duty. Years later, I would see those others whom the Army had discarded, often hanging around street corners in their worn Vietnam uniforms, often unemployed and, too often homeless, no longer remembered by the Army as an institution.

Today, another generation is once again discovering all this, and we must address the full needs of our veterans and their families. Combat experiences can cripple as well as kill, emotionally and physically. Painful newspaper exposes have already revealed the tragic neglect of wounded soldiers struggling for long term treatment at Walter Reed Army Hospital. But the problem is not that limited. Veterans' care, especially mental health needs, have been woefully underfunded, and extraordinary efforts will have to be made to provide for our veterans coming home from Iraq and Afghanistan.

Today, our army is made up entirely of volunteers, and we have worked hard to maintain its cohesion. So far, despite the stresses of repetitive tours in Iraq and Afghanistan, the army has held together remarkably well. But there are worrisome signs with recruiting and retention, and protection of the volunteer force remains a critical concern. We simply need a much larger force to meet the demands placed on it. And we must face up to the needs of the Guard and Reserve elements, especially, who, when they come home, face problems regaining employment and securing health insurance. These men and women are fighting for us. And if we don't take care of them, we'll lose them, defeated not on the battlefield by the enemy but by the politicians at home.

SEVEN

~

BUILDING A FORCE

The bright winter sun of February 1980 danced off Cheyenne Mountain in the distance as the troops stood in formation that cold morning, waiting expectantly. These were the men of 1st Battalion, 77th Armor—550 soldiers, organized into a powerful fighting force. The battalion comprised five subordinate headquarters: a headquarters company, three tank companies, and a combat support company, with the latter made up of scout, mortar, and antiaircraft platoons. These men had all enlisted as volunteers, drawn to the army from across the country. They had a wide variety of personal backgrounds, and more than half of them were married. As I approached them, they were relaxed in the at ease position: feet spread shoulder width apart, hands clasped behind their backs.

This was my new command: a tank battalion. You were given command of a battalion only once, and with that command came all the responsibilities for mission accomplishment and for the welfare of the troops and their families. That meant, in a more immediate and day-to-day sense, that I would be responsible for the soldiers as well as for their equipment, their barracks, their budget, their reenlistment, their training, and even their off-duty conduct and any problems they might have with their families. If they had a car accident, I was responsible. If they lost a weapon, I was responsible. If they got in a bar fight downtown, I was responsible.

I'd been placed in command the day before, on February 11, 1980, and it was time for me to speak to the troops. This would be an important and a tough moment for all of us.

There's an old saying in the army that you'll never have more influence with your men than what you will have in your first speech to them on your first day in command. These men had doubtless heard other battalion commanders before me, and I had never given such a speech. But the organizational impact of my taking command could be most important.

I knew the men in this battalion had worked hard over the last few months, but according to the army's measurable standards, they had not succeeded. The previous battalion commander and his wife had been well liked, but the men felt frustrated by their repeated failures. The pervasive attitude that swept through them was that of losers, and their morale was in the dumps. Whatever else I might do, I knew that had to be turned around. In my first speech, I wanted to be brief, straight, and inspirational.

"Men, I'm proud to be with you. This unit has a great combat history, from World War II, from Korea, from Vietnam, and now from here at Fort Carson, Colorado. I want you to know that I fought in Vietnam, and I have served in Germany, and now I'm here with you at Fort Carson. And I'm proud to be here with you. Together, we will make a great team. You can count on me to give clear instructions, firm orders, and to do the best I can to get the job done as well as to take care of each of you. But I will also expect a lot from you . . ."

The next day, a young soldier I'd never met sent me a letter that read:

"You're inspiring us like some kind of Clint Eastwood, and we won't let you down."

I had been put in command early because this particular unit was in real trouble. They simply weren't making the grade in taking care of their equipment. In a tank battalion, taking good care of your equipment—which especially means your vehicles—is the basis for everything else. The situation was much the same as that which, back in the nineteenth century, would have faced the commander of any cavalry unit: In order to effectively perform his mission, he had, first of all, to make sure that his men took good care of their horses.

Tank battalions, of course, are organized around the use of tanks. In the 1st of the 77th, the tanks were M60 A1s, sixty-ton monsters armed with a 105mm main gun and two machine guns and moving around on two tracks. And they were just as lethal as they looked. As my platoon sergeant had told me when I was training in Germany as a cadet, "Tanks are killers, and they don't care who they kill." They could kill by design, but they could also kill by accident. The battalion's wartime mission would be to attack or defend against the Soviets if they crossed the border into Germany, and we had to be trained and ready for that. And the fundamental task in our preparation, of course, was keeping the battalion's fifty-four tanks operational.

Part of the problem was that this particular battalion had been pushed really hard over the previous year. They had spent a lot of time in the field running the tanks in maneuvers, and the tanks were already old to start with. In an effort to save on unnecessary wear and tear, the battalion had been testing the concept of leaving some of the tanks in a kind of ready-to-use storage and then having the crews share the remaining equipment.

But that hadn't been all, for there was also required tank gunnery training, individual soldier training and testing, and comprehensive command inspections.

Under this regime, the officers and men of 1–77 Armor were being driven at what was simply an unsustainable pace. Just like a horse that's been ridden too hard for too long, the battalion had broken down. Morale was in the pits and a mood of angry resignation had set in. One of the more glaring results of this unit funk was that the troops and their leaders had failed to adequately repair and service their equipment. Engines were leaking oil, steel was beginning to show through wear spots in the rubber bushings on the steel tracks, and the drive sprockets that transferred the power from the 750 hp diesel to the tracks were simply worn out. Gun tubes were just plain overcooked, and some were even loose in their mountings.

And those were just some of the more glaring problems with the tracked vehicles. But the battalion's three hundred wheeled vehicles fared no better. Truck driveshafts were worn out, bolts were sheared off, and the protective rubber boots on axles were torn. There was snow on the ground, and the outdoor motor pools, where most of the work on the vehicles had to be performed, were bitterly cold. It was obvious that little was getting done, and when the division's annual inspection team came down to spend a full week inspecting the equipment and the procedures of the battalion, the results were predictable: They flunked. Badly.

Late in the afternoon on the day I took command, I had walked to the motor pool where the tanks were parked. More than half of them had their back decks off, and the engines and transmissions had been removed for repairs. Oil was still seeping from some of these massive hulks, and the canvas tarps that were supposed to protect them were too often either missing or badly torn. Snow and ice covered some of the tanks, and here and there tools were just lying on the ground and rusting in the snow.

This was now my problem.

"You've got six weeks to get the equipment in shape and pass a reinspection," my boss had told me. "I'll get them to leave you alone until then."

I knew he wasn't happy, because the battalion's poor condition reflected on him, too.

This was the real post-Vietnam volunteer army. We were all learning together, generals, colonels, captains, sergeants—experimenting with new tactics, bringing in new equipment, trying to develop more cost effective ways of training. And to keep our ranks filled, we were also trying to recruit the best possible volunteers, and to encourage those who served with us to stay on and reenlist. The army had hired an advertising firm, which had come up with a catchy slogan: "The Army Wants to Join You!" But that didn't seem to work too well, so they replaced it with another: "Be All You Can Be!"

During those first few days, I talked to each of the five company commanders separately. I first heard their assessments, and then I enlisted their support. And at the time, they all seemed to be earnest and determined. But somehow they just hadn't gotten the job done. I also heard a lot of remorse from them." Sir, we let your predecessor down," one said candidly, "but we won't let you down."

Leadership is about performance and about competence. You have to deliver. Whether it was tank gunnery or maneuvers, I'd pretty much learned the hard way. As a battalion operations officer in Germany, I served in a troubled unit, plagued by personnel turnover, lack of strong operational procedures, and a staggering workload. When the battalion in Germany wasn't training properly, I'd had to fix it, personally writing training tests for soldiers, supervising the companies' training, and working to coordinate training with a number of sister units. When it came time for our big maneuver tests, I'd had to create and brief the plans. When my crew and I almost failed tank gunnery qualification, I'd had to really master the fine points of the equipment. As a brigade executive officer at Fort Carson, I worked once again with technical manuals and experienced technicians to master the equipment. This was going to be my fourth successive job out of the last five where I would be replacing someone who hadn't gotten the job done.

To be effective, you have to organize, you have to study, and you particularly have to master details. You must push your team hard and motivate them to attain high standards. And you don't get style points. It wasn't about posturing or about who could best relate to the boss. Successful leadership in the army, I believed, was measured purely on performance.

One of the first things I did in my new battalion was to set up a system of equipment inspections and get a tight grip on subsequent repairs. After the crews and mechanics had checked their tanks, identified the faults, and ordered the spares, I asked the commanders to check them again personally. Then, after they were satisfied, they were to bring each tank to me, and we would inspect it together. I wanted them to really know the equipment.

One evening I was with the A Company commander. He was a fine officer, and had been one of the top cadets in his class at the academy. Together, we crawled up on the front slope of his tank, and I reached down into the telescope well with my arm, checking to see if the telescope was securely mounted. The telescope was the secondary sight for the tank, and it was held in place by a mounting bolt deep inside the well. As a young officer myself, I'd learned on the tank gunnery range that if it wasn't mounted securely, then that tank couldn't "hold bore sight." In other words, you'd never hit a target, because the telescope wouldn't remain aligned with the gun tube.

This tank was missing the required bolt. Obviously, someone, sometime, had removed the telescope, and then, because the bolt was hard to reach and hidden in the well, had simply neglected to put it back in and mount it correctly. I turned to the company commander.

"Rollie, do you know what a telescope wedge bolt is?"

"No, sir."

I had him stick his arm down and feel the hole and threads where the bolt belonged, and then grip the telescope and watch it move in its mounting. It was loose.

"Do you see?" I asked.

"Sir, it'll never happen again. I promise you the next time I bring this tank back here, I'll know how to check every component, and there won't be any mistakes."

He was as good as his word. A few weeks later, he and his company, and the rest of the battalion, passed the reinspection with flying colors. I was really proud of them. They had mastered details. They could "grip" their units, and make the wheels and gears work. We began to call it "command grip"—the skill and insight required to know how things worked in detail and just how to make them work.

A few days later, the officers and I were sitting in the Officers Club with our wives for the Friday night Happy Hour. It was an army tradition. After a hard week, the wives joined the husbands for an hour or two at the club. I'd found it essential for morale and team building to bring the wives into the circle and try to break the performance pressure on their husbands. People could unwind a little, joke, and tell stories about the week and each other. And if you did it right, the officers and their wives left feeling appreciated and respected as part of the team.

But it was also a time for looking ahead a bit. As we sat around the table, I brought up the subject of Ironhorse Week. The division and its support organizations—all 26,000 troops—would set aside one week in May each year for sports and military skills competition. Battalions had to field football, basketball, softball, track, marathon, swimming, tennis, and golf teams. There was competition in marksmanship, in marching, for best squad, best tank crew, and best scout and mortar crews. And there were "combatives," like tug-of-war, horse-and-rider fights, even wheelbarrow races.

Ironhorse Week was designed to draw in every soldier in the division, even those who weren't particularly athletic. The idea was to emphasize excellence, break the hard daily routine, and raise morale. Medals were presented at a daily awards ceremony, special big round discs that hung from ribbons and were worn around the necks of those who had won them for the rest of the week.

Battalions could also win a trophy, and, I was told, it was the ultimate Fort Carson measure for "bragging rights." For the last couple of years it had been won by an infantry battalion. Infantry battalions were larger—averaging over 750 troops—and maybe a little rougher than tank battalions. At least, that's what they thought.

If you wanted to bring a unit up to its best, you had to set a high mark on the wall, and we certainly couldn't rest for long on the success of that maintenance reinspection.

"So we should think about Ironhorse Week," I said, over the pitchers of beer on the red gingham tablecloth. Most of the commanders had been through it before. I hadn't.

"What was it like?" I pressed. "What do you think we need to do in order to make a good showing?"

As they began to talk and share ideas, enthusiasm mounted, and people began to commit themselves emotionally. The B Company commander, who would soon be reassigned and leave Fort Carson, had been one of my students at West Point. He looked at me hard.

"You're going to do it, aren't you, sir? You're going to help us win Iron Horse Week."

This from the guys who had been in what was widely considered one of the worst battalions in the division. And now they were talking about making a mark high on the wall of Ironhorse Week.

"No," I said. "I'm not going to do anything. Rather, it is what *we* are going to do. *We! We!* It's all of us!"

They absorbed that, were a little louder, and more confident. They had finally begun to believe in themselves, and you could feel their energy level rise.

Bill Frederic, the operations officer, drafted a detailed plan, assigning specific responsibilities for each event to one company or another. Battalion-wide tryouts would be held for some of the teams, and time would be set aside for preparation and organization.

One day, Staff Sergeant Carmona, a tank commander from A Company, came into my office holding a yellow T-shirt, with the battalion's motto, "Blackhawks!" emblazoned across the front. These were the first distinctive unit T-shirts anyone had ever seen at Fort Carson. Carmona was a free spirit, and he'd spent his own money to have a bunch of shirts printed up. We were picking up momentum.

By Ironhorse Week we were ready. Soldiers knew their assignments and had their T-shirts. Commanders had organized their teams, practiced, and, when they were among the top athletes, were participating themselves. At battalion, we were tracking the multiple simultaneous events, backing up the companies' efforts, providing water and transportation to move troops from one effort to another. I picked up responsibility for the swimming team.

At the first evening awards ceremony, we started picking up medals. Our troops and their loud cheering was punctuated by company guidons jabbing toward the ceiling of the big tent. By Wednesday night's ceremony, we were actually winning, earning more medals than any of the other twenty-five battalions. The boss, four-star general Bob Shoemaker, from Atlanta, was there to present awards and see the spirit. It was the big night, and 1–77 Armor walked out having shown their winning spirit. Best of all, our troops felt like winners, and they had earned that feeling because they *were* winners. You could feel the energy among the troops.

But by Thursday night the superior numbers of the infantry battalions began to tell: They just had more athletes. Ultimately, we finished second in points, but having begun as "maybe the worst battalion on post" in January, we'd definitely turned things around.

At the Officers Club that Friday night, a couple of the new battalion commanders, preparing to take command of their battalions, cornered me in the bar.

"Wes, we saw what you did," they said. "We can do it, too, and we'll smoke your ass next year."

But this was one of the problems—if the environment is too competitive, then cooperation suffers. I had seen this mistake too often in Army units. What might look to senior officers like a little friendly rivalry might actually be a bitter, destructive competitive struggle which could really drive units apart. The key was to set high standards for performance and then build teamwork to meet those standards, not to set units against each other in win-lose competition. I resolved to avoid those kinds of head-to-head competitions in my units if at all possible.

Over the next two years, the battalion went on to success after success in the competitive peacetime environment of Fort Carson and the 4th Infantry Division. Tank gunnery, maneuver training and evaluation, no-notice readiness tests, maintenance inspections, deployment to Germany, reenlistment competitions—we excelled in all of them. We became a consensus pick as one of the top three battalions on post. And we actually won Ironhorse Week each of the following two years, which meant we had beaten all of the much larger infantry battalions in the competition.

Troops, like all Americans, like to compete and win, and good leaders find ways to help their men become winners. It was a lesson drilled into us again and again, from our first days at West Point. But the best leaders understand that you have to make all the troops winners. It's no good to have just one great unit, or one great leader.

But turning a unit around is much like a business turnaround. It is a matter of changing people's image of themselves while building strong foundations for performance, and then putting in enormous effort to actually assure the performance.

First, we established clear tasks and priorities. There were positive priorities, like "Qualify all crews in tank gunnery"; and there were negative priorities, such as "Lose no weapons," and "Reduce the numbers of AWOLs by 50 percent." So you have to prioritize. And we did. And what was lower priority we sometimes didn't do as well. But I had learned that some events and occurrences are so damaging that they must be avoided, and positive effort must be expended to prevent these things from happening—you can't just hope for the best. So these became our "negative priorities," things we didn't want to happen

We briefed everyone on our tasks. They were simple, direct, and measurable. And we measured ourselves at every opportunity. It wasn't always pleasant to see yourself marked on every action, but it did promote "command grip". We pressed the tasks downward to soldiers, tank crews, and mechanics, so everyone knew what they had to accomplish— or avoid—every day.

Second, we established strong, regular, personal communications. Once a week, I had a lunchtime meeting with the company commanders, and each morning they met with their platoon leaders and first sergeants to discuss the work that day, the following day, and the people available. In the motor pool, every mechanic received assigned tasks twice a day, and a supervisor was responsible for these tasks. And all of this was done in a unit that was constantly moving in and out of the field, receiving new personnel at the rate of twenty-five to forty per month, and, on one occasion, deployed to Germany for six weeks.

And third, we built a command climate where soldiers were important, with everything from Best Soldier programs, giving recognition to the outstanding soldier during a particular week, and Ironhorse Week, to a lot of personal time listening to troops and taking their suggestions. And we worked hard to keep "command energy," pep, and enthusiasm alive with these programs. I also learned a lot from listening to soldiers, and tried never to repeat old practices that had failed, unless I could understand and explain why "this time" would be different.

Across the army, scores of battalion commanders like me were implementing similar programs, inspiring soldiers and leaders, and building stronger teams. You could feel the rising level of confidence in the phone conversations and flow of letters, and in the rising quality of the new soldiers coming in and the steadily improving rates of reenlistment.

Today, in my business activities, I see many CEOs tackling the same issues as they build new companies or resurrect those that have fallen on hard times. It always starts with a clear vision, well-defined priorities, and good communications both ways. And you have to keep a sense of humor and never allow yourself to get arrogant. It sounds simple, but believe me, it isn't easy.

One Saturday morning, I'd come into Battalion headquarters to catch up on paper work. There was no one around but the Staff Duty NCO, and I'd come in wearing my "civvies"—khaki pants and a golf shirt. One young soldier was pushing a broom in the hallway, his punishment for having started a fight with another soldier. After a few hours, I left, but came back later to check for messages. Inside the latrine, an unexpected one was scrawled in the freshly paint cubicle wall: "In civvies, Lt Col Clark ain't s___." And that was true—the authority I carried was by virtues of the U.S. Army. It wasn't personal. We were all, in that respect, equal. It was a message I've never forgotten, and it has served me well.

Organizational leadership is the bread and butter of America's working culture. That's what has given us advantages in business as well as in battle, and it has to be studied, practiced, learned and relearned. Each situation and each set of personalities is different, so the ability of the leader to learn, to observe and critique himself, to correct dysfunctional gestures, patterns, activities, and to create both a bond and a certain distance from his or her teammates, is critical.

But these skills are also eminently teachable. And there's probably no better learning laboratory for leadership than the armed forces, where men and women are placed in so many different stressful situations. I'd just like to see our veterans get more credit for these skills from their potential civilian employers.

EIGHT

REBUILDING THE ARMY

In midsummer 1982 I learned that I had been selected for promotion to colonel. I could barely believe my good fortune. Selected early for major, selected early for lieutenant colonel, and now I was selected for promotion to full colonel at the age of thirty-seven, the youngest and, so far as I could tell, about the most junior officer on the list. Little did I understand what I was about to face.

By historical standards, of course, I wasn't so young, for in time of war American officers of the past have often been promoted at a young age. George Armstrong Custer, for instance, was promoted to brigadier general during the Civil War at the age of twenty-three. But by contemporary standards, considering that the average age of the officers then promoted to colonel was in the early forties, I was young. Very young.

Then, in what seemed to be a complete reversal of fortune, I was twice not selected for the next step up the ladder, which was command of a brigade. In the ways of the army, you never actually learn why; your name just isn't on the list.

The first year of eligibility for the selection, I was studying at the National War College in Washington, D.C. Upon graduation in June 1983, I was initially assigned to Headquarters, Department of the Army, Office of the Deputy Chief of Staff for Operations and Plans. I would be one of several hundred officers in that office. Then, after the "second look," in which I was considered but not selected to command a brigade, I was given an opportunity to go back to the field. Or perhaps I should say that it was as close as I could get to the field as a colonel without commanding a brigade, and that was an assignment to the National Training Center at Fort Irwin, California.

The post-Vietnam Army put a high premium on selfless service, meaning that it did not want its officers looking first for their own glory, and it did not want them to "use" their troops to advance their own personal ambitions. But that was a bit tricky, as the Army *did* want its leaders to be ambitious for their troops and units. It also wanted its leaders to seek opportunities for duty; it just never liked "show-boating". And in 1984, the National Training Center was about as far from "show-boating" as you could get.

NTC is a training area for Army units in California's Mojave Desert, uninhabited land on which dozens of tanks and their supporting mechanized artillery and other armored vehicles can maneuver together at the same time. Here they can stage war games, in which a unit undergoing training can maneuver against an Opposing Force and truly test the skills they would need in time of war.

This was the so-called "high desert". Fort Irwin is thirty-five miles from the nearest town, its training areas a land of rocky mountains, arid valleys, and dry lake beds, right on the edge of Death Valley. It is not an assignment for the weak.

It was 113 degrees that day in August 1984 as we drove over the hill and saw Fort Irwin. Through the haze and dust along the two-lane road to the cantonment area, the buildings looked like dollhouses, a small cluster of civilization lost in miles and miles of ocher desert, sweltering creosote bushes, and stony, craggy mountains. We'd been there briefly fifteen years earlier, and Gert knew exactly what we were getting into. The only difference was that we hadn't been there in the full afterburner blowout, sunbaked heat of summer. And that made everything different from what we had experienced earlier. Much different. The house trailer they had for us was air-conditioned, but the only other cool place on post was the "beverage locker" at the PX, as the post exchange was commonly known. Gert joked that she seemed to want to spend a lot of time looking at cases of Coca-Cola and 7-Up during the first couple of days.

I was to be the commander of the Operations Group at the National Training Center. As an army officer who valued above all else the training of soldiers in peacetime, this was my dream assignment—to run the training and evaluation system for the army's new training center.

I had a thousand square miles of desert and five hundred officers and NCOs to work with. Rotating through the training each year would be fourteen brigades, each with two maneuver battalions and artillery and engineers units. That meant a package of about four thousand troops would be arriving for unit training every twenty-seven days. My job, then, was to plan the scenarios, oversee the most realistic live-fire training ever, direct observer/controller teams, create the lessons learned, and by constantly coordinating and implementing the entire process, to truly help build a fighting army.

When we got there, the National Training Center was just ramping up. Much of the system was still being improvised, and that meant I'd be there on the ground floor. As we drove onto the post, I couldn't wait to get started. This wasn't about just training a battalion or a brigade; it was about training most of the army's battalion and brigades. In other words, it was about training the army.

Over the next few days, I took stock of my new command. I had 3 lieutenant colonels, 28 majors, 102 captains—all of them previous company commanders—and about 400 lieutenants and NCOs. And bit by bit their stories came out:

"Sir, I was told I either had to come here or retire."

"Sir, I've been passed over for promotion, but they said if I came here I might make it next time."

"Sir, I was told I wasn't good enough to teach at West Point, or recruit, or go to ROTC."

Well, I knew how they felt. We all wanted to soldier, and here we had a great opportunity to do just that.

Over the next few months, under the guidance of the new commander, Brig. Gen. Ed Leland, we trained units at a punishing pace, constantly innovating with new wrinkles on the scenarios, new measures of evaluation, greater reliance on high technology scoring, more realism in the artillery and air engagements.

And it was both difficult and inherently dangerous work. We had hundreds of heavy vehicles and thousands of exhausted soldiers engaged in challenging operations. Operations were continuous, running for twenty-four hours per day with men driving over rough terrain at night under black-out conditions, all of this conducted on a very demanding tempo. Our intention was to stress the organizations to the breaking point, identify the risks they were running, and strengthen them at their weakest points.

On the first rotation in early October, an armored personnel carrier from a unit in Georgia ran off an embankment and rolled over in a ditch in the early morning darkness. But when that happened, a spare machine gun barrel that was loose inside the vehicle struck a young soldier in the head, and he was killed. He was the battalion commander's son.

During the next rotation, a tank driver from a unit in Kansas set his brakes and climbed out to retrieve a map that had fallen off the fender. But the tank's brakes weren't fully set: they released, and the tank rolled forward and crushed the driver. He was nineteen years old, married, with a child.

During the third rotation, we had another, even more bitter tragedy. The senior observer/controller for the live-fire team was Maj. Frank King. Dragon 3 was a great field leader, I thought. He juggled all the details, controlled his team, called for targets, evaluated the battalion task force, and had a tremendous instinct for danger. Ed Leland and I usually accompanied these live-fire attacks, each of us in his own jeep, just to provide oversight and call a halt if anything went wrong. So far, this day, everything seemed to be going just fine.

But as the next series of targets came up and the unit opened fire, something went wrong: As the forward tanks opened fire, so did either an engineer armored personnel carrier, commonly referred to as a "track," or an air defense track, not up front but several hundred meters back in the formation. Large-caliber bullets—hundreds of them—spewed in several cones of fire toward the targets, the sounds merging with the deeper *craack* of the tank cannons. It was an impressive display of coordinated firepower.

But what the gunners on one or more of those tracks couldn't see was the O/C jeep that was moving off to the left side of the lead platoon of tanks. They may have thought they were shooting a safe distance away from the tank platoon moving forward, but, hidden from view by the rolling terrain, was Major King, in his jeep.

"Cease fire! Cease fire! Dragon 3 is hit." Lt. Col. L. M. "Mac" Johnson was riding in Frank's right seat, just reporting in after completing his battalion command tour to become the first of our battalion-command experienced senior observer/controllers. "Cease fire!"

The cease-fire was immediately passed from the O/C net to each of the radio nets in the battalion. Firing stopped immediately, and the vehicles halted. General Leland and I drove down off the observation post to find Frank King.

In the three or four minutes it took us to find him, other O/Cs had already driven over to him. I pulled up from behind and saw Frank's head, tilted back, leaning against the seat. Mac was standing beside the jeep, holding the radio handset, helping call in medevac. I jumped out and ran over to Frank, bumping into a captain who was turning away, sobbing.

"He's dead. He's dead . . ."

Frank was dead. His head slumped back, eyes closed, a hole the size of a fist in his throat where the big bullet had blown through, raw red, his field jacket drenched in his lifeblood, his skin already a pasty whitish-green. A medic stood beside him, helpless. Frank had been killed instantly.

It was a bone-chilling, raw cold that morning on the high plateau, the sun showing weakly through thin, high clouds. And it was deathly still. There was no sound but the distant thump-thump-thump of the medevac chopper flying in. I looked at Ed Leland. He was swallowing hard, and his hands seemed very pale as he radioed in a report that would go to the Forces Command commander in Atlanta.

We both knew we were responsible. Frank King had been in charge, but I was Frank King's boss, and Leland was mine. We both had approved the training, and we'd watched it proceed, just as we had many times before. There were many safety measures built in, and anyone could have called a cease-fire had they seen the danger. We could have halted the exercise, but we hadn't. I don't know how Leland felt, but I felt a terrible sense of failure, of responsibility, of guilt, and of shame.

Gert was at the hospital on base by the time Frank King was brought in, waiting to be with Frank's wife. Also there was OPFRO Commander Colonel Jay Hamby's wife, Wanda, who was highly respected by everyone.

The accident hit us hard, and Frank's loss was emotionally devastating to the entire community. The families knew it was difficult and sometimes dangerous work: Their men would be gone for days at a time and then arrive back home dirty and exhausted from the extreme exposure. They knew that soldiers from the units that rotated through the training cycle were occasionally injured or killed. But they hadn't realized the risks our own men took as well.

After this tragedy, everyone's "fear factor" went way up. I counseled and consoled team members, and we reviewed procedures, examined details, strengthened safety measures, and double- and triple-checked each other. Slowly, we rebuilt the team's confidence and determination. We were able to restart live-fire training a few days later—it was simply too important for the army to give up.

In early February, Col. Jay Hamby was out before dawn inspecting positions on a freezing morning. He wanted to be sure his units were ready to meet the Blue Force, the unit that had rotated in for the training. But driving in blackout conditions, the driver couldn't follow the rough terrain. He ran the left side of the vehicle over a rock, and the jeep flipped onto its side. Somehow Jay fell out and was crushed and pinned by the vehicle.

The dust-off call came over the radio and I got word to Gert. An hour or so later, Gert was in the hospital again with Wanda, but this time it was Wanda's husband who had been lost.

The peacetime army wasn't supposed to be like this.

We tightened down on discipline. No loose equipment in vehicles, better maintenance checks, tougher safety briefings, more emphasis on leader responsibilities. On each subsequent effort, we found more ways to improve safety and reduce risks without compromising training. In fact, we found our actions not only improved safety, but also improved overall unit performance.

The truth was the force that had come to Fort Irwin for training, the Blue Force, usually lost its battles with the Opposing Force, whose personnel were stationed there and went through this training repeatedly. The observer/controllers were there watching each battle, monitoring preparations and planning, listening on the Blue Force's radio frequencies, and being assisted by analysts located miles away in an operations center, who were themselves watching the battle unfold on TV and through telemetry. After each battle, the O/Cs assembled the units and sought to account for what had happened, thus helping the Blue Force improve its proficiency. This was all important, for we wanted to use the NTC to fix the army. But if no Blue Force could defeat the OpFor, that made me very uncomfortable.

We continued the after-action review system, and we began to change the process in a very significant way. We were no longer measuring units by whether they conformed to the army's fighting doctrine. Instead, we were asking, "What happened?" "Why?" and "How can we do better?" It was "discovery learning," a collective pursuit of the truth. No war stories; we knew what happened, but we had to ask the units to help us discover the why.

It was a brutally honest process. Mistakes were uncovered, and commanders had to explain themselves in front of their teams. This required total candor; no cover-ups, no excuses. "Why did you issue the order so late?" "Why didn't you rehearse clearing the obstacle?" "Why weren't the tanks bore-sighted?"

Each battalion fought six or seven battles against the OpFor while brigade and division commanders often sat in on the after-action reviews. They carried the lessons home at all levels, and bit by bit the army changed. There were still a few senior officers who wanted to fire people when a mistake was uncovered, although one by one they, too, began to recognize that we were creating a "learning organization."

We were making improvements, and creating a very open atmosphere. But after several months, I could no longer suppress a troubling question: If every one of the mistakes regularly made by the visiting Blue Force was avoided, would they then win the battle? There were an almost infinite number of mistakes a Blue Force could make, but even though the OpFor also occasionally made mistakes themselves, they still won. Why, I wondered, was that?

I watched one day as an OpFor tank crew in battle came up out of their defensive position. The tank commander had a way of standing up in his turret and looking over terrain while his vehicle was still concealed. When he saw that he could pull off an effective shot, he brought his tank over the rise and out of hiding, quickly aimed and took a shot, then backed down and disappeared. The tank commander was intense, wanting most of all to win, to defeat this supposed enemy. And he was savvy.

His tank knocked out several Blue Force tanks without being spotted, and when it was time to pull back, he used smoke to cover the retreat.

And then it hit me: Only soldiers win battles. The top leaders can lose by making mistakes, but the winning is done by the troops, by their skill, cunning, discipline, intuition, and motivation. It was obvious, and like many other obvious but previously unseen factors, it was a bombshell in its implications, for we had clearly invested far too little in the most critical element on the battlefield: our soldiers. Not the commanders, but the soldiers. Commanders could lose a battle, but only soldiers could win.

I laid out my theory to General Leland, and we presented it to every visitor and in every briefing. In no time it was all over the army. We had cracked the code: In order to win, focus on drills at the crew and platoon levels. Again and again. To win you had to be better at the soldier, crew, and small-unit level. You could lose a battle higher up, but you couldn't win one.

For the Army, placing more emphasis on individual soldier skill, motivation and discipline has been the key piece in building a better force. Over the years, we steadily increased the command focus on this level of the organization, even though it was the least "glamorous" and the most difficult. During the late '80s and early '90s we made great strides, but unfortunately, it has taken the losses of Iraq to gain the budgetary priority needed to begin to adequately address all the needs of our soldiers.

And as I reflected on our experience at the time, I realized that you usually only see the faults that you're looking for, and only correct the mistakes that you anticipate. Because we were all officers and senior NCOs, we were focused too much on fixing our own skill set. It was "lucky" intuition to recognize the overwhelming contribution of the individual soldiers. And because it cut across the grain of vested interests long term institutional bias toward high-tech solutions as the expense of individual soldiering, it was even tougher to fix.

Soon army leaders were putting in place a training center for light infantry forces. They began discussing their use of computer simulations to bring a similar training experience to the division and corps commanders, the two- and three-star generals who hadn't yet been tested in battle.

Then, to my great relief, my name came out on the brigade command list in my third year of eligibility.

We left Fort Irwin in January 1986, but we left behind a much different organization and a much different training process than we had found. We also left close friends—we'd been through a lot together in the High Mojave Desert.

I went on to command a brigade of the 4th Infantry Division at Fort Carson, Colorado, where I had a chance to put into practice all that I had learned and tried to teach at NTC. We practiced tight discipline, taught a lot of officers' classes, and emphasized soldier skills. We took our training seriously, and our division commander, Gen. Jim Hall, and his assistant division commanders gave us the support and resources we needed.

Because I had previously commanded a battalion at Fort Carson, it was a bit like coming home, for Gert and young Wes as well as for me.

Mom and Dad were living in Hot Springs, Arkansas, long retired and enjoying a small house on scenic Lake Hamilton. They would occasionally visit us on our assignments, and we tried to visit them at least once a year. But Mom wasn't doing well. She'd had her first heart attack when she was sixty-four. Then at age seventy-one she had an operation for carotid artery disease, and some years later she told me her legs just continued to ache. She was handling these things well, however, for she told me one day, "Wesley, you'd think at seventy-eight I'd had a good, long life. But nobody wants to stop."

She and Dad couldn't make it to the brigade change of command ceremony in April 1986, and I couldn't make it home for Mother's Day in May. Then on Saturday, May 10th, Dad later told me, she was just arranging the Mother's Day flowers I'd sent her when she cried out and fell to the floor—dead, of a massive heart attack.

No one can love you the way your mother does, and you can't really love anyone else the way you love your mother. I still feel the pain of her death.

Meanwhile, my son was swimming, playing on the lacrosse team, and getting ready to graduate from high school. Gert enjoyed our colleagues and their families on post, and we all enjoyed living in Colorado once again.

Then, all too soon, my brigade command was over. The army chief of staff decided that I would stay with the training effort and take over the fledgling effort to create a Combat Training Center for division and corps commanders.

The idea was to put the generals and their staffs under the same kind of pressure as lower units and produce training and learning effect at their levels of command just as we had at battalion and brigade. The concept was to have observer/controllers, an opposing force, realistic war-fighting scenarios, and candid after-action reviews. Of course, there was at least one key difference: We had to resolve the combat not with real troops and lasers but with some kind of war-game simulation. It was simply impractical to deploy tens of thousands of troops just to train the division commander and his staff, and since I had helped develop the National Training Center, I was assigned to bring those lessons and procedures to them.

And there was another difference: Generals liked losing even less than colonels did. Everyone warned me that there would be resistance. This was a sensitive area, as senior officers, many for the first time, found themselves in a win-lose maneuver battle in a realistic scenario against an enemy force capable of defeating them.

During this period, we trained and evaluated twelve divisions and one corps. And with every iteration, the training became tougher, more realistic, and better evaluated. The army chief of staff, Gen. Carl Vuono, was there for many of the after-action reviews, for this was his personal program. And the program moved forward.

For the first time since maybe the Louisiana maneuvers of 1941, the army had the tools to train, exercise, and really examine command and control of large formations and top-level leadership in preparation for war. Ideas and insights flooded out—for new hardware requirements, new procedures for decision making, new emphasis in training and preparation.

This was perhaps the final step in rebuilding the active-duty army after Vietnam. We had converted from a draft to a volunteer force, in which soldiers had to be inspired and motivated to stay in. We'd recognized that families weren't a nuisance but the essential backbone of the whole army concept, and they had to be respected, resourced, and listened to. We'd brought in new, up-to-date equipment. We'd revised our approach to warfare by recognizing that battles were won by soldiers, not by officers grease-penciling colored lines on map overlays. We had changed organizational behavior significantly by creating a climate in which mistakes were recognized, admitted, and learned from. And we had built functional integrity into the force, from the bottom, now, all the way to the top.

We reformed the army by creating a "change engine," in this case a simulation in which organizations were required to prove their mettle under realistic conditions. And the simulations were so realistic, and so powerful, that they became the focus of most of the organization's efforts.

The process has applications far beyond the military. We need simulations like these throughout government to deal with urgent issues like homeland security, disaster assistance, and nonmilitary intervention in failed states. It's a growth market, but we must have leaders who are not afraid to push their teams hard—even to the extent of failing in the training scenario—in order to gain the needed lessons!

We should be modeling disasters in coastal cities, for example, and then bringing together all the teams responsible for mitigation and causing them to "play it out." We might have prevented Katrina's most severe consequences had we done so. Or we could model economic and legal development in Africa, for example, showing how changes in private property laws, or national taxation policies, can impact years later, and working with leaders in those countries to help them understand the implications of their choices—or their failure to make choices.

For the army itself, these efforts provided a true reform in organizational climate and focus. All of our top leaders have now grown up through the training center process of tough missions, an opposing force, a realistic environment, after-action reviews, and candor. But in large organizations, I discovered, you need a kind of continuing revolution. You have to keep reexamining and reinventing, because the excellence is usually not just in the processes but in the thought that goes into the processes. You don't win simply by following the rules; you win by understanding and revising the rules.

As for the Clarks, in the five years since we'd left the high-level work in Washington, we'd moved three times and been at the very center of the efforts to transform the army. For me it had been incredibly satisfying. Gert and Wes had put up with the dislocations and upheaval, and he'd won an ROTC scholarship to Georgetown University.

In September 1989 General Vuono invited us into his office in the Pentagon, where he and Gert pinned on my first star as a brigadier general. We were moving back to Fort Irwin to command the National Training Center, which was, we believed, the best brigadier's job in the army. We arrived in October, 1989, in the middle of a training cycle.

"Sir, you and Mrs. Clark are due at the Officers Club in a half hour. You're hosting General Sir Peter Inge and Lady Inge, and then taking him out to the battle tomorrow morning."

Well, at least things hadn't slowed down at NTC!

When we arrived at Fort Irwin, much had changed in the almost four years since I left. Many of the most promising officers in the army were now requesting assignment to NTC in order to truly learn their chosen profession. The rotation schedule had stabilized at twelve brigades per year, which was a little more bearable pace, and "Lessons Learned from the NTC" were prominent topics of discussion across the army. But for us, everything just looked brand-new, and of the highest quality.

Hundreds of millions of dollars were being spent on new barracks, motor pools, headquarters buildings, an operations center, and, fortunately, on amenities for families—new family housing, new schools, a new convenience center and shopping facilities. Fort Irwin was now a showcase for the army. It was on every prominent military visitor's itinerary, and we had a full-time staff organized to host them all properly.

For me, it meant a welcome command, unusual at the one-star level, plus the chance to continue to push realistic operations, leader development, and lessons learned and to allow the lessons we learned to alter doctrine. But the biggest change would be that I would now have responsibility for the entire community: ten thousand people, homes, stores, utilities, schools, the hospital, operating budgets of over $300 million, and one thousand square miles of Mojave Desert. Now I would have the opportunity to take care of soldiers and families the way I'd always believed that it should be done.

I began by hosting an off-site convocation just a few days after assuming command. We pulled all the senior leaders together at a conference center in a hotel in the Victor Valley area, where we discussed our priorities and started building the community teamwork we would need.

As I stood in the line going in for registration, I already knew most of the officers, and their wives, but one woman behind me I couldn't place. I introduced myself, then asked

"What do you do here?"

She introduced herself, and then asked,

"And what do you do?"

A couple of people standing nearby chuckled at her expense. After all, I'd had the assumption of command ceremony, and then my picture appeared in several newspapers, including the post newspaper, and it had been all over the community for the last few days. But I got the message: most of us are a lot less important than we think we are. Even when you're the Commanding General, and everyone's taking your picture and yessir-ing you, you have to understand that most of the folks wouldn't recognize you and don't think much about you. She helped me keep my new command in perspective.

Gert had always been active in the Wives Clubs or Spouse Groups, where we were stationed. She collected ideas, sensed problems, and helped me think about better ways to take care of the troops and their families. And she was strong and outspoken. So was I. We had to be. There was a backstory.

On the first day of school in September 1976, when I was with the 1st Armored Division in Germany, I happened to be at home in the German village of Gundelsheim when the army school bus pulled up in front of the house to let Wes off after his first day of classes. As Gert and I watched from the window, the bus door opened, but no one emerged. A minute later, Wes bounced off the bottom step and landed on his behind in the street. His lunch box was tossed out after him.

Somewhat upset, I went out to pick him up and speak to the driver, but the bus was already roaring off down the street. I pursued it for several miles in my car before finally losing sight of it.

As a result of this incident, we became the unofficial watchdogs of everything and anything associated with the American school. School bus monitors, after-school activities, playground supervision—Gert was always there. According to the school, Wes was too advanced for first grade, because he had been taught to count in kindergarten. They recommended advancing him immediately to the second grade, where he would become the youngest and one of the smallest children. So we became curriculum experts because we worried about what our son was learning.

When the division's top school specialist came to Bamberg to address the PTA, the local commanders knew they would hear a lot of criticism. One of them even asked Gert not to say anything in the meeting, but that was a mistake. As Gert said, "Who does he think he is, asking us to be quiet so he can protect his career when our kids are in jeopardy?!"

She lowered the hammer on the local school and the command climate in the PTA meeting. Eventually, we got a new school principal in Bamberg.

We also learned that a little after-duty socialization goes a long way in keeping units happy. In every assignment we worked the Friday night happy hours, the monthly hail-and-farewells, and the annual holiday parties. From the constant buzz of community dialogue we took our tasking efforts.

At every assignment, I was responsible for the on-post conduct and off-post welfare of the soldiers and families under my command or supervision. We visited apartments, had discussions with landlords and creditors, met with PX and commissary leaders, and complained to the post engineers about the quality of on-post housing and upkeep. At Fort Irwin, Gert had worked for the Red Cross, counseling young families about budgets, trying to help them deal with their overwhelming expenses on scanty army salaries, and then helping them get loans to see them through. Over the years, we learned a lot about how communities were supposed to operate and what needed to be done to keep them on track.

One of the most important of our new directions at Fort Irwin was enhanced community involvement. We initiated town hall meetings, held in the community center with several hundred people attending and broadcast over cable television to every home. This was my idea of democracy in the military. On the stage were each of the principal staff officers or leaders affecting the community: the engineer responsible for grounds and housing, the school principals, the PX and commissary managers, the commander of the hospital, and others, all prepared to present their programs and respond to concerns expressed by community residents.

The first meeting began innocuously enough, with the presentation of brief summaries of the latest projects and priorities. Then the floor was opened for questions.

"General Clark, what are you going to do to reduce the waiting time at Burger King?"

I gave that one to the PX manager, but there was more.

"General Clark, why can't we plant flowers in our yards?"

"Engineer, what do you say to this? Who has said, 'No flowers'?"

The engineer deferred to his grounds expert, who was seated in the audience. "General, we sent out a flyer to all residents of the new quarters explaining the drip irrigation system. It delivers just enough water for the shrubbery that we've planted. We asked them not to plant flowers because we can't trust that they'll water them, and then they could rob our shrubs of water."

He meant well, but this was just the kind of bureaucratic paternalism I'd been fighting against for twenty-five years. So it was about trust, was it? That was easy. "Well, let's authorize everyone to plant flowers so long as they water them, and then, when we're out checking neighborhoods, we'll watch the shrubs and watering. You all, please water your flowers!"

Applause rang loudly through the hall. Then this:

"General, I brought my child into the hospital emergency room a couple of weeks ago. He's nine years old and was running a high fever, and we asked to see a doctor. They made us wait outside, and we had to stand out on the loading dock in a forty-mile-an-hour wind for over two hours while we were waiting to be seen, and my boy got even sicker, and that's just not right!"

"Doctor," I turned to the hospital commander, "who would have done this? Surely we can do better?"

The hospital commander sat up straight, arching his back defensively. "Sir, I did that! That boy may have had a communicable disease and there was no way I was going to risk infecting everyone else waiting in the emergency room. I'm not going to risk the health of my staff and other patients for something like this!"

It sounded pretty awful.

"Ma'am," I picked up, "we'll fix this and do better next time. I'm real sorry about what happened, and if there's a way to prevent needing to do this, Doc and I will fix it." Doc and I had a long talk afterward.

After a couple of sessions like this, communication opened up, people understood their opinions were respected, and everyone on the staff understood better that their job was to serve the community. It had taken me twenty-five years to gain the authority to bring people together as a community, and it was one of the most satisfying aspects of all my military service. Then it became a matter of solidifying the vision that was emerging: soliciting good ideas, generating greater community commitment to their schools and activities, and presenting this more engaged, dynamic community to our senior leaders, including those in Congress, so that it could become fully funded.

It was not long after I took command that Saddam Hussein's Iraqi forces invaded Kuwait. Word ricocheted through the army that a deterrent force might be sent to Saudi Arabia, and my boss at Forces Command in Atlanta, Gen. Ed Burba, happened to be out with us observing the training.

"Sir, if we do send forces, I'd sure like to find a way to help. I'd love to go."

I was wheedling, and felt a little bit embarrassed. But I'd spent my entire career preparing for something like this, and I wanted to be part of the team.

"Wes, it's probably not going to happen. If we need you, we'll call. You've got a very important job here."

A few days later, the first troops deployed. I then found myself having to relay General Burba's refrain to the dozens of others who came to me requesting to be sent on Operation Desert Shield.

During the next few weeks, we did some important work, building replicas of the Iraqi fortifications and obstacles and planning and practicing how to attack. We created an Iraqi threat, and let the 1st Infantry Division practice against it before they deployed to Saudi Arabia. We experimented with mine plows and dozers, even flying B–52 bombers over the minefields we had emplaced to mimic those of the Iraqis and dropping bombs to blow them up. We made TV tapes of the techniques, showing how best to attack the fortified positions, and traveled to Saudi Arabia for a four-day troop visit in early December to brief our findings to the force preparing for the invasion. It was all we could do to help.

Not that it was easy.

The army, my army, the armored force, was going to war. Jim Wilson, Pat O'Neal, and I were going back to California. The only thing worse than being in war, I figured, was to have the army go to war and not be there to help.

~

The world was changing. The Berlin Wall had come down in 1989, and a Bundeswehr officer had explained that Soviet troops would be leaving. What had been East Germany and West Germany was going to be reunified into one German nation. U.N. peacekeeping operations were starting to make news, and conflict was simmering across former Yugoslavia.

For the troops and families at NTC, it had been an exhausting and frightening few months. A few soldiers had been pulled out and sent to war, but most of us had just worked seven days a week trying to train and certify forces here, while the families anxiously monitored the foreboding news broadcasts and worried about what the future might hold.

But by May 1991, the peacetime training schedule was in full swing again. There were new commanders and troops that had not gone to Kuwait who had to be trained, and then there was training of the units when they returned and cleaned up, too. The NTC had become one of the great engines driving the army.

Gradually, the army returned to normal, and we resumed the grinding rotation schedule, determined to continue to help shape the army. Our work to support and care for families wasn't unique, as leaders all over the army pulled together to help it become more and more of a family institution. The men and women we want to serve value their families, and their children's education, more than they value the next pay raise. And so it has made eminent good sense to dedicate resources to the family side.

From the outside, the armed forces may appear to be all about weapons and orders and discipline. But from the inside, it's very much a community, and the best of our leaders do all they can to make it more like this. There may be no elections, but if they are good leaders, they are campaigning hard for the understanding and support of the families, as well as the troops themselves.

In America, and in the armed forces, people don't follow authority blindly. Rather, they have questions, see problems, and have suggestions. Better listening by leaders not only makes the institution better, but also makes it more appealing to the higher quality people we want within the service. Especially now, in the midst of the major combat commitments of the past several years, America's military families need to be listened to, and supported. And better listening encourages more initiatives from the families themselves.

Promoting families extends across a broad range of efforts that includes the provision of larger and more modern military housing and customer-friendly hours at the post exchange and commissary. It means schools that really take an interest in the kids and in their parents, and a predictable duty schedule for the soldier that avoids last-minute deployments or unexpected weekend duty. It calls for a robust, proactive medical system, adequate pay and allowances, and assistance in helping military spouses find meaningful employment. These are also the issues of modern America, of course, in cities and towns that dot the nation.

But there are also some unique military requirements. For example, soldiers are often away from home, so their spouses must be given broader authority to act in the soldier's absence. Most children never quite understand the military family member's absence, especially when they are sent to war. This makes the children a little more emotionally vulnerable in school, and it raises the stress of the spouse who stayed home enormously.

Families need information, reassurance and support. And unlike many non-military families, they are often far away from their friends and relations who could provide a safety net. This makes every kind of family problem more difficult. And when soldiers return from war zones, they are often highly stressed and face a welter of uncontrollable, unpleasant images and emotions. Post-traumatic stress disorder, as it is called, now afflicts about one-third of the returnees from Iraq and Afghanistan. They need continuing professional help. Every returning soldier should be professionally evaluated for the disorder because the soldiers often don't recognize it in themselves. But above all, soldiers and military families cry out for understanding by America. They are living in relative isolation, especially during times of war, yet they are serving and sacrificing for us.

Another group that deserves special consideration is our National Guard and Reserve forces, their ranks filled by men and women who are incredibly dedicated. Just imagine giving up a weekend a month for years, and two weeks every summer, and then being called to active duty. Such service could mean immediately losing the means to support your family, in the short term, and then returning home and possibly discovering that your old job is no longer there.

Today, it is clear that guardsmen and reservists and their families should have the same access to Tricare and dental insurance as the active-duty forces—because we expect our reservists to be medically prepared for duty on short notice. To ease the financial burdens of service, we should further consider establishing programs to terminate military active-duty pay gradually, over a year or more, as the forces transition back to the civilian sector.

These family programs—along with avoiding the kind of endless commitments to hazardous deployments like Iraq—represent the two best means of avoiding a return to the draft. And whatever the social merit of conscription—and there may be some—our nation's army is far more effective if it is comprised of skilled, motivated, and experienced *volunteers!*

NINE

IN SEARCH OF A MISSION

It was a Friday afternoon in May 1991, and I found myself in the Pentagon with an hour free. How could I best use the time?

Paul Wolfowitz was number three in the Pentagon, the under secretary of defense for policy. He'd come out to Fort Irwin in early January to observe our new training methods, and we'd driven around the desert together. We had talked about national strategy, and he invited me to drop by to see him when I came through Washington. Because of my work for General Haig, we seemed to know a lot of the same people.

I found the big wide stairs and navigated my way to his third-floor office.

"Hi," his assistant said to me. "I'm Scooter Libby. Paul will see you now," and he opened the door and led me in.

A little distracted, Wolfowitz looked up.

"Congratulations on the war, Mr. Secretary," I picked up. "You must feel really good about the way it's all worked out."

Saddam's forces had been pushed out of Kuwait, American casualties were light, our troops were coming home, and there was tremendous public support for our action.

"Hi, Wes. Well, thanks, but not really," he said. "We screwed up and left Saddam Hussein in power. The president believes he'll be overthrown by his own people, but I rather doubt it."

I had read about this criticism, but I was out in the real army, and out of the loop in these kinds of discussions. I listened intently.

"But we did learn one thing that's very important," Wolfowitz continued. "With the end of the cold war, we can now use our military with impunity. The Soviets won't come in to block us. And we've got five, maybe ten, years to clean up these old Soviet surrogate regimes like Iraq and Syria before the next superpower emerges to challenge us."

I tried to engage a little.

"You mean China? We would have to act that rapidly?"

"Maybe. We could have a little more time, but no one really knows."

The conversation drifted off into pleasantries, and I excused myself. But the discussion lingered in my mind. The cold war, was it really over? A new U.S. strategy? The use of force? More missions in the Middle East? I had a lot of questions, and I didn't have any answers.

Then I returned to the desert and continued training troops for a few more months. I could put aside those questions. Others did not

On the other side of Europe, one of those who was quick to recognize new possibilities was Serbian strongman Slobodan Milošević. A brilliant functionary inside Tito's Yugoslav Communist Party, Milošević was an English-speaking lawyer who, by his early thirties, was managing one of Yugoslavia's largest industrial conglomerates. He then moved steadily up the ranks, and with Tito's death in 1980 had gradually positioned himself as one of the leaders in post-Tito Yugoslavia. As a Serb, he was a member of the nation's largest ethnic group, the one that dominated the military and government. And he found himself able to heighten his power and influence by accentuating the historic animosities between Yugoslav ethnic groups. Without the threat of a Soviet takeover or of an intervention by Tito's strong hand, factional forces, envies, rivalries, and even naked hatred, began to build

On June 28, 1989, Milošević rallied nearly one million of his followers in a large field in Kosovo to commemorate the six hundredth anniversary of one of the great Serb tragedies. Though the historical accounts differ, on June 28, 1389, at the Field of Blackbirds, or Kosovo Polye, Serbian forces had been defeated by those of the Turkish Ottoman

Empire. The defeat led to centuries of Turkish occupation of the land and oppression of the Serbian people.

Although Kosovo was once a center of Serbian culture, this largely rural area was gradually populated hundreds of years ago by Albanians, a people who speak an entirely different language and had been converted, over time, to Islam. The reaction of most Serbs as the Albanian population mushroomed was to move north into more urbanized areas, thus abandoning Kosovo to the Albanians. And although it is true that Albanians make up some 90 percent of the population of Kosovo, that region remains a raw nerve to many Serbs, who compare their relationship with Kosovo to the relationship of the Jews to Jerusalem.

Those present on June 28, 1989, say that when Milošević took the stage, his voice boomed out in apparently impromptu rhetoric, delivering a strongly pro-Serbian rant that could only stoke historic animosities. And among his massed and fervent Serbian supporters, he lit a fire. Soon, groups of Serbs were meeting privately, remembering their heritage, drinking, singing old songs, arming themselves, and preparing to refight the old battles, particularly the one when Croats had sided with Germany in World War II, while Serbs had fought against them with the Soviet Union.

These age-old vicious enmities had all been kept quiet under Tito, but they were kept alive. There was silence, but no forgetting.

The Europeans as a whole could see the emergence of a post–Cold War world, too, and many were asking whether NATO and the American troop presence in Europe were still needed. French diplomats reportedly reminded the United States that what might be happening in Yugoslavia was a European problem and that Europeans could handle it without American help.

And it wasn't only Yugoslavia. The whole world was stirring. Old perspectives seemed out of date, alliances seemed obsolescent, commitments seemed unnecessary. Governments were overthrown, and alignments were changing. In Romania, longtime dictator Nicolae Ceau_escu was captured in vicious fighting and subsequently executed on Christmas Day 1989. East German, Czechs, Hungarians, and Poles were throwing off the Soviet yoke of the Warsaw Pact, which was officially dissolved on July 1, 1991. Even the long-repressed Baltic republics were rising up, seeking independence and fending off the last vestiges of Soviet imperialism.

In August 1991, I watched on CNN as Russian president Boris Yeltsin mounted a tank and turned away a feeble coup attempt aimed at saving the old system. The Soviet Union itself was dissolving.

And in faraway Afghanistan, new forces were moving to fill the power vacuum when the Soviets departed, leaving their puppet regime fatally weakened. These were the Taliban, militant Islamists, using the name of God and the magnetic power of faith to take over a war-ravaged country. It had been the Soviet Union's Vietnam, and now thousands of victorious fighters were seeking to consolidate their power.

Elsewhere, old cold war conflicts lingered, even after the super-power competition was gone. Africa had been wracked by war, and now the entrenched hatreds and the legacy of war fueled continued fighting within and among nations. From Ethiopia and Eritrea in the east, through Sudan, Somalia, Tanzania, Namibia and Angola, up to Liberia, and Sierra Leone, and into the heart of Africa, in countries like Rwanda and Burundi, almost everywhere there was violence, conflict, or open warfare.

I tried to follow the news and would occasionally see someone I knew among the newsmakers, like French General Cot, on assignment to the new United Nations mission in the Balkans. But the events were distant and poorly reported, the actors were largely unknown, and the origins of conflict often obscure.

In these years Gert and I were living near vibrant civilian communi-ties—Colorado Springs, Kansas City, the Los Angeles area, and not far from Austin, in central Texas. Around the army posts there was new con-struction, and increasing signs of prosperity. The old coffee houses and topless bars of the Vietnam era were largely gone, and many of the pawn-shops and cheap secondhand stores were vanishing as well. Even the fast-food shops were being dressed up. Wherever we lived, we made local friends, visited the local attractions, and felt at peace in America.

In the early 1990s most everyone was caught up in their day-to-day lives. The days when America felt threatened, even close to nuclear war, were gone. It was over. President George H. W. Bush was calling it the New World Order; historian Frances Fukuyama wrote a book whose title stuck: *The End of History.* And in no place did we find any real awareness of what was happening abroad. People were patriotic and proud, and of course we'd done our duty against Saddam Hussein's aggression in Kuwait. But for most Americans, the rest of the world was a long way away.

~

By September 1991 Gert and I were saying goodbye to Fort Irwin. It had been our home twice, and each time we'd put our whole heart and soul into every aspect of the mission. We loved the people we served with, and there were a lot of tears driving back to Virginia for my new position at Training and Doctrine Command.

It was a two-star position. Major general. I would be one of the key staff members for Gen. Fred Franks, helping him embed the lessons of the Gulf War and the NTC in army war-fighting doctrine and in our materiel requirements. We moved into a big house, and I met my staff of three hundred military and civilians. It was all day, six days a week, and two briefcases of work every evening at home.

After a month or so, I ran into the former Army Chief of Staff, General Carl Vuono, now retired, at a briefing.

"Wes, what are you doing here? You're supposed to be commanding a division somewhere!"

A few days later the new army chief, Gordon Sullivan, called. "Don't hang any pictures. You won't be there long," he said.

A few weeks later, we got orders to report to the 1st Cavalry Division, at Fort Hood, Texas. I would become a division commander of one of the most storied divisions in the army. It had been formed on horseback in 1921 to patrol the Mexican border, deployed to the Pacific without horses for World War II, helped liberate the Philippines, occupied Japan, fought in Korea, converted to the 1st Air Cavalry Division for Vietnam, and finally returned to Fort Hood in 1972 to be reorganized as an armored division. The unit had just fought in Desert Storm under Maj. Gen. John Tilelli, and after I took over command from him, I would get them ready for the next problem.

But in late March, Dad called to tell me he was going in for open heart surgery. After my mother had died in 1986, Dad, though he was my stepfather, had assumed her role as my booster, counselor, and confidant.

Dad had the surgery, and his recovery at first was fine. He was still in the hospital, and was cheerful enough. But he was an old man, and he had just been through major surgery. In addition, he had apparently had a minor stroke, then caught pneumonia. Week after week, his condition swung back and forth: now in intensive care, then back on the ward. I visited almost every weekend.

In May 1992, our son Wes graduated from Georgetown. He had made a strong record in the School of Foreign Service and had taught English in Czechoslovakia for two summers. But he had really enjoyed ROTC, where he made good friends with other cadets and thrived on the field training exercises. When we arrived for his graduation ceremonies, he met us in his new army uniform.

"Oh, he looks so good!" Gert exclaimed. Yes, he truly did.

I administered his oath of commission, then Gert and I, one at each shoulder, pinned on his gold second lieutenant's bars. Gert beamed and cried; I hadn't seen her so happy in many years! I was proud of him, but also a bit concerned, knowing how much the uniform I wore and the army life our family led may have influenced him in his choice of profession. But he was young, and whether he stayed in and made the army his career or not, I knew that a few years in uniform could only do him good.

Then it was back to Arkansas, where Gert and I spent our time between assignments with Dad as his struggle continued. At last it was time for me to report to Fort Hood, but I assured him that I'd be back soon. I'd been gone only three days when the hospital called.

"Your Dad passed away this morning."

At first, I was stunned. Then, I was confused, angry, and terribly sad. His death was a heavy blow.

Life is precious, so precious, and people fight for hope. And while there's hope, they fight to live. No matter what they may look like on the outside, elderly and infirm, inside they're a young person, at once loved and yet alone in a terrible ordeal.

Dad's death closed an important chapter in my life. The love from my parents was now something I could only remember and hold in my heart. I had to pass that love on to my son, and Wes was far away, pursuing his own army career. Gert and I put our hearts back into the army and the army families.

And with my division, I practiced all the leadership lessons I had learned over the years: morale building, command team socials, frequent dialogue within the top levels of command, off-site meetings to thrash out vision and command philosophies, annual and quarterly briefs to establish objectives and tasks, periodic performance counseling two levels down, and lots and lots of walking around, talking, and making myself available. We took the training we had developed for the reserves during the Gulf War—the "lane training"—and built on it to focus on the small-scale teamwork that wins battles. Repetitive rotations to the NTC had finally gripped the whole Army. Noncommissioned officers knew their duties, and they were prepared to take command in the field; battalion commanders now brought real training center or combat experience as company commanders to their duties. And the Army focused tightly on correcting any problems detected in "the last war".

All the generals knew this wasn't enough. But it was where we had to start while we tried to understand the major international forces at play in this new era. And we had to take care of our people, too. If they weren't retained, motivated and developed, we'd have no army left. So I had to work community responsibilities as well, including support for the schools and various housing areas.

When I visited the Fort Hood high school for the first time, I asked the principal what the main problems were. It soon came out that teenage gangs were the untreated, and so far untreatable, wounds in Fort Hood society. I asked who the gang members were, some clots of teenagers on the playground after lunch were pointed out to me. So I walked over to them, smiling my friendliest smile. One young woman turned to face me as I approached, so I spoke first to her:

"So what does your father do?"

"In the army," she said, through clenched teeth. "He's in Hawaii. I hate him." She was fifteen, petite, attractive, Hispanic. And angry. She lived with her mother and stepfather (also in the army). There were fights in the home, and she needed her friends, she said, gesturing around to the small group nearby. The principal had already warned me that the girls often pack knives for the boys to use, but this girl was no threat to anyone. I kept her engaged, and we talked neighborhoods, activities, and how to make things better. Then she drifted off, and I moved on to the others, seeking their feelings, trying to see their world.

We identified the parents by name, counseled them, and made them more aware of their children's behavior. We worked hard to provide more activities for teenagers on post, and cleaned out the brushy areas between neighborhoods where the older kids would hang out at night. Bit by bit the violence, and the fear, went down.

I'd learned over the years that this linkage between parents and kids was crucial. Parents should really know what's going on in school. That means that when a student receives notice that he has to report to a teacher or other official for guidance counseling, the parent should be given the time off from work so they can be there. We picked two schools, got the parents together at a PTA meeting, and explained the new program.

From the back, one of our sergeants asked, "So, you don't trust us to know what's going on? You want to force us to be there?," "No," one of my staff explained, "we want to make it possible for you to be there, no matter what the conflicting duty requirements may be."

The program was a success, and soon it was adopted by every school at Fort Hood, and later, across much of the army. Parental involvement was recognized as the key to improved education. When the parents heard things about the behavior of their child in school straight from the teacher, they were able to ask questions, and then to team up with the teacher to help their child reach his or her potential. In education, there is no measure of accountability more important than a parent's love and a teacher's commitment—teamed together—to prepare a child for life.

With the disappearance of the Soviet Union, the world had changed. Now it seemed the army was being used as more of a humanitarian relief mechanism abroad. One U.S. Army division was tapped to go to Somalia to help deliver relief supplies, despite warnings about what that country would be like. Within the military these were called Operations Other Than War—OOTW—or sometimes Military Operations Other Than War—MOOTW. Whatever it was going to be called, we watched from the sidelines as tragedy ensued, and struggled to understand the implications for the army. Fighting had begun in June 1993 when a local warlord ambushed a United Nations column. The security situation was deteriorating, and now U.S. units and equipment were being deployed.

By August 1993, we were getting strange requests and directives, like, "Have two OH58D Kiowa Warriors ready for airlift by 0900 Sunday. You may send one maintenance tech, but no crews."

But there was a major lesson here being ignored, a lesson our army had learned many times over: When you deploy, send cohesive units, don't pick units to pieces, and don't go into combat, or near combat, with patchwork outfits. Why do we have to relearn old lessons at the expense of our soldiers, I wondered.

And there was a new president. From Arkansas. One Saturday morning, as several of us were out riding horses, the corps commander, LTG Pete Taylor, leaned over and said, "So the president's a friend of yours?"

It was said casually, but there was a bit of accusation, too.

"He asked the chief at West Point last week if he knew 'my friend Wes Clark'?"

Well, we had met once, in college. But not at Oxford: I left a couple of months before he arrived there. And we'd had dinner together once when I passed through Arkansas several years before. With the army's permission, he'd appointed me to serve, along with about thirty other people, as one of his commissioners for the White House Fellows program. Still, I wouldn't have thought he was a friend.

But a few months later Gert and I were in Washington for the introduction of the new class of fellows, when the president walked right over to Gert, called her by name, took me aside to meet the vice president, and invited us upstairs for dinner. The invitation was unexpected, and I was surprised.

It had happened in October, a few days after eighteen American soldiers were killed in Mogadishu, Somalia, and soon we were upstairs in the White House, in a dining room wallpapered with pictures of West Point cadets. It was so ordinary, and yet so overwhelming. This was the President of the United States, and Gert and I were sitting at his table and eating supper with him and his wife, and some others from Arkansas, including the Oscar-winning actress Mary Steenburgen. Then the talk at the table turned to our response in Mogadishu.

"What do you think we should do?"

He, the president of the United States, was asking me. I felt a little disoriented as I tried to answer; this was far beyond the leadership, discipline, training, tank repair and family welfare issues I was working every day at Fort Hood. But I would give him my view. I recounted the options I saw: withdraw, hold steady, or reinforce, and told him, "Reinforce with at least a division, and clean them out. Please don't let them get away with this kind of attack against our soldiers."

He didn't do that, however, for he found a way to reinforce offshore to pose a deterrent threat while taking no action, and soon our troops were withdrawn.

The post–Cold War world was increasingly unfamiliar—and would tax the imagination, skills, and characters of soldiers and political leaders alike. Institutions like the U.S. military—and the U.S. government—have a difficult time adapting to new environments.

We had already confronted this problem before, when we were rebuilding the army in the mid-seventies. But the problem then was the Soviet threat: "how to fight outnumbered and win"; "how to defeat the second echelon forces"; "how to manage rear area security and protection against the Soviet special forces." Now there was no Soviet threat. We had spent twenty years working this problem. During that time, we had designed new organizations, built new equipment, revamped training, created new disciplines of study in organizational art and leadership development, opened new facilities and changed our ethos and our mind set. We had recruited a whole new cadre of noncommissioned officers, the sergeants who are the backbone of the Army, and built a system of schooling to educate and train them throughout their twenty-plus year careers. We had become an army of "professionals," skilled and dedicated warriors, increasingly focused on the use of powerful weapons to destroy a powerfully equipped armored enemy force.

So what was the purpose of our military institutions? And what would motivate the men and women and their families to serve, to move, to sacrifice, year after year? That is the perennial question, and it must be asked over and over again.

We took pride in the outcome of the Gulf War, for Saddam's legions never had a chance. But was this all the purpose we had in mind for the army we were building? Or would there be more? And what would we need to do to our army to enable it to win the first and last battles of that next campaign? We sensed then that these were questions that would take years to answer, and decades more to learn if our answers were right.

Now, we are hopefully going to emerge from the latest wars in Iraq and Afghanistan, and the War on Terror. After these wars—and there will be an "after"—the army will again have to pack away some vested interests and pick up their new tasks, whatever they might be. We should put down a marker now, for the army must stay abreast of a changing environment. Study it, report it, and develop military requirements from it; that will always be required. But when change comes, we must not be too reluctant to drop old ideas, requirements, and materiel.

And it won't just be the army; it will be the nation. We will be in a new environment, and we'll have to adapt as a nation. It is always a daunting prospect.

TEN

A NEW STRATEGY

"The J–5 should be able to drive the staff," General Shalikashvili explained as he interviewed me a few months
later. "Will you be able to do that?" John Shalikashvili, the
son of a noble family from Soviet Georgia, immigrated to the United
States in the early 1950s and rose to become the chairman of the Joint
Chiefs of Staff, the top officer in the armed forces.

Shali was enormously admired and respected. Having arrived in the
United States at age 16, he earned an ROTC commission and rose
steadily on the basis of his sound judgment, keen insights, hard work,
and even temper. He had made it up the ladder, through every "station
of the cross"—one of the 75 percent of captains who make major, one of
the 60 percent of majors who make lieutenant colonel, one of the 50
percent of lieutenant colonels who make colonel, one of the 5 percent of
colonels selected for brigadier general, one of the 50 percent of brigadier
generals selected for major general, one of the 10 percent or so of major
generals selected annually for lieutenant general, one of the two or three
lieutenant generals selected annually for four star general—and finally,
the one four star selected every four years, from among all the generals
and admirals of all the services, to become Chairman of the Joint Chiefs
of Staff. And people liked him too.

Yes, Shali posed the right question. Could I really do the job? And he and I both knew that we wouldn't know the answer until I got to the Joint Staff in the Pentagon and tried. The J–5, director of strategic plans and policies, was the bridge to the national security planning process, to the United Nations, and even, substantively, to Capitol Hill. All the big issues passed through the shop and its three-hundred-plus officers and civilians. The question was, Would we make any difference, or would we just be the transmission line, in effect, passive observers?

Shali chose me to try.

In late March 1994 we said our goodbyes at Fort Hood. I'd ridden in a cavalry charge with the horse cavalry platoon, saber drawn and galloping across a half-mile-wide field, then vaulting over a ditch. The change of command took place in front of division headquarters, and Gert was given a bouquet of yellow roses. General Denny Reimer, commander of the Forces Command, took the colors from me and passed them to Maj. Gen. Ric Shinseki, my replacement, and then he pinned on my third star, as young 1st Lt. Wesley Clark II stood watching.

When I became the J–5, we also moved into a house at Fort McNair in Washington, D.C., a big, white-pillared colonial with a picturesque view of the Potomac River and Haines Point. And if I looked for it in the distance, I could even see the Washington Monument from my backyard. I could run the one-mile loop around post or hit golf balls across the parade field in front of my home. And it was only a seven-minute drive to the Pentagon. No one, I thought, ever deserved to live this well.

But the job also came with some big problems. My deputy, marine major general John Admire, came in to brief me on my first day in the office. Our staff work is compromised, he explained. Barry McCaffrey's been gone for months, and before I arrived, we had been "picked apart" by the Joint Staff principals and in the interagency.

So, this was what Shali implied about driving the staff. Okay. I thought I understood. Then my executive officer, Col. Tom Banks, pushed a stack of three-ring binders across the table at me.

"Sir, here are your prep books. You'll need to study them in preparation for your testimony before the Armed Services Committee next week."

The binders were stacked a foot high and filled with acronyms, names, places, issues, and problems.

This wasn't NTC, or the Cav. It was a whole world that I would have to master to be effective; literally, a whole world. The J–5's breadth ran across every continent, and to every war plan and to every policy, treaty, and issue in the U.S. government that had national security implications, even to issues like recommending approval of requests to export defense-related technology. I'd always said I wanted to work on national security issues, and so far I'd had great preparation in understanding the army, from bottom to top. Now I'd have to learn a considerable amount in a wide range of new areas.

Meanwhile, in the wake of the collapsed Soviet empire, others around the world were also exploring the new environment. In the Balkans there was open warfare. Serb dictator Milošević had seized control of the Yugoslav government and army, and the other ethnic groups, in their former respective areas, were forced to fight for their own independence.

Slovenia had made it, easily repulsing the Serbs. Croatia had fought back as well, and was free and recognized by the world as an independent state, but divided by continuing ethnic warfare. Bosnia had also declared independence, but under attack from both paramilitaries and Serb forces, as well as deeply split ethnically, the country was in its third year as an active war zone. Its countryside had been ravaged, the capital Sarajevo was besieged, and thousands of U.N. peacekeepers were struggling to restrain and contain the conflict.

In the Caribbean, the Duvalier regime that had long controlled Haiti was gone. A democratic election had placed Jean-Bertrand Aristide, a Catholic priest, in charge, but the military had soon staged a coup against him and taken over the government. Most of the governments of the western hemisphere, led by the United States, were protesting and attempting to pressure the coup leaders into accepting Aristide's return, but to no avail.

On the other side of the world our old nemesis, North Korean dictator Kim Il Sung, had turned away international inspectors and might be preparing to reprocess spent nuclear fuel in order to manufacture nuclear weapons, a direct challenge to the U.S. security umbrella in northeast Asia. Pakistan also had engaged in nuclear activities and was under U.S. sanctions.

In the Middle East, our new president had already struck Iraq with cruise missiles, but he had also worked out a promise of agreement between

Israel and the Palestinians. And he was keeping Iran in the deep freeze with a policy of "dual containment" of both Iraq and Iran while sustaining ties with traditional friends in the Middle East like Saudi Arabia.

In Africa, we were still coping with the aftermath of that brief flurry of combat in Mogadishu that had burst on us the previous October, while trying to structure a way to conclude our mission there and remove our remaining troops. There were occasional reports about mujahideen from Afghanistan in the area, but nothing specific enough to raise an alarm. And among other African conflicts, there was the festering struggle between two rival tribes, the Hutu and the Tutsi in the central African states of Rwanda and Burundi.

Outside of Russia and the Balkans, Europe was in turmoil. There was fighting between government forces and rebels in the former Soviet republic of Georgia, and in Tajikistan, and also between Azerbaijan and Armenia in a disputed region called Nagorno Karabakh. And in addition to NATO, there was a multiplicity of institutions struggling with problems, an alphabet soup of overlapping memberships, ambitions and bureaucracies: the Partnership for Peace (PFP), the European Union (EU), the West European Union (WEU), the Organization for Security and Cooperation in Europe (OSCE), and many other smaller organizations as well. And even within the EU, not all members were equal in the latest quest for European integration.

Inside the Pentagon and in Washington there was a continuing concern over the size of the U.S. military, and especially the nuclear-armed missiles, submarines, and bombers left over from the Cold War.

Many of us in government would be working on these issues, for they were the concerns of many agencies and leaders, from the president down. But my team in J–5 was responsible for shaping the military's perspective for General Shalikashvili and communicating it to the others, while defending our military interests as policy was being formulated.

Still, I was singled out by a *Washington Post* gossip piece a few weeks before I arrived that said I could drop by the White House and have lunch with the president at any time I wanted. While that reputation gave me a lot of heft as I met people within the interagency process, it also singled me out for targeting by partisan Republicans on the Hill. Not that it mattered in gossip-hungry Washington, D.C., but it just wasn't true.

Gert listened to my brief descriptions of what I was up against and said, "Well, this is what you wanted." And, as usual, she was right. I did want this job. I was on the varsity team.

But unlike most sports, there was no off-season in which to get ready. Crises and problems hit from my second day on the job, and the onslaught continued every succeeding day, including almost every weekend. The two presidents of Rwanda and Burundi were shot down as they flew into Kigali the previous night. Were they shot down by one of our lost Stingers from Afghanistan? Two days later, the French and Belgians invaded Rwanda to rescue their citizens, and the fighting was on CNN. What should we do about it?

The next morning, a Saturday, we were discussing the upcoming trip to Korea by the secretary of defense, but we had to face some salient new questions: "Does the war plan need to be updated?" and "What will North Korea do if we go to the U.N. for sanctions?" On Sunday, it was "What are the appropriate air rules of engagement to enable us to generate maximum pressure on the Serbs over Bosnian airspace and still remain within international law?" And on Monday morning, one of my assistants, who'd been out of town the previous week, reported that he was part of the group preparing plans to invade Haiti.

"Haiti?" I asked.

But I was impressed with the team of officers I was working with in the Joint Staff. A few years earlier, Gen. Colin Powell, then chairman of the Joint Chiefs, had put out a call for higher quality in the Joint Staff, and Shali had kept up the pressure. The results of their efforts were plain to see, for these officers could keep up with anyone, in government or outside. They all had advanced degrees, loads of energy, could write and brief well, and were formidable at the table in the interagency process. No wonder you could hear occasional grumbling about the primacy of civilian control from the various secretaries' offices on the third floor of the Pentagon. But all the way down, they were an impressively competent group of uniformed officers, all capable of handling the most sophisticated issues, arguments, and positions. They would have been outstanding leaders in any American business or industry.

However, in that spring and early summer of 1994, our government seemed to be lurching from crisis to crisis, problem to problem, finding stopgap solutions at the last minute and growing steadily more fatigued.

You paid a heavy price for the nonstop weekend meetings, I discovered. This was not only because they took energy, but also because they consumed the time normally devoted to the reflection and preparation that would result in momentum during the workweek.

Washington, I found, was a one-issue, never-stop town. Whatever was current dominated the press and so hogged the dialogue on the Hill. The administration would find itself too often in the response mode, trying to coordinate testimony, issue press statements, and attend to urgent-response and long-range considerations simultaneously. There were morning meetings of the deputies' committee in the White House situation room to prepare for afternoon meetings of principals, and simultaneous interagency working groups trying to look ahead to the next day's problems, with Sunday morning calls to coordinate before the Sunday talk shows.

After I had been in the job only a few weeks, during which I had already made a trip to Korea, Shali pulled me aside. "Wes, we hired you to be the strategist, so what is this strategy that has us facing a crisis every weekend?"

He said it in a nice way, but I knew he was being pounded by the administration and by critics on the Hill.

What was the strategy? Congress was hammering away, with a seemingly endless series of issues, questions, and concerns, and first on their list was one simple question: Did the administration have a strategy? There was also a provision of the 1986 Goldwater-Nichols Act that called on the Pentagon to write a National Military Strategy, though one had not been written. And why was that?

In fact, the United States was lost in the post-cold war world. Our country was adrift, and if not in immediate danger of annihilation, then certainly in danger of losing its way, squandering its resources, and failing to secure its vital interests.

In the cold war, we had had a strategy. It was formulated step by step, over two different administrations, but it was an American strategy. The first principle was that we wouldn't withdraw from the Old World, as we had after World War I; rather, we would remain engaged abroad. We helped create the United Nations. Then, as the Soviet Union began to be recognized as an adversary, we provided assistance to countries like Greece, who were resisting Communist subversion. American diplomat

George Kennan, an expert on the Soviet Union, published a seminal article in *Foreign Affairs,* entitled "The Sources of Soviet Conduct," suggesting that if we just contained the Soviets, their system would ultimately collapse.

In keeping with that concept, when North Korea invaded the South, we sent U.S. troops into the fight, battling to contain Communism on its periphery. We also sought and gained legitimacy and international support for our purposes and interests. We tried to build international law and act within it; we pushed de-colonialization; we tried to act not simply in our own interests but also in support of others.

Spurred by the Soviets and the Korean War, the U.S. rearmed, built alliances in Europe and across Asia, and, on occasion, used covert means to block Soviet expansionist efforts. But Eisenhower also rejected the concept of preventive war against the Soviets. He refused to go along with the roll-back of Communist gains in Eastern Europe, and stood firmly for decolonization and against British and French intervention in Egypt. He also supported dialogue, even hosting the Soviet leader, Nikita Khrushchev, on a 1959 tour of America.

The cold war strategy seemed to encompass every aspect of America, not just foreign policy and the military. New incentives were given to strengthen American industry, and especially its research and development. School curricula were updated to strengthen language, math, science skills, and physical fitness in the face of the Soviet challenge. American universities opened their doors to foreign students to expose them to our ideas, libraries were built around the world to explain America, and even American multinational corporations were playing a role in spreading our ideas and values. And while Democrats and Republicans always had a somewhat different take on the value of power and strength versus the value of dialogue and legal agreements, nevertheless, there was a broad and bipartisan consensus on major elements of our approach.

General Powell and Lt. Gen. Lee Butler, his J–5, had seen the problem years earlier. They had created the "Base Force," a rationale for hanging on to most of the military even though the Soviet threat it had been built to defend against was gone. In essence, the argument was that the United States was a major power with worldwide interests to protect, so we needed to retain a large force. But this formulation wasn't really a strategy, except maybe a strategy to hang on to military spending.

To be sure, Powell had a point, because you could eliminate military capabilities in a matter of months. As chairman of JCS, for example, he'd led the effort to pull back and eliminate the army's chemical and nuclear artillery capabilities, which were now gone. But when you started cutting units, dismissing troops and officers, and eliminating base structure and industrial production, these were cuts that, if those forces were needed again, would take years and years to overcome.

But the question remained: What is the threat? And could it be used to drive a strategy, akin to that of the cold war?

Ted Warner, one of the assistant secretaries of defense, worked with the White House and State Department; he and I and others began to use a standard formulation of the four dangers: (1) regional instability; (2) proliferation of weapons of mass destruction; (3) transnational threats like terrorism, narcotrafficking, and organized crime; and (4) the threat of a resurgent Russia should it change its orientation toward the West. Yes, I thought, those four pretty well captured the range of problems.

A visiting Chinese general described their study, which showed that now there would be more conflicts within nations than between nations. U.N. peacekeeping was running at record levels, with over 70,000 Blue Helmets deployed. We compared perceptions with other nations in staff talks, normally with harmonious results.

Still, none of this constituted a sufficient threat to drive an overall national strategy, at least nothing to replace the cold war strategy. There would be no magic formula that could be applied to work the post-cold war world. If we were to create a strategy, it would be based on our actions, on how we dealt with each problem, rather than on some abstract theory we might look to for guidance. During the course of 1994, 1995, and into 1996, this was difficult, challenging work.

But there was no shortage of ideas. Almost everyone in the State Department, it seemed, had a pet idea on how the military could be used. And the normal Joint Staff response, I learned, was to throw the problem right back on "the suits" at State: Tell us precisely what you want us to do, and we'll tell you what we will need and what it will cost to do it. But even so, because it had funds that could be diverted as well as transportation, communications, and other logistics that could be commandeered for "non-military" purposes, the military quickly discovered that it was the "go-to" agency.

For its part, the administration was hard pressed, and one major issue was Africa. Faced with a deepening civil conflict and reports of large-scale massacres in Rwanda, the administration temporized and worked through the United Nations. As the principal staff office working U.N. policy issues, we were involved in fashioning a response. Madeleine Albright, the U.S. ambassador to the United Nations, wanted a plan, and so I tasked my Middle East chief, Col. Perry Baltimore, with crafting a military response that could insert a force to stop the slaughter. Then I took the result to my boss, General Shalikashvili.

"Sir, here's the plan." I held out the briefing papers and map for him to scan. "U.S. logistics, intel, command and control, and some troops on the ground—maybe 20,000—will take a couple of months, cost upward of $2 billion," I continued.

We couldn't go in halfway and fail. When the United States did something, it had to do it right, I believed. If there was one single principle to hold on to, the major lesson of Vietnam, this was it: Be slow to go in, and make sure you have enough power and capabilities to do the job. Otherwise, don't go in!

"Wes, do you seriously believe anyone in Congress will support such a plan now, in Africa, eight months after Mogadishu?"

"Probably not," I admitted.

"Neither do I. Give it to me. I'll take care of this."

That was the last I heard of the plan. Discussions and briefings continued in New York, and the Rwandan Tutsi army, which had building its forces in Uganda, launched an attack to recapture the country. This time, it was the Hutus on the receiving end. The French launched a stabilization mission, ostensibly to stop the fighting and protect refugees, but they actually provided support to the Hutus. Then the United States put together its own humanitarian operation in western Zaire to provide water and relief to several hundred thousand Hutus who had fled Rwanda.

Over the next year, the terrible stories of the slaughter trickled out of Rwanda. Teachers had slain their students; priests had turned on their parishioners. It was pure genocide against the Tutsis, usually accomplished by machete. Parents were begging murderers to shoot their children instead of chopping them up and then, if their grisly request were granted, the parents were forced to pay for the bullets. One man received permission to throw his children down a well and jump after them. The stories of horror were endless and gut-wrenching. The United States could have taken action, and we could have made a difference. But we didn't. We had failed, and I had been part of that failure.

On North Korea, we did better. While the interagency was busy preparing for the worst, President Clinton had secretly dispatched former president Jimmy Carter to see the North Korean leader. Carter negotiated a sketchy agreement that may well have saved the Koreas from a dangerous crisis, if not a highly destructive conflict. But all that had been done was to open a door to an alternative. It still had to be formally agreed to and approved by both parties. Ambassador Robert Galluci, assistant secretary of state, took charge of the negotiations, and, working as part of the interagency team, my staff and I helped craft the U.S. positions as the negotiations progressed.

As usual, there were varying positions on the issues. How much would the North Koreans give up, and when? Would they turn over the spent uranium fuel rods? When would we commence construction of the two light-water nuclear reactors that had been promised? I worked my way into the technicalities of the issues and studied the records of previous negotiations with the North Koreans. And in all cases, I found that the North Koreans had been incredibly tough-minded, stubborn, and graceless. They didn't see compromises the way Westerners did. But if you looked at the conflict from their point of view, as a small, isolated country, you could see their rationality. They weren't crazy, just hard-nosed and fearful.

I joined Galucci in arguing for an approach that recognized North Korea's interest in hanging on to the fuel rods as long as possible. This was their negotiating leverage; force them to give it up too soon, and they would have to walk out. They would see no more reason to trust us than we had to trust them. To be successful, then, the negotiations had to give each side something it could consider a win.

Eventually, the negotiations produced something called the Agreed Framework. The United States, South Korea, and Japan would provide North Korea with two light-water reactors for power generation. Controls would prevent any diversion of nuclear materials, and the United States would also supply thousands of tons of fuel oil in the interim, while the reactor was being built. In return, the North Koreans would cease their nuclear work at their existing reactor and the spent fuel rods would be "canned," or placed in safe storage but not reprocessed, and would be surrendered at a later time as the two nuclear reactors were constructed.

None of us believed the Agreed Framework was the end of the matter, however. What for us was one problem among many was for North Korea a matter of regime survival. But for now, we had averted a crisis.

Everything seemed to happen simultaneously in the post-cold war world. Problems weren't sequential, and even while we delivered relief supplies to Rwanda and worked the negotiations with North Korea, conditions were prompting our engagement in Haiti. The total economic embargo of that Caribbean nation led to a further deterioration inside Haiti, a great and growing number of refugees seeking escape in small boats, and an almost unmanageable effort to rescue them at sea and intern them at the U.S. military base at Guantánamo, Cuba. A White House decision was made to invade, using a combination of airborne and sea-landed forces, as authorized by the United Nations.

Then, at the last minute, as the troops were in the air, negotiations in Port-au-Prince between a top level U.S. delegation and the coup leader, Gen. Raoul Cedras, led to his capitulation and acceptance of asylum in Panama. The airborne assault force turned around in the air and returned to Fort Bragg, and the other force, under Lt. Gen. Hugh Shelton and Maj. Gen. Dave Meade, came ashore the next morning unopposed.

In J–5, we were deeply involved in this effort. From the moment I first saw the plan, in July 1994, I could see a looming, slow-motion disaster. That afternoon I went to see General Shalikashvili.

"Sir, your plan for Haiti has a real problem," I began.

Shali looked up from his desk:

"And what is that?"

"Sir, there's no exit strategy. Once we're in, we're in, and, we'll be in the same fix in which we now find ourselves in Somalia."

It was a military-only plan, tightly classified, and it had no plan for what to do after our troops got in and took over. He took a second to think, but only a second.

"Yes, you are right. Fix it," he said.

Over the next few days I went to New York City with Ambassador Albright to help negotiate a handover of the mission to the United

Nations after the first six months. Bhoutros Bhoutros-Ghali was simmering across the table, but his head of Peacekeeping Operations, Kofi Annan, was more accommodating. We eventually got our U.N. Security Council Resolution and turnover plan accepted.

I then formed an interagency group to explore the ramifications of the planned takeover and to bring in the other necessary agencies. Soon everyone was coming to the second-floor conference room, expressing concerns and offering ideas. Richard A.Clarke was there representing the National Security Council staff, Walt Slocombe and Ted Warner from OSD, Mark Schneider from State, and many others.

A principal issue was public order and policing. Who would do this if we took out the Haitian armed forces, the so-called FAdH, in our invasion, because the Haitian organization was all the police there were? I had explicit instructions from Shali: We don't do police work—a seemingly obvious lesson from Somalia. The Department of Justice could do police training to create a Haitian police force. But they couldn't even start planning until the operation was under way, because they had no money. I explained the problem to Shali, whose response was immediate:

"You become the police training officer, "he said. "Fix it."

Eventually, Deputy Defense Secretary John Deutsch ended up calling nations to beg for "police monitors," and we got them. We suggested the Atlantic Command host an interagency rehearsal before the invasion, and then we turned over the working group to Richard Clarke at the NSC. They were the ones who should be tasking other departments of government, I believed, not the Joint Staff.

I began extensive liaison with Haitian president Bertrand Aristide, whom we were restoring to the office, and his assistant, René Préval (now president), as well as with the U.S. Atlantic Command, which was in charge of the intervention. Finally, as the operation unfolded and it was time to "insert" U.S. forces rather than have them "invade," Slocombe and I rewrote the operational directive at 10:00 P.M. that Sunday night in my office.

The landing of the U.S. troops went smoothly, but on the first day of the operation, some of them stood by as a Haitian was beaten to death in front of TV cameras. That night, on White House instructions, Slocombe and I rewrote the rules of engagement. U.S. military forces didn't do police work, true enough, but we weren't going to stand by as crimes were committed and allow disorder to spread. Too bad the lesson wasn't retained for use in Iraq.

~

At the same time, Bosnia was becoming a principal concern for me. A U.S. peace effort had stalled, fighting was continuing, and every battle-field reversal prompted a new crisis. And inside the Pentagon, Bosnia was kind of an orphan on the staff. No one from our staff had been there, no U.S. troops were present, and it was a continuing series of crises for the United Nations and the Europeans.

That's how I came to make my first trip to the former Yugoslavia, in August 1994 and was able to meet both Bosnian and Serb leaders, including the then unindicted but plenty-evil Gen. Ratko Mladi_. That visit enabled me to write an informed strategy document on the conflict for the NSC staff and the interagency group.

Nothing much changed with respect to Bosnia during the autumn of 1994. But the administration was clearly gaining a grip on its foreign policy, to the evident disappointment of the politicians on the other side of the aisle. The Republicans had seen the muffs and blunders of 1993, and believed they'd found a key opening for partisan politics.

Meanwhile, Gert had accepted a volunteer position with Republican Sen. Kay Bailey Hutchison of Texas. Kay had heard of Gert through friends at Fort Hood and asked her repeatedly to come in and help. Eventually Gert agreed, but on the condition that she should help only on military family issues, and only as a volunteer.

But the hallway rumble in Congress was unmistakable, and Gert couldn't help overhearing the plotting and scheming in Republican partisan circles.

"We're going to get him on foreign affairs," they said. "Clinton is weak, confused, and he doesn't know what he's doing. He's vulnerable."

This is the way our political system works: The opposition party spots vulnerabilities in the presiding government and offers the electorate an alternative. In this case, the Republicans had found what they believed was a glaring weakness, and they would exploit it. That's elementary in principle, but in practice, it is often not so clear.

As a senior officer working on important issues, I became part of the political environment. And this was true even though I was scrupulously nonpolitical and my best connections were with the old defense intellectual crowd of Republican administrations. But if the military work coming out of the Pentagon succeeded, that meant President Clinton succeeded, and Republicans would have no issue to pick with him. That made it very easy to understand why I became one of the targets for Republicans.

At one hearing, as I was waiting to testify, one of my assistants noticed a staffer who worked for Republican leader Trent Lott going around the room, handing out papers to each Republican senator or their staffer. My assistant went up to say hello to the staffer and discovered he was passing out a note advising that I was a Rhodes scholar from Arkansas and my military testimony was not to be trusted. A few weeks later I called a West Point classmate, a federal judge in Mississippi, to have him ask Senator Lott to call it off.

"Aw, Clinton's ruined it for all those Rhodes scholars," the senator reportedly replied to my friend. However, he did agree to stop the attacks on my experience and judgment. But at another point, some staffers were circulating a petition to have me fired, and it dutifully was sent to Senator Hutchison's office.

"No, I don't think so!" her chief of staff said. "His wife works here!"

It was not really a rude awakening for me, as I knew the political knives in Washington are sharp and swiftly wielded, often in the dark. No, it really all came down to what General Shalikashvili had told me once: "If you want to make a difference in this town, you've got to be prepared to take the heat."

But it was also true that, no matter how nonpartisan the senior military attempted to be, the Chairman of the Joint Chiefs of Staff was the principal military advisor to the President and the Secretary of Defense. That meant the top military staff could hardly be divorced from the success and failures of national security policy, and these outcomes, of course, carried political consequences. This meant, among other things, that the basic premise on which the Army had been rebuilt after the Vietnam War, the notion of pure military professionalism, a warrior spirit divorced from the other elements of U.S. power—law, diplomacy, marketplace economics—was simply too narrow to be effective.

As for our purposes, step by step, we were answering that question: What is our strategy? We would stay strong and stay engaged, use force only as a last resort, fight with allies at our side if we could, or by ourselves if we must. But somehow we had to take this response ordered by the Democrats and make it bipartisan, and then take a bipartisan strategy and gain public support for it, thus converting it into a national strategy. And then, eventually, we had to create the means and modify the forces to make it work. There was a lot to do to come to terms with the post–Cold War world. So far, we had the ideas, but we didn't yet have a publicly understood and accepted strategy.

ELEVEN

LIVING THE STRATEGY

Sure enough, just as had been predicted by experienced Balkan watchers, in May 1995 the Bosnian Muslims struck out from Sarajevo, then under siege by Serbian forces. The Serbs struck back, further squeezing Muslim enclaves isolated east of Sarajevo and nominally under U.N. protection. The British and French reinforced their U.N. troops and for the first time provided some long-range artillery. It was a welcome step, because these U.N. troops, the blue-helmeted peacekeepers, were so poorly equipped and lightly armed that they couldn't actually confront the Serbs and their armored vehicles, artillery, and air force.

But the Serbs were on the move. First, the enclave of Zepa fell. Then, despite international protests, an over-flight, and a couple of bombs dropped by a NATO jet, the Serbs persuaded a Dutch battalion of Blue Helmets that resistance was futile in the enclave of Srebrenica. Dutch soldiers put down their weapons, and a Serb force entered and seized the Muslim population. Men were separated from families, and the women and children told to move out, back to the Muslim-held territory. Under the watchful eye of Serb General Ratko Mladi_, some 7,000 Muslim men were loaded on trucks, taken a few miles away, and murdered in cold blood. At the time, NATO suspected what had happened but, except for some imperfect aerial photography, we lacked comprehensive evidence.

Though we didn't know all the facts at the time, the Serb action against the safe areas was nevertheless deemed unacceptable. Various international leaders met in London to prepare a stronger diplomatic response and military options if Serb aggression continued.

In Washington, Defense Secretary Bill Perry called some of the military and civilian leaders within the Department of Defense who were tasked with these issues over to his town house in Alexandria on a Sunday night in late July 1995. National Security Advisor Tony Lake is putting together a new plan for negotiations, Perry explained, and we might be involved. U.S. ambassador Richard Holbrooke, now assistant secretary of state for European affairs, would probably lead the talks. Should the Department of Defense put people on the team, and if so, whom? Perry inquired.

I looked over at General Shalikashvili. We both knew Holbrooke well, and I'd already had a run-in with him over NATO enlargement. He was one of those at State who continued to advocate for more use of the military. This set of negotiations would definitely be a problem for the Defense Department. For that reason, it was determined that Deputy Assistant Secretary of Defense Joe Kruzel and I would participate in the negotiations.

Shortly thereafter, new fighting erupted in the Balkans as a revitalized Croatian military force attacked the Serb-held region of eastern Croatia. Dubbed Operation Lightning, the Croatian offensive achieved immediate and dramatic success. Now it was the Serb civilians who were fleeing their homes and seeking protection in Serb areas of Bosnia. Meanwhile, the Croatian forces continued their military campaign into the traditionally Croatian regions of southern Bosnia.

The U.N. mission had finally failed, a victim of inadequate authority and under-equipped U.N. forces, and actively sabotaged by the warring factions in Bosnia, and by outside governments as well. It would be war now, and the U.N. troops were themselves at risk.

With the flames of conflict spreading across Bosnia, Tony Lake, our interagency team leader, led the first phase of the new U.S. plan. With Tony was Deputy Assistant Secretary of State Bob Frasure, National Security staffer Sandy Vershbow, and from the Pentagon Joe Kruzel and me. I was especially close to Kruzel, an Air Force Academy graduate with a Harvard doctorate and long experience in Eastern Europe. We traveled together in a small government jet to meet top leaders and discuss the Balkans. Lake explained to our European allies that this was America's plan, and they had to support it. In return, we pledged to deploy up to 25,000 U.S. troops in Bosnia under NATO control and to take over the mission from the United Nations. This was important, for the U.N. peacekeepers had already shown themselves to be powerless in the face of Serb threats to the civilians there. Our plan called for a separation of combatant forces, a territorial division of ethnic groups within Bosnia, and elections for a new Bosnian government. And the U.S. troops would return home within a year.

It was London, Paris, Bonn, the Crimea, and Ankara in five days. Then Richard Holbrooke literally came off his honeymoon, met us in London, and took control, bringing with him air force colonel and NSC staffer Nelson Drew.

Our first stop was Split, Croatia, to meet the U.S. ambassador there, Peter Galbraith, and organize our efforts. As we drove up along the coast, the view was spectacular, with glistening limestone cliffs and the deep, clear green of the Adriatic in the late summer afternoon. Staying at the Tower Hotel, tucked right beside the water in a small harbor, we noticed a third-floor balcony protruding out over the water. Yes, the proprietor told us in rough German, hotel guests sometimes got drunk and jumped from the balcony into the water at night. It was only about twelve meters high, he said.

Joe and I looked at each other, and our faces were split by wide grins. What a perfect way to build team spirit! And why wait? Let's all jump!

Richard Holbrooke demurred, others declined, and eventually only Joe and I climbed up the railing. But as we climbed, the water dropped farther and farther away. And when we reached the balcony, the water was way down there, and we were way up here. Maybe we had been a bit too eager . . . But no, the fat was in the fire now, and we really couldn't back down.

So I jumped, and Joe followed. It was a long drop, but after we surfaced, we were truly gleeful. We swam across the harbor to a rocky quay, and when we pulled ourselves out of the water there, we kept smiling and laughing as we told each other *"Not bad for fifty!"*

The next day, we began in earnest, first off to see Croatian president Franjo Tudjman, then into Belgrade to meet Serbian president Slobodan Milošević, and finally back to Croatia.

And as I watched Holbrooke work, my respect for him grew. He was smooth and eloquent in moving a complex diplomatic dialogue forward, and he wasn't afraid to tackle tough issues within the team. He was very bright, and a real workhorse. We were clearly feeling our way forward, but in him we had a good pathfinder.

Milošević was unable to guarantee that we could gain unimpeded access through the Serb siege to visit the president of Bosnia, Alija Izetbegovic, and his prime minister Haris Siladzic, in Sarajevo. So, on a Saturday morning we caught a lift on a U.N. helicopter to the top of Mount Igman, U.N.-secured territory overlooking Sarajevo. There we were met by a U.S. Hummer and a French armored car for the trip through the battle zone into Sarajevo. Tension was high because the Serbs often engaged U.N. traffic on the mountain with antiaircraft fire, and had destroyed a vehicle on our route just a few days earlier. I asked Holbrooke to ride in the HMMWV with me, and we put the rest of the team, including my assistant, Maj. Dan Gerstein, in the French armored vehicle. Then we started down the mountainside.

We halted on a narrow, cliffside road, trying to slip by a column of French trucks moving up the mountain. They had the inside position on the dirt track, and I could look out over the sharp drop off beside us and see Sarajevo thousands of feet below. Then the French truck driver halted opposite us was gesturing and pointing. A buzz seemed to go through the stalled French column. Holbrooke, speaking French, was trying to make sense of it. Some drivers were dismounting their vehicles, pointing up the road behind us. "Something about an armored personnel carrier going off the road," Holbrooke muttered.

We looked behind us. Nothing. Then it hit is. They were talking about our armored personnel carrier! We got out and ran back to where the French drivers were pointing down the steep mountainside. Yes, there appeared to be some broken tree limbs. But was there a vehicle down there? What were we seeing? Our escort officer, a U.S. Army lieutenant colonel who'd picked us up in the HMMWV and led the French vehicle, slipped down the steep mountainside to investigate and disappeared into the undergrowth. Then there was the sound of small arms-fire and a muffled explosion or two from farther down the mountainside.

The French were mystified. "Mines," they said, pointing down the mountainside. No one had communications, and Holbrooke and I were frantic. That armored car had been filled with our team members! Finally, I could wait no longer, and I started down the mountain.

"Wait, come back," Holbrooke called.

At that moment, a Bosnian general appeared, but he spoke no English. Through my poor Russian and sign language, we learned that the road switched back. This meant that if we kept going down the road, we would find the fallen vehicle from below.

Holbrooke and I took off on foot, running down the road, my army green dress uniform coat flying. The Bosnian was right, and a mile or so farther down the road, as it circled back in a horseshoe bend, we saw a cluster of halted vehicles. Someone spoke broken English, but no one could explain what had happened. I scrambled hand over hand up the steep mountainside, and soon found a medic with a dead French soldier. Two more, he pointed. That's all. The dead soldier could have been from our vehicle, but I couldn't be sure.

I slid back down to the road and saw a stretcher was being brought up from farther below, bearing an American who was barely conscious, moaning in pain. Someone pointed down below, where a column of greasy black smoke was rising.

I just started running, breaking through the brush as I stumbled and fell down the mountainside. A couple of hundred meters down, I saw the vehicle, turned on its side and burning. A Bosnian fighter leaned against a tree nearby. Stay away, he cautioned with his hands. But my men might be in that vehicle, and I couldn't stay away. I used a log to pry open the hot metal door, and it was like looking into a furnace. Two of our men were there, clearly dead, the flames licking only inches from their still faces.

I quickly looked around for something with which to put the fire out. I found nothing, so I ran back through the brush, scrambling up toward the road, hoping to find a fire extinguisher. Every soldier I'd ever lost, every accident I'd ever seen, every trace of guilt I'd ever felt, they all came back to me now. I would have done anything to rescue those men.

We put the fire out and recovered the bodies of Ambassador Bob
Frasure and Colonel Nelson Drew. Then we combed the area and
learned that two of our team had crawled out of the vehicle before it ex-
ploded. Dan Gerstein had survived by wedging himself into a corner as
the vehicle flipped and rolled some twenty times coming down the
mountain. He had helped a massively injured but still alive Joe Kruzel
get out of the vehicle, and both were taken to a hospital. Within hours,
we learned that although Dan lived, Joe had died from his injuries. Joe,
the Air Force Academy guy who jumped off that balcony with me. In so
doing, we had so openly celebrated life. And now he was dead. It was a
grievous loss and a serious setback. Richard Holbrooke and I returned to
the States and attended a memorial service at Fort Meyer to commemorate our three colleagues. After that, we received guidance from President
Clinton: Build a new team, go back, and get the job done. The guidance
was clear, and strongly delivered.

Over the next three months, we did our best to follow the president's orders. Along the way, we met numerous times with each of the
Serb, Croat, and Muslim leaders as well as with a number of European
diplomats. We took advantage of NATO air strikes against the Serbs
to gain a cease-fire and Serb withdrawal of heavy weapons from Sarajevo. We also worked to secure Russian support for the process and
slowly crafted a draft agreement. The details would be hammered out
in final form through direct talks among the parties and with our help
at a secluded location: Wright-Patterson Air Force Base, in Dayton,
Ohio.

As Holbrooke mused one day, "I don't know whether we're negotiating or mediating."

It was true, our role changed from time to time as we adapted to
whatever it took to push the process forward, sometimes carrying messages between the parties, other times trying to talk them out of their
views. At one point, I found myself arguing with Adm. Leightin Smith
on the need to resume air strikes, and at another time negotiating with
Milošević to turn over a captured French pilot.

My role had changed, too, as Holbrooke brought me more tightly
into the process. With help from Joint Staff colleagues, I prepared and
negotiated the military annex for the agreement, drove the inclusion of a
police annex, and with Jim Pardew, Joe Kruzel's replacement on the

team, helped work the territorial division that separated the warring factions. At one point, I was in Moscow, pleading with the Russian foreign ministry; at another I found myself delivering a late-night briefing to the assembled NATO ambassadors in Brussels. In the end, I negotiated the final details on the map that would divide Bosnia.

Holbrooke and I and the others on our team had spent hundreds of hours arguing with some of the worst, most difficult people in the world, including indicted war criminals Radovan Karad_i_ and Ratko Mladi_, all the while weighing arguments, watching body language, and working to generate sufficient common interests to move each element of the diplomatic process forward. Eventually, we succeeded in winning the agreement of all parties. Like all diplomatic agreements, it was imperfect, and all parties had reservations. But the fighting stopped, and NATO troops entered Bosnia.

As Holbrooke once observed, diplomacy wasn't about finding final solutions, it was just about stopping the killing. This was what most of us hadn't understood, especially those from the military. We were looking for final solutions: unconditional surrender, or some similar formula. But reality is usually more complicated. The essential thing is to move from fighting with weapons to fighting with words. There would always be arguments, and that, after all, was why there would always be a need for diplomats.

Along with Holbrooke and the others, I had spent the last four months working at the intersection of diplomacy and force. We spent a lot of time talking about the future of the Balkans with Milošević. Serbia would be, he said, a small but reliable ally of the United States; Serbia would be one of the seven gateways of Europe; Serbia would like the Balkans to have no national borders whatsoever. He was looking ahead, trying to work past the conflict.

Some of it was a game he was playing with us, there was no doubt of that. But I also began to see that through changing people's minds and opening the door to an alternate vision of the future, you could gain "strategic consent," in other words, their willing cooperation.

As Milošević warned, "General Clark, do not have NATO become 'occupying power'; 'occupying powers' do not do well here." It was a threat, he would compare us to the WW II Nazis. And, like all effective threats, it happened to be accurate. The key, he explained to us, was to treat people with respect. For all his evil, Milošević was an acute observer of human nature and an astute practitioner of power diplomacy.

This experience drew on all my military knowledge and leadership background and confirmed all I'd studied of diplomacy. These were the principles of power politics among nations. But to work, it was clear, they had to be exercised through personal relationships. Ultimately, diplomacy wasn't about trade-offs; it was about persuasion. To succeed, you had to link the hard calculus of cost and benefits to charm, new opportunities, and the promise of a better tomorrow. Success was 90 percent persuasion, backed up by 10 percent coercion.

Inside the administration, we finally completed the national security strategy of the United States, *A National Security Strategy of Engagement and Enlargement.* It was dutifully issued in February 1996, but received little of the fanfare required to offset the previous years of partisan criticism that seemed invariably to come from the party out of power. We would remain engaged in the world, supporting friends and those who shared our values. If force was to be used, it was to be used only as a last resort, and even then alongside allies, if possible.

We also issued its national military strategy companion piece, *A Strategy of Flexible and Selective Engagement.* We would maintain our strong nuclear deterrent and forward presence forces, and we would use our military as directed for peacekeeping or humanitarian purposes, though they would remain organized and prepared for war. And, just a few weeks before I left, we published *Joint Vision 2010,* a key document in laying out how the armed forces would actually operate. It stressed high technology, modern communications, and precision strikes—all of which, rolled together, constituted much of the vision we took from Operation Desert Storm. But we added to it the concept of "full spectrum dominance," the need to prevail at any level of contest, from peacekeeping and hostage rescue to full-fledged warfare, which emphasized land forces and incorporated lessons from Somalia and Haiti. It proved to be a pity that the incoming Bush administration either neglected or discounted these ideas; they could have saved much grief in Iraq.

What we had done in practice was establish the idea that a robust military was essential in peacetime. We could use these military assets to build relationships, supplement or empower diplomacy, and head off impending conflict, as well as to simply go to war. It was a much more active form of deterrence than we had had before, and some were calling it peacetime engagement, or preventive diplomacy.

Abroad, the effect of our actions was to reestablish America's leadership. At the end of the cold war, as Europe sought integration, some people in France were working to reduce America's cold war influence. By its initial abstention from the surging conflict in Yugoslavia, the United States had partially abdicated its leadership role in the world. President Clinton and his national security team took the lead again. The Dayton Peace Accords had demonstrated American competence as well. From this experience I drew a lesson in leadership: set the objectives and principles; discuss, listen, and work to build consensus, which means to accept allied suggestions and; retain responsibility; and then make it happen. Each of our allies was rational and political; they had their own domestic concerns that impacted policy, just as did we. Successful leadership internationally required not America's dictation, but America's consensus building. It was the art of the possible, just like domestic politics. Forging consensus was about building relationships, listening and learning, handling people on their own terms, and taking risks, professional and personal, including physical risks. This was the meaning of international leadership in the post–Cold War world.

The U.S. military had become the go-to agency of rapid response within the government. The combination of large, in-place capabilities, worldwide communications, and ready financial resources that could be reallocated enhanced the Pentagon's stature far beyond its war-fighting responsibilities. Other branches of the government had not been reformed to accommodate the implications of the new strategy. The State Department didn't create cadres of "political developers," nor did Commerce discover how to create jobs overseas, nor did Health and Human Services take over the public health responsibilities of nations we were assisting, nor did Justice acquire the capabilities to implement legal reform and police and public security assessments and training in advance of an operational deployment. All this was largely left to the military, or to pure dumb luck.

By late 1995 it was clear that we were not succeeding in Haiti. It was one of the relative failures of the administration. We could restore a government, and even organize elections, but we couldn't seem to heal a broken society, transform a social order, or create self-sustaining economic development. And when we intervened, we inevitably became responsible, not just for installing a new government, but for the enduring welfare of the whole society from which a functioning government should draw its support. That, unfortunately, was simply beyond our means, skill, and level of commitment. And this limitation would become even more devastating as the George W. Bush administration plunged into Iraq in 2003.

As for the services, especially the army, there was little patience with the practical aspects of these ideas. The army had sharpened its focus on the war-fighting mission alone. The engines of NTC and the Battle Command Training Program, along with the long shadows cast by the public adulation of General Norman Schwarzkopf and Operation Desert Storm, and the need to keep the force funded seem to obscure for most army leaders the shape of things to come. Never mind the deployments to Rwanda, Haiti, and Bosnia; the army didn't seem to accord these missions much respect. There was little emphasis on the cultural awareness or language skills that might be needed in the future, but a whole lot of emphasis on rebuilding the "warrior spirit." Shali saw the problem, observing often that "real men don't do MOOTW—these Military Operations Other Than War."

By the end of 1995, the first NATO troops were in Bosnia, and much of the responsibility shifted to the J–3, the operations shop. I had more than enough other work to do, especially after having spent almost four months continually overseas.

But it was also time to consider the future. In the army, promotion to three and four stars is for a specific position only. At the time of promotion, therefore, the officer signs his own request to retire, two years hence, unless extended or given a new position. And the end of my two years was fast approaching.

I spoke with my friend, Lt. Gen. Dan Christman, about my problem. We had been together off-and-on for over twenty years of assignments. Dan was serving as assistant to the chairman and saw General Shali regularly every morning. "I'll talk to him," Dan said. "He at least should tell you something."

~

Over the next three months, I received a new assignment. The army controlled the nominations, but the approval went through Shali to the secretary of defense, then to the White House, and on to the Hill. Pure army assignments tended to be left solely to the army, but assignments to Joint positions were considered more broadly: All services nominated someone, and ultimately the secretary would decide, presumably with the advice of the chairman.

As it happened, Gen. Barry McCaffrey was asked to take a Cabinet-level position as director of the Office of National Drug Control Policy. That move opened up his billet as commander, U.S. Southern Command, in Panama. The army nominated as replacement a Spanish-speaking three-star who had previous experience in Panama, but he failed to pass muster at the higher levels. As part of my J–5 responsibilities, I was familiar with the command and its issues. Secretary Perry took a close look at me on a brief trip with him to Chile, Venezuela, and Panama, where I distinguished myself by getting very sick. Regardless, he selected me for the position and promotion.

Leaving one station and moving on to another was always hard for both Gert and me. But this time, Gert had some special goodbyes to say, as she had carved quite a niche for herself while working for Senator Hutchison. Handling military family issues, as well as helping to organize Kay's weekly breakfast for constituents, Gert saw a different slice of Washington. She befriended staffers, saw the truly selfless effort and dedication that most members of Congress put forth for good government, and also watched the partisan nature of much of the business on the Hill. She achieved her own kind of special status there, taking phone calls and offering advice. Above all, she saw the extraordinary trust and faith that Americans place in their government. She and Kay parted life-long friends.

As for me, promotion to full general was more than I had ever expected. I had had some close calls, as when I'd rolled a car, been shot and almost killed, and experienced the partisan opposition to Clinton's government gunning for me. I had undoubtedly been too outspoken for my own good, and perhaps some officers had watched enviously as I rose through the ranks. But I was truly gratified by the opportunity, for now I'd have at least one more chance to contribute, this time as commander in chief, U.S. Southern Command.

~

"Wes, I would like you to look at two issues," Secretary Perry said to me as I was leaving the Pentagon to take command, "and come back and talk to me about them. First, tell me about the counter-narcotics mission; is it doing any good? What should we do with it? And look at the situation in Panama, and tell me, if it's even possible, would we want to stay there after we turn over everything to the Panamanians after 1999. And if not, what should happen to the command?"

The word on the street was that the Southern Command was the military's secret. It over-watched a little-understood but fascinating region, with enough troops, resources, and military missions to be interesting, and it sat in the same time zone as Washington, D.C.

General Shali explained it to me, "Wes, you are going to an important area, but it tends to be overlooked in much of the dialogue and deliberation in this town. You must represent your region to Washington."

It was quite a region—all of Latin America except Mexico, and all of the Caribbean as well. Thirty-three nations. Four hundred million people, and everywhere countries were breaking out of the pattern of military coups and repressive governments to establish real democracies. Chile's economy was thriving, Argentina had ended inflation by pegging its peso to the dollar, and in Peru Alberto Fujimori was infusing new economic vitality into the heart of the Incas' storied kingdom, albeit with a rough hand.

The United States maintained a few thousand troops in Panama to assist in training and exercises—mostly civic action projects like road building and medical teams—throughout the region. We also operated warships, flew AWACS planes and manned a few ground-based radars in Colombia and Peru to assist local governments in what was known as "source zone interdiction" of the narcotics trade.

Gert and I plunged full force into the assignment, meeting government officials and other opinion makers, visiting exercises, and learning the culture and perspectives of the region. I learned to speak Spanish, and we entertained frequently in our home, making strong friends among the Panamanians and hosting many visiting U.S. officials. And I constantly promoted the region to Washington, extolling its importance and calling South America the Continent of the Future.

The region was large, wealthy, and incredibly diverse. We visited almost every country. I met with presidents, ministers, and generals, reinforcing American interests and goals, such as democratization and free market economics. But I listened carefully, and did not preach. I knew these leaders talked among themselves, and reputations had a way of spreading. Gradually, I gained their perspectives and their trust. And they sought that understanding.

The Chilean minister of defense, seeking U.S. permission to buy F–16 fighters, explained it to me in Santiago one afternoon. "You Americans don't understand; you believe there are no threats here, that we're just making things up. But let me tell you, in 1978, these Argentineans almost went to war against us over the ocean boundaries off Tierra del Fuego. It took the intercession of the pope to stop the war. And then they turned around and went to war with Great Britain. I'll tell you," he said, "a country that will go to war with Britain is liable to do anything!" Each country was distinctive and there was a long history of enmity, struggle, and conflict between some of them. Though Chile's government sought the approval to buy the American-made fighters, it also wanted the understanding and respect of the United States.

~

My travels in South America produced widely varying experiences. I argued vigorously with a French-educated Brazilian general commanding forces in the Amazon who was training them to repel a potential American invasion. I felt the ravages of land-locked Paraguay's long isolation. I saw the terrible poverty of La Paz, Bolivia's capital, and its suburb, El Alto, and worked to strengthen the interdiction activities in Colombia, Peru, and Bolivia.

While I was traveling with the narcotics police in the Bolivian Amazon, I encountered an Indian woman in the jungle and was heartbroken when she explained in Quechua that her five-year-old son's belly was penetrated by worms, and he was dying.

"Indians don't live long down here," the translator explained. The family was living on a ten-foot-square platform that was raised on stilts to keep it above the rain-soaked jungle floor. Their shelter was a large piece of blue plastic sheeting. The translator pointed to the older son's blistered feet, and noted there was no father in this household. "Cocaleros," he said, as the poor farmers who subsisted by raising coca were called. But what I saw was a family struggling to survive, against impossible odds.

Out of sight of America, away from the video games and malls, life was a struggle for shelter, food, and clothing on an income of less than a dollar a day. What progress were we making? I asked. And where would I have found myself had I been born here? Why couldn't we do more, when so little would mean so much?

I briefed Secretary Perry on the counter-drug missions and recommended we explore with the Panamanians whether there could be an extended role for the U.S. counter-narcotics effort in the country. With the secretary's approval, we began drafting a major enhancement of training and assistance to enable the Colombians to better deal with the narco-traffickers, later enacted under my successor, marine general Charles Wilhelm, as Plan Colombia.

The State Department tasked veteran diplomat John Negroponte to work with me on extending a U.S. presence in Panama. It was a delicate dialogue. The Panamanians certainly appreciated the U.S. role in ousting the dictator Manuel Noriega. But they were also very proud of their sovereignty, and their scheduled assumption of authority for the Panama Canal was anticipated by the Panamanian people with great relish.

We had made a strong beginning, but then it was time to say goodbyes once more. I was nominated by the new secretary of defense to move to Europe to take over from Gen. George Joulwan, as commander in chief, U.S. European Command and Supreme Allied Commander, Europe.

It was considered the top command in the U.S. forces, consisting of more than 100,000 soldiers, sailors, airmen, and marines, over the greatest span of territory—eighty-nine countries in Europe, the Middle East, and Africa. It also had most complex mission, including the ongoing peacekeeping mission in Bosnia. And it had the most complex organization, for it was really two commands, a U.S. command and a NATO command, each with separate headquarters, troop units, and missions, united only in the person of the commander himself.

Somehow, after I departed, the U.S.-Panamanian dialogue died away. The American presence ended on December 31, 1999, and the U.S. Southern Command is now headquartered in Miami, Florida, while its army component is located in Texas. Today, Panama is at peace, and prosperous. Very proud of its successful stewardship of the canal and what it has achieved on its own, Panama is perhaps the best friend of the United States in all of Latin America.

In Latin America, as elsewhere, I found a hunger for America's attention and respect, and an opening for much good work. There 400 million people live in bustling economies with proud cultures and traditions and tremendous natural resources, and they offer emerging markets for U.S. trade, technology, and investment. These nations could become our closest partners. And no, these countries wouldn't bow down before an empire, nor should they, for if we want strong friends and allies, we should respect their own domestic concerns and recognize the political forces that give rise to their policies. But what I had confirmed, once more in my own mind, were the great common interests that all human beings share: love of family, respect for one's own culture and upbringing, personal courage, determination, and competence. There are profound differences in language and upbringing, religion, and professed beliefs, but there is a common humanity. And on that basis profound common good can be achieved, if we would all work together.

The difficulty, of course, is always implementation of new ideas. I reconfirmed in Panama what I had already discovered in Washington: when it came to a strategy of "engagement," almost all the resources were military. There were no national deployable "reserves" of doctors, lawyers, accountants, auditors, city planners, forestry experts, agricultural extension services, or police trainers. Instead, we hosted a handful of military exercises each year, with perhaps a few hundred National Guardsmen who could build or repair a few miles of highway, or perhaps a team of Army reserve medical personnel with a few doctors who could treat medical emergencies or conduct vaccinations for a week and a half before going home. While this was useful for the local people, the purpose of the exercise was military training for our people. The idea behind the engagement was "military" relationship-building.

Unfortunately, this was only a small fraction of the support these countries needed. And the support was purely military, leaving the impression of U.S. military power as our dominant theme. Of course, there were many non-U.S. government charities, relief and assistance groups in the area, but their actions were not part of any official "strategy". Not could they make up for the lack of U.S. government non-military official "outreach."

Still, I had learned a lot from the experience in Latin America, and I was anxious to try out my ideas in Europe and Africa.

TWELVE

WAR AS A LAST RESORT

I would spend much of my command tour in Europe operating against Slobodan Milošević and his schemes to secure his gains from the war in Bosnia and his endeavors to continue amassing power through ethnic cleansing. Sometimes it was open warfare, as in his campaign to expel the Albanian population from Kosovo; sometimes it was shadowboxing with his cronies in Bosnia or Montenegro.

"General Clark, you say you are simple soldier, but you are not. You are a strategist," the Serb president challenged me on one of my first trips back to Belgrade to see him after assuming command in Europe in July 1996.

"Mr. President, I am just a soldier."

I suppose I was a strategist, too, one of many worried about Europe and the Balkans. But why make it easy for Milošević? I suspected he was monitoring my conversations in some way, perhaps when I met with commanders in Bosnia, or maybe with Russian help. And he had moved a long way from his more helpful stance during the Dayton negotiations two years earlier.

But, insofar as I would have to deal with President Slobodan Milošević, I held a distinct advantage: I knew him well, from hundreds of hours of observation, conversation, and study. I knew him far better than he knew me. This also gave me a key asset in strategic leadership in the command, for I had "special knowledge" and credibility

In fact, Milošević had gotten the breather he wanted from the conflict and now was busy guarding his base of support and considering his next move. Rather than turning over indicted Serb war criminal Radovan Karad_i_ to the International Criminal Tribunal for prosecution, he was dodging the issue. At the same time, his intelligence agents were stirring resistance to the NATO and U.N. mission in Bosnia and reaping millions in payoffs from his fellow Serbs.

As both the commander in chief, U.S. European Command Europe and the NATO Supreme Allied Commander, I found myself in an interesting place organizationally. Above me, there was a dual chain of command, insisted on by Eisenhower to give heft to the command when NATO was a much simpler organization having a much simpler mission. Yet the command arrangement had a unique strength, as I could speak for the Americans to the Europeans and for the Europeans to the Americans. It just depended on keeping both sets of superiors reasonably happy, which was the continuing challenge for every Supreme Allied Commander.

～

The NATO mission in Bosnia had begun in late 1995, using the Military Annex to the Dayton Accords. The idea was to give the military broad authority, endorsed by the Serbs, Bosnians, and Croats—the so-called strategic consent of the major parties engaged in the conflict—but to carefully limit what the military was actually obligated to do under the terms of the agreement. No disarmament of the armed forces fielded by the Serbs, Bosnians, and Croats. No policing. Just to separate forces and provide opportunities for voluntary turnover of armaments. NATO was to go in big and heavy, intimidating any potential opposition. But then, if necessary, NATO could take whatever actions were necessary to protect and enforce the Dayton Accords. All of this was the exact opposite of the failed U.N. mission that NATO was replacing.

More than 20,000 U.S. forces, built around the U.S. 1st Armored Division, crossed the Sava River from Croatia into Bosnia and took up their assigned sector. Forces were separated, some weapons were turned in, and all fighting stopped. There was no active opposition to the 60,000-strong NATO force.

But there was violence, particularly in Sarajevo as Serbs turned over territory to the Bosnian Muslim-Croatian Federation. Large swaths of Sarajevo were torched by them as NATO, whose troops were authorized, but not required, to take action, stood by watching. Slowly it became clear that many of the goals outlined in the Dayton Accords would remain unfulfilled because of the squabbling and stubborn political resistance of the former warring factions, the Serbs in particular. Repatriation of refugees wasn't happening, indicted war criminals remained at large, and the political, economic, and juridical aspects of the accords remained unfulfilled, all largely due to Serb resistance.

On the day I took command, British special forces operating under the NATO umbrella seized an indicted Serb war criminal. The capture was successful, despite U.S. misgivings about the expansion of military actions.

The next day I was called in by NATO Secretary-General Javier Solana who told me to promote the success of the civilian side of our mission, not just the military. As Solana put it, "NATO cannot succeed in its mission if the international mission as a whole is not successful." He was making me responsible, indirectly, for the overall implementation of the Dayton Accords, for the refugee repatriation, the election, and the development of the government and the economy.

Solana was my boss in the Allied chain of command. He was the full-time political chief of the alliance, subject, of course, to the heads of state of the alliance's member governments and their on-scene representatives, the NATO ambassadors. But I was also responsible as commander of the U.S. European Command to the U.S. Secretary of Defense William Cohen. Cohen had a different interpretation. A former Republican senator, he had not supported the Dayton Accords, remained deeply skeptical of our mission there, and privately sought to withdraw our forces from the mission, often against the expressed desires of the State Department and the White House.

~

After the detention of an indicted war criminal in Bosnia, the Serbs raised the stakes with a series of riots and mob-style violence against small groups of NATO forces and unguarded property. Serb radio made provocative statements, including allusions to the Nazi occupation of Yugoslavia during World War II. There seemed to be White House pressure for a strong response to this renewed violence, so I returned to Washington for consultations with General Shalikashvili and Secretary Cohen.

Over the next few weeks, the Serbs' game of chicken with NATO continued to result in sporadic violence. The British surrounded a Serb Special Police station in Banja Luca, and ordered it evacuated and closed. I directed our new NATO on-the-scene commander, army general Ric Shinseki, to order the Serb Special Police to register their individual weapons and turn in their heavy weapons. A Serb riot in Brcko resulted in a U.S. soldier injured and a tactical redeployment that was misread by some as NATO weakness, though the United States ended up occupying high ground and surrounding a key Bosnian Serb communications relay site. The Serbs then demonstrated against the new U.S. position, threatening our troops with violence and demanding we evacuate their site. It was the kind of "crisis-in-a-bottle" that doesn't look terribly significant from halfway around the world, but can carry enormous strategic consequences for a mission as a whole.

As that contest broke out, I was caught on an aircraft flying back for meetings in Washington. Even from my command aircraft communications were sometimes poor, and it was difficult to follow what was happening. But it was clear that this confrontation between a few hundred Serbs and a company of U.S. troops on a remote mountaintop was shaping up as a struggle that would define NATO's strength and credibility in the Balkans. Would NATO have to bow to Serb intimidation, as the United Nations had?

New to the theater, Ric Shinseki had delegated to his subordinate commander, Maj. Gen. Dave Grange, the authority to negotiate the handover of the mountaintop site to the Serbs. As I read the proposal that had been agreed to, it was clear that we had been outmaneuvered politically, and I could see that this was going to be read as another defeat. I ordered Shinseki to withdraw from the agreement. But if he were to do so, he and his authority risked being compromised. In the end, we modified the agreement and avoided the worst of the political fallout.

But it was an important lesson learned: Military authority can be delegated; political authority must be carefully reserved.

The Serbs would continue to cause problems, however, and they planned a major demonstration against a NATO-friendly Serb faction in Banja Luca for Monday, September 8, along with a coup attempt against a local Bosnian Serb leader, Biljana Plasi_. Hundreds of buses would carry the self-professed "brave" Serbs, armed with staves and timbers, and converge on the city under the guise of a preelection rally. Working through the State Department, we secured U.N. help to delay the rally, and with Ric's troops, we slowed the bus caravans, eventually leaving the radical Serb leaders isolated in a hotel in Banja Luca and under siege by the local Serbs who disagreed with them politically. This was a major political defeat for Milošević's Serb forces. Achieving it took help from the State Department, NATO, and the United Nations, as well as the forces on the ground. The success was a product of effective policy coordination and skilled implementation.

Our next step was to follow through on NATO planning to be prepared to shut down the provocative Serb media. At the request of Carlos Westendoerp, the U.N. High Representative for Bosnia and Herzegovina, and with the approval of Solana and U.S. Defense Secretary William Cohen, I ordered Ric to seize four TV and radio relay sites, shutting down the Serb propaganda operation against NATO and the international community. NATO troops responded flawlessly: French, Italians, Norwegians, and Swedes alongside British and Americans. It was NATO's first-ever ground offensive action.

The next morning, I found myself in front of the alliance's defense ministers assembled at Maastricht, Holland, for a scheduled briefing, and I was pleased to report on our successful operation. Now we had the political upper hand on the ground. We had shown we were competent and not afraid to use our authority. We had used low-level military actions—only a few hundred troops, with no casualties suffered—to gain superior strategic effect, just as we had envisioned doing when we wrote the Dayton Accords.

Over the next several months, we continued our operations in Bosnia in an effort to break Serb resistance to implementation of the agreement. We were able to close certain police stations and stage carefully planned operations that detained suspected war criminals. Our actions heartened

the international mission in Bosnia and drove back the sense of inevitable
Serb takeover that was fueling the Serb supporters. We were able to move
forward with the first refugee returns, elections, and other political and
economic reforms. But to do so required careful attention to the unfold-
ing situation in Bosnia.

I agreed to meet with the new Croatian member of the Bosnian
tri-presidency, which also includes a Muslim and a Serb, in Mostar.
"Meet me at the bank," he suggested. When I arrived, I noticed a
shiny new metallic green BMW parked out front. "Nice car," I observed to him casually as we sat down." Yes," he said, "it is mine. And
welcome to my bank."

It was his bank. He was the president, and, yes, the government was
doing business with his bank. "And why not?" he asked. Well, for several
good reasons, I thought, including conflict of interest. Conflict of interest—a cardinal violation of the principle of good government. Public
servants must work for the public good, not the private good. And in the
Balkans this juncture of private enrichment and public office was a way
of life. We began to insist on financial disclosure statements for the promotion of generals and for other public officials as well. It was an important weapon in the fight against corruption and for good government.

Meanwhile, Gert and I were fully engaged in all the other aspects of
command—working the diplomatic issues associated with military relationships among eighty-nine countries, working the allied headquarters,
visiting national capitals, preparing to bring Hungary, Poland, and the
Czech Republic into the alliance, and looking after the readiness, training, and welfare of the 100,000 U.S. soldiers, sailors, airmen, and
marines assigned to the command, plus another 150,000 associated families and civilian workers such as teachers and managers. Gert and I implemented teacher-appreciation days, worked to improve quality of life
for the single service members, and worried about school boards and
school curricula. Gert put her talent for listening and caring to work in
various spousal and service organizations. Leadership, even at the highest
levels of command, was still about troops and families and building
strong communities.

We had an absolutely top-notch team of U.S. and international officers, a total of nine four-stars working within the United States and allied
command structures. The Supreme Commander title, which General

Eisenhower had picked up during World War II and carried into NATO, had always sounded a bit over the top, but with nine other four-star commanders reporting to me, I came to appreciate that if people gave you a title like that, you probably needed it.

Dealing with the Balkan issues was always risky, but I had spent hundreds of hours participating in the discussions and working the Dayton Accords, building relationships with the principal participants, and, in some cases, sizing them up as potential adversaries. The combination of military and diplomatic requirements was, somehow, what I had been preparing for my entire career, beginning at West Point. And we were succeeding in Bosnia, moving the whole mission forward, because we had effectively used military forces to achieve political leverage over the Serbs inside Bosnia. We were able to do that because Milošević was trapped by his signature on the Dayton Agreement. Whenever he objected to something, we pointed at the agreement. This simply raised the stakes for him and frustrated his ability to use the kind of on-the-ground intimidation, threat, and violence he had successfully employed against the United Nations.

Moreover, the legal underpinnings of Dayton gave strength to the alliance. The ambassadors could use the language of the accords to retain support from their governments and public back home, despite the threats and risks the accords would be ignored or violated, primarily by the Serbs. These were legal commitments, and there was no backing away, provided military leaders were willing to use the authority granted. And I was. Again and again I saw the power of international law. However much we in the military had for years debunked it, in this situation, the rule of law was critical.

This successful exercise of authority also further strengthened my personal credibility. And as I had begun to recognize at the level of strategic leadership, it is one thing to have a title and quite another to have real authority. Such authority had to be earned, step by step, through performance.

As we traveled throughout Europe, Gert and I perceived again the magnetic attraction of the United States, especially for those who had long been oppressed behind the Iron Curtain. There was no doubt that NATO's appeal in Europe had something to do with a strong, residual fear of Russia, particularly in the East. As the Bulgarian foreign minister explained, "Today Russia is weak, but someday it will be strong again, and before then, Bulgaria must be a member of NATO."

But it was also respect for what we represented as Americans: the freedoms, the opportunities, and, most of all, the ironclad, politics-free protection of the rights and liberties enshrined in our constitution. We were a superpower, sure. But it wasn't just that we weren't Soviets, but, rather, that we weren't like the Soviets. We had laws, principles, and due process. We treated our allies with respect, not as dupes. We consulted; we listened; we tried to build consensus. We even supported lofty goals like European integration, which was manifestly against what some in Europe believed were our selfish interests of perpetuating European division and thus its financial and political weakness.

One day, I traveled through Bosnia with the incoming Russian military chief, Gen. Anatoliy Kvashnin, who had commanded a division in Afghanistan in the 1980s. We talked about warfare and weapons, about the hopes and fears of nations. We were two professionals, former adversaries, now exploring issues that might make us colleagues and perhaps even friends. It was the high-water mark of U.S.-Russian military relations, at least in Europe. Soon General Kvashnin would be more tightly surrounded and thus under pressure by the Russian intelligence apparatus, and even on this occasion, I learned later, my NATO interpreter, who sat between us, was likely a spy working for the KGB.

Gert and I were enormously proud to represent the United States in Europe. Respect for America had soared as a result of progress in implementing the Dayton Agreement and the decision to enlarge NATO. Europe still saw events from the perspective of East versus West, and the West now clearly had the upper hand. But we had to be careful, because the Russians still had considerable influence, were smarting from their Cold War failure and the subsequent sense of humiliation as their forces withdrew from the Eastern Europe states. And we had no desire to make enemies of the Russians.

When I landed in Skopje, Macedonia, on a Saturday in early March, 1998, U.S. ambassador Christopher R. Hill was on the phone. He was a friend and colleague from the Dayton negotiations and a rapidly rising star in the Department of State. This was his first embassy.

"Wes, can you come over and see President Gligorov now? He'd like to talk to you."

During the shuttle diplomacy preceding the accords, Richard Holbrooke had brought us to Skopje once to meet Kiro Gligorov, the sitting president of the former Yugoslav Republic of Macedonia. He was a wily survivor, a 1939 graduate of Belgrade University who had been a Communist partisan during World War II and became a longtime top official in former dictator Tito's Yugoslavia. Fluent in English, he was also a scarred survivor of a recent assassination attempt, with an inch-deep hole in his forehead. He knew the local scene, and especially knew Milošević. And he had excellent political instincts.

Chris was already meeting with him when I arrived. Gilgorov welcomed me and then cut to the heart of the matter.

"Serb special police in Kosovo have just cornered and murdered some sixty members of the Jashari family. It is Milošević's way of dealing with his internal security problem, but it will lead to war. Albanians," Gilgorov explained, "are not like Bosnians; they won't be intimidated. They will fight back. And Milošević will use force. He will say he will negotiate, but he won't. All he really respects is force."

Kosovo was some 4200 square miles in size, a pastoral valley of rolling hills and farmland surrounded by rugged mountains. Albanians made up a strong majority of the population, but Kosovo was ruled by a small Serb minority empowered by Belgrade. It was going to be the ultimate Balkan powder keg. War there had been staved off in late 1992 when President George H. W. Bush had used the threat of force to warn Milošević not to unleash his police and military on the Albanians.

"So what about President Bush's Christmas warning?" I asked. "Won't Milošević be deterred?"

Gligorov said no, the warning had been made too long ago, and too much had happened since then.

It was a grim message. As I completed my visit to our troops in Task Force Able Sentry, who were then patrolling the border between Macedonia and Serbia, I kept thinking of Gligorov's news. Another war in the Balkans would undercut NATO's guarantee of security and stability in Europe and likely trigger massive refugee movements. If Milošević took forceful action here, it would embolden the Serbs in Bosnia to further resistance. Like it or not, we would have to consider our options.

I faxed a letter to the Pentagon the next evening describing my visit and Gligorov's warning, and suggesting the Christmas warning from

President Bush be reissued. But I soon learned that the Pentagon leadership was unhappy to receive the letter. As Air Force General Joe Ralston, the Vice Chairman of the Joint Chiefs of Staff, explained, they already "had a lot on their plate." I was told they didn't need anything else to worry about. It was, frankly, an outrageous response, but I bided my time.

My concerns reflected the broad consensus of informed European leaders, and over the next few weeks, as the clashes in Kosovo escalated, I began to be quizzed by the Europeans: What was our assessment? What could be done? Could we use airpower? Should we insert a stabilizing force? Of course, they had their own ideas, but they were looking to the United States for leadership. Eventually, with United States concurrence, the NATO political chiefs tasked my headquarters to investigate the options in staff analyses that were to continue over the summer.

In early June I returned to Washington and briefed Gen. Hugh Shelton privately on what I believed might work: a renewed threat of NATO air strikes to empower a serious diplomatic effort to engage and weaken Milošević. I knew Milošević and his genuine respect for U.S. airpower. With Shelton's go-ahead, I briefed Cohen and National Security Advisor Sandy Berger.

Good officers, I'd always been taught, didn't just bring a problem, they also brought a recommended solution to their boss.

The White House bought my approach and essentially adopted it, even as the Pentagon choked a little on the concept. Secretary Cohen wanted no deeper involvement in the Balkans, and once again, several days after I'd done the briefings in Washington, Joe Ralston brought his message.

"But if we threaten him, and he doesn't stop, then do we bomb? And if the bombing doesn't work, then do we invade?"

Well, yes, there were no guarantees in this business. But the alternative was to stand by and do nothing, and then, after being accused of failing, get drawn in under even more adverse circumstances. The other question, the question that should have been asked and wasn't, was: How do we take advantage of a military threat to strengthen diplomacy? What we were looking for was an attention getter to enable us to achieve a diplomatic solution, and nothing more. In diplomacy, I had learned, sooner is better than later, and a little now counts for more than a whole lot later on.

But the summer of 1998 was a tough time in Washington, as domestic politics were again encroaching on foreign policy. The Republicans were charging President Clinton with weakness on the issue of Saddam Hussein's defiance of the U.N. inspection program. The Pentagon, on the other hand, craved Republican support for an enlarged procurement budget, while some in the administration recognized the continuing distraction of Kenneth W. Starr, the Whitewater investigation, and now Monica Lewinsky. But it wasn't just the administration ; it was the town, the media, and the nation. Europeans were simply amazed—and appalled—at our national penchant for distraction.

In spite of these distractions, we began to squeeze Milošević with an air exercise. Dozens of aircraft flew within Serb radar range along Yugoslavia's southern and western borders, an implicit NATO warning. Meanwhile, I was busy working the follow-on military options while tracking Chris Hill's diplomatic efforts. At the time, Richard Holbrooke, the logical man for the diplomatic work, had retired to private life. The lead responsibilities thus fell to Chris, a Dayton veteran himself.

Milošević read the situation and took full advantage of it. He noted all the reservations of the French and German foreign ministers, who were publicly declaring that NATO could do nothing without a U.N, Security Council resolution, which Russia opposed. Milošević steadily escalated the violence and repression in Kosovo. By the end of the summer, 300,000 to 400,000 Kosovars had been driven from their homes and were living in the forests. NATO was already looking weak, the East Europeans warned me.

Meanwhile, I had been working through the various military options: forces to be deployed to watch borders, air strikes against targets in Kosovo and Serbia, and even a couple of options to invade, one directed at Kosovo, another directed at Belgrade. These weren't really plans, however, just brief sketches of operations that cited the forces required, matched the operations to political aims, and examined the pluses and minuses.

In NATO, no military planning can be done without authorization from the political authorities, and on these issues the governments of NATO were moving very cautiously. I had to fight against disclosing every potential target in advance to the hundreds of people associated with the national missions that constituted NATO. There was acute

political sensitivity at every step, since the alliance was caught in a political trap inherent in the nature of democracy itself: In attempting to
coerce Milošević, NATO governments risked frightening their own
voters. But in trying to avoid frightening their citizens they gave the
international community and, worse, Milošević, the impression of in-
decisiveness and weakness.

There was one last chance to salvage NATO's reputation and stop
Milošević short of war, a NATO defense ministers' meeting at which real
decisions could be made. I traveled to Washington, where I explained
our circumstances to Secretary Cohen and asked him to respond to
Milošević by pushing for a formal NATO warning.

Here I was again, asking for help. Secretary Cohen probably didn't
welcome my assessment and recommendation, since the Republican majority in the Senate opposed Clinton's work in the Balkans and wanted
no deeper involvement. But he ultimately agreed to press the Europeans
to issue a real threat to Milošević. At the defense ministers' meeting,
Cohen carried the day: NATO issued its activation warning for an air
campaign against Serbia.

This activation warning, or ACTWARN, which ordered NATO nations to identify the forces they would commit, caused a huge stir in Europe. It was accompanied by U.N. Security Council Resolution 1199,
which called on member states to use "all necessary means"—the famous
Chapter 7 of the Charter of the United Nations authorizing the use of
force if necessary—to deal with the humanitarian crisis and calling for
excessive Serb forces to be removed from Kosovo. Milošević was told to
withdraw his extra troops and police from Kosovo, and Richard Holbrooke, still a private citizen, was dispatched to use the ACTWARN as
leverage against him. Holbrooke also used a more threatening AC-
TORD, an actual order to activate the air force elements for the air campaign, and finally won Milošević's acceptance of an unarmed
international "observer force" to mediate the disputes.

The pace of diplomacy was grueling, with late meetings in Brussels,
classified messages day and night, endless calls with Washington, and
one of our own officers traveling in the negotiations with Holbrooke.
This was exactly the way such crises always consumed the energies of the
participants. But I had also learned this about diplomacy: have a back-
stopping team. Your representative makes tentative agreements, but you

reserve the power to commit or cancel. Working this way, we were able to supplement Holbrooke's ground observers with new aerial overflights and liaison teams.

Still, it wasn't enough. Milošević had tried to wriggle through the negotiations without actually removing his excessive troop and police presence, as NATO had expected and, on October 15, he had agreed to do. I brought the evidence to Solana and the Chairman of the NATO Military Committee, General Klaus Naumann from Germany, and we agreed to confront Milošević personally. We did. But his resistance continued, and with White House approval, I made a second visit on October 20. This time, as Milošević continued to backpedal and dissemble, I asked him to step into an adjoining room and talk to me privately, without his normal entourage.

When we were alone, I looked Milošević in the eye and said: "Mr. President, let's stop fencing about this. You are going to have to withdraw all your excess forces from Kosovo. And if you don't withdraw, Washington will tell me to bomb you, and I will bomb you good."

"Well, General Clark, NATO will do what it wants to do."

"Get real, Mr. President. I know you don't want to be bombed."

There was a pause, and before he answered me, he blinked.

"No, General, I do not."

"Then tell your generals to be cooperative and get those forces out of Kosovo."

Another brief pause, then, "Okay, General, I will tell them."

That was a key verbal concession. Finally, on a third trip, General Naumann and I were able to get a written withdrawal agreement from him. Even then, however, cagey lawyer that he was, Milošević tried to wriggle out of the agreement by having subordinate generals sign it rather than signing it himself. I knew that when we later challenged him on his failure to live up to it, he would say that he hadn't signed it and therefore he wasn't bound by it.

"I don't see your signature here, Mr. President." I said disapprovingly as the typed document was shown to us.

"Is not necessary." Milošević whined.

But eventually, he did sign.

That afternoon, General Naumann and I returned to Belgium, thinking we had succeeded. But by late the next morning, no Serb forces had left Kosovo. In frustration, I called the U.S. embassy in Belgrade on an open line, knowing the Serbs would be monitoring all calls, and discussed moving aircraft and preparing to bomb. Almost by magic, a little while later Serb vehicles began moving out. Within days, hundreds of thousands of Kosovars returned to their homes.

We had succeeded. NATO had used the threat of air strikes to force the Serbs to back off their ethnic cleansing against the Kosovar Albanians. I had staked my reputation on our ability to coerce Milošević by this threat, and it had worked. Now all we had to do was follow up with a diplomatic settlement before another round of fighting began.

This showed that NATO's nations could be pulled together in a crisis, though it was not easy. We had halted ethnic conflict, given diplomacy a chance, and proved that NATO had an important role to play in the post–Cold War world. At the same time, we were continuing the peaceful implementation of the Dayton Agreement in Bosnia, training our forces in Europe while responding to the threat of terrorist attacks on them, and preparing to bring three new nations into the alliance. It had been a busy year.

But of course, you can never be certain that diplomacy will work. In November 1998, the diplomatic effort ran into trouble almost immediately. Ambassador Chris Hill went to Belgrade hoping to come up with some formulation that could end in a peaceful and gradual manner the destructive repression of the Muslim Albanians inside Kosovo by the Serb military and police. But Milošević wasn't buying into this. Citing Albanian infractions of the agreement we'd just reached, he instead prepared for a new round of ethnic cleansing.

On a Saturday in January 1999, U.S. diplomat Bill Walker, the newly arrived head of the international observer mission in Kosovo, called me to report a massacre: The bodies of over fifty unarmed Albanian farmers had been found in a ditch, all shot at close range. This was the very kind of incident we feared. We had even been ordered to prepare a Tomahawk missile reprisal against the Serbs, a strike that would be ready on call in case it was needed. But we didn't want war. I called both Solana, who was visiting his family in Spain, and the Pentagon to inform them.

NATO sent me and General Naumann back to Belgrade to confront President Milošević and find a resolution that would bring his repression to a halt. We met with him nonstop for over seven hours, but he was stubborn and defiant, unwilling to admit to the massacre or to allow a proper U.N. investigation of the incident. We took that bad news back to Brussels, but NATO still worked to avoid conflict. French president Jacques Chirac offered to host formal negotiations between the Serbs and the Kosovar Albanians in a palace at Rambouillet. This was to be a French-led Dayton-like peace agreement. But two extended sessions over a four-week period produced only the Albanians' agreement— Milošević's Serbs walked out in defiance of the efforts made to preserve peace.

Meanwhile, we observed the new buildup of Serb police and military forces in and around Kosovo, including some of the top armored forces of the former Yugoslav military now being used by Serbs. We estimated their number at perhaps forty thousand troops, maybe more. This was going to be the Serb equivalent of the Powell Doctrine; they were building the capabilities to use overwhelming force against the Albanian population and the few hundred lightly armed Kosovar fighters they might face. Simultaneously, they would deploy sufficient troops to guard their borders against a NATO intervention. The international observers saw the ominous buildup, and they realized that they themselves were increasingly at risk. In the end there was nothing that could be done but prepare for the worst, and the international observers were told to leave immediately.

I had been working behind the scenes both to help defuse the conflict and to prepare for it. On several trips to Washington I had both consulted with and warned the Pentagon and certain members of Congress of what was coming. I also urged that the greatest effort be made in the negotiations, and tried to identify some of the ancillary factors that could prove troublesome, such as Russian interference.

Without political authorization to do more, the military planning for use of both American and NATO forces against Serb forces and installations was limited. This was particularly the case because of periodic reports from U.S. and European diplomats that negotiations between the Albanian Muslims and the Serbs were making some "progress". The implication was that force would not be needed, and no one really wanted to think about military planning while there was still hope for peaceful resolution of the issues.

In the U.S. channel, we were still building target lists and answering White House queries about what was shaping up to be a carefully calibrated and limited bombing campaign. In the NATO channel, some member states expressed great concern that we not make things worse by threats of air strikes or any other military action. Nations were jittery, and they would only become more so as we got closer to action.

The Chairman of NATO's Military Committee, German General Klaus Naumann and I were deeply concerned about what would happen once NATO air strikes began, because with airpower, as with diplomacy, there is no guarantee of success. Airpower attacks and destroys targets, but its real impact is more psychological and political. If we wanted to be certain that we could stop ethnic cleansing in Kosovo, we'd have to put troops in there on the ground as well.

I talked it over with General Naumann, and with Solana, the master of political sensitivities of the allies. Solana explained it clearly to us: "Wes, you know the nations cannot deal with this issue at this time." In other words, if I insisted on doing the full range of military planning, it was likely that NATO would do nothing, not even bomb, and the Serbs would get away with their ethnic cleansing. "Now, what is it you want to do?" Solana asked me. General Naumann got the same response, and we were stymied.

I knew that the initial planned air strikes might not succeed in stopping Milošević. If that happened, we would need to escalate our military efforts, but those were plans that would have to be developed as we went along, for it wasn't politically possible to do the advanced military work that we would have wanted to do. I had to swallow the risk.

Secretary of State Albright asked me to meet her in London in early March to discuss the options.

"Do we have to follow through with the use of force?" she asked.

There was no wiggle room in NATO's demands, or the threat of air strikes if these demands weren't met.

"Yes, we must take action," I affirmed.

And we both worried about what might happen militarily.

Washington couldn't help much, either. Although the Joint Staff was working with us in the development and advance approval of bombing targets, the subject of Kosovo had become a political football among the Joint Chiefs themselves, as they argued about whether our national interests in southeast Europe justified military action. And these concerns, of course, fed into partisan politics on the Hill. Some members of both houses of Congress had legitimate doubts about the use of force in Kosovo, while others just did not understand the region or the stakes involved. Both groups were joined by those who simply smelled an opportunity to inflict a political defeat on the administration.

On Saturday, the twentieth of March, the Serbs struck in a classic ethnic-cleansing operation. The army surrounded a large village, then police searched homes, arresting anyone who might become a resistance leader. Then paramilitary thugs went from home to home, demanding gold, taking occasional hostages—especially young women—and then running people out of their homes. By mid-afternoon, the TV screens around the world were showing thousands of people fleeing for their lives.

Ambassador Holbrooke returned to Belgrade for a last diplomatic tussle with Milošević. But that proved fruitless, and word of the failure soon reached both the NATO member states and Washington.

That Tuesday night I received a call from Solana, telling me the air campaign would begin within twenty-four hours. The Pentagon called and asked me to telephone some senators and congressmen, seeking their support. Here I was, a nonpartisan military officer, asking for political support for my mission, which, if granted, would enable a Democratic president to succeed and his Republican opponents to be proved wrong. This was going to be a political and military fight on several fronts, including that of Washington, I thought, but we are going to stop the ethnic cleansing and defeat Milošević.

I had come a long way since I arrived at the Joint Staff in 1994 and handed Shali that plan for intervention in Rwanda. Within the limits of my political guidance from the civilian leaders, I was pushing for the United States to do what was right, not just what was easy. I had felt the blood lost by those Rwandans—we had let them down. I had seen the devastation in Bosnia, where, had the United States had acted forcefully in 1991, three wars might have been avoided. So if this was going to take a fight, I was ready.

It would be a personal campaign. I was identified personally with the policy, starting with my 1994 visit to the Balkans, my work with Richard Holbrooke, and my advocacy for diplomacy backed by a threat to head off the conflict looming in Kosovo. I laid my professional reputation on the line. I had succeeded in October, in gaining concessions by threatening force. Now, I would have to prove that the alliance could make good on its threat. I couldn't fall back on the Pentagon, for it had become quite clear to me that they didn't fully support our engagement in the Balkans. And I couldn't fall back on the Europeans, for they were following, not leading. No, this was why I had the big title, I slowly understood: As a supreme commander in war, you either win, or you're fired. Wars are authorized by political leaders—but they are symbolized by generals. I had always sought responsibility; now I had it. But would I receive the authority necessary to win?

"Feet dry." was the radio message we got from our pilots when they came in from the sea and reached land on the way to their targets, the signal we had awaited. It meant our aircraft and missiles were on the way in for the first strikes. This was the cap on a very busy day, with the formal U.S. authorization to attack coming from the president and repeated in a telephone call from Hugh Shelton, a contemporary of mine who had taken over as chairman of the Joint Chiefs in October 1997.

That first night, we struck with a wave of Tomahawks, which are jet-engine-powered cruise missiles launched from ships. We also launched stealth aircraft, plus fighter-bombers, at them: altogether a total nearly 1,000 bombs in two waves. I clung to the secure phone in my study, eyes glued to CNN and the computer screen.

The reports were good. By 3:00 A.M., all our aircraft were out safely. We wouldn't know the results for a few hours, but the air campaign was on. None of us, of course, knew what would happen next.

For the military, the campaign was a series of interrelated processes, dominated by the following three stages: Identify targets; prepare, launch, and recover aircraft; and disseminate information. Thousands of soldiers, sailors, airmen, and marines were involved, their efforts coming from bases and intelligence centers in the United States and across Europe, from aboard ships at sea, and from various other headquarters and command posts. Each of these processes had to function effectively, and then they had to be fit together: Pilots had to be briefed on targets; reconnaissance had to confirm target effect; classified and declassified information had to be provided on the operation.

This is what the military trained for, everything from weather forecasting and imagery interpretation to aircraft repair, shipboard navigation, communications exercises, and seminars and studies at places like the Air Command and Staff College and the Naval War College. On the first night the entire complex organization ran smoothly and functioned sharply. It felt good to all of us inside the process.

But all the organizational excellence was nothing unless the strikes achieved their purpose, which was to shock Milošević into halting the ethnic-cleansing campaign. How to link the process of striking targets with this political objective became the overriding issue of the campaign. What would it take to break Milošević's will? Or would we break NATO's political consensus first? As the NATO Supreme Allied Commander, and the person inside the alliance who had spent the most time with Milošević, I had unique responsibilities here, too.

After the first night, some expected that Milošević would give in. But all through the next day, we heard nothing from the Serbs. I made a call to their chief of defense, General Dragoljub Ojdanic, asking him once again to withdraw his forces from Kosovo. He refused, so we struck again the second night. The following day, alliance political leaders were growing uneasy. The Hungarian prime minister sent his ambassador to warn me: "Do not lose."

On the third night, bad weather caused us to cancel some strikes. On the fourth night, a Stealth fighter was hit over Belgrade, and we aborted some strikes. We did rescue the pilot, but it was clear to everyone by this point that a night or two of strikes would not be enough. Those who had believed that such a brief bombing campaign would give Milošević an excuse to surrender, an excuse he wanted and would grab at the first opportunity, were proven wrong.

I wasn't surprised. Though I hadn't been able to rule out an early surrender, I hadn't expected one, either. Milošević was rational, yes, but he was also very stubborn. He believed his interest in Kosovo was greater than ours, and he probably thought he could ride out the strikes while the NATO allies argued among themselves and eventually called off the action. Sure enough, some within NATO were discussing whether we should pause the bombing to give Milošević a chance to reconsider.

In strategic leadership positions, as in every leadership position, you have to be nimble or flexible enough to change a plan, and honest enough to know and admit it when it's not working. I went to Solana and asked for permission to strike targets in Belgrade. It was time to escalate, not to pause, and I put all my effort into gaining the authority to do just that. Solana saw the need, and we altered the plan.

Two nights later, our cruise missiles slammed into military headquarters in downtown Belgrade. That attack was precise, and it showed an escalation of NATO's determination.

But the Serbs were fighting back. They intensified their campaign against the Kosovars. They also mounted a strike effort against U.S. forces in Bosnia, which allowed us to shoot down two Serb MiG–29s while also turning back several Serb ground-attack aircraft. Still other Serb aircraft flew over Kosovo, threatening to strike Albania. And they attempted to destabilize the government of neighboring Macedonia by flooding the country with Kosovar Albanian refugees.

Milošević, in other words, was not passively waiting for our air attacks to cease.

There are two basic theories about air campaigns in modern times. The first is now called shock and awe, and its proponents say you should go in big, strike unexpected but politically significant targets, and put maximum psychological stress on enemy leaders. Such an approach, it is argued, will clearly show the enemy leaders how powerful we are. This not only might frighten them, but also force them to give in.

The second approach simply calls for striking targets whose destruction materially weakens the capabilities of the enemy state, thus forcing the leaders to give up because they lack the means to attain their objectives. Ideally, of course, the same set of targets would have both effects, though it seldom works out that way.

Inside NATO, we would spend the next eleven weeks analyzing, debating, and struggling to reconcile what we wanted to do with what we were capable of doing. We knew we could strike bridges, bunkers, and buildings and hit them with almost every bomb. But we didn't believe that any single one of these targets would be decisive, and each would carry the risks of injuring innocent civilians.

Nor was the destruction of any or all of these targets likely to limit Milošević's ability to attack the Kosovars. To actually affect his capabilities in that area, we would have to strike his forces: his tanks, trucks, artillery, soldiers, and police. This would be much more difficult than striking buildings or fixed structures, of course, primarily because we lacked observers in place to detect, identify, and call in the air strikes. But if we could succeed in making such attacks, then we would achieve the trifecta of minimizing the risks of harming innocent people, safeguarding the Kosovars, and directly impeding Milošević's military aggression.

In the United States, there was a lot of faith in the strategic bombing approach,

that is, punishing Milošević and the Serbs by striking the high value targets such as buildings and bridges. In Europe, political leaders wanted us to attack Milošević's forces. To hold the alliance together and to advance the campaign, therefore, I had to make sure we did both.

The fixed targets had to be approved at the political levels in Washington, London, and Paris. It was a constant fight, with air commanders pushing me for more targets and politicians asking questions about unintended consequences while trying to weigh benefits versus risks. Political leaders knew the alliance would lose its public support if our strikes resulted in a significant number of casualties among innocent civilians. But knowing this, the Serbs made sure that many of their key military assets, which were our most important targets, were located near houses, apartment buildings, hospitals, schools, or churches, any of which might be inadvertently damaged when we struck. I came down on the side of hitting more targets closer to Belgrade and taking more risks. We had to put the squeeze on Milošević, and we had to ratchet up the pressure relentlessly once the strikes began. But almost every night there was a painful back-and-forth as we sought political approval to hit targets such as bridges, TV stations, or command and control installations. It was a continuing struggle, in other words, to persuade the political leaders to keep increasing the pressure on Milošević.

At the same time, I was pressing the air commanders to do more to attack the Serb ethnic-cleansing machine on the ground, and to do so without losing aircraft. We began to put B–52 bombers over enemy encampments and put our strike planes in orbit over Kosovo. Soon, we were able to use Predator unmanned aerial vehicles to help us spot the enemy, and even the AC–130 gunships made attacks along the borders.

It was a real technical challenge to go after Milošević's forces on the ground, and we were learning step-by-step. And that was my job as well, to emphasize our successes and to encourage innovative tactics as we sought to do something that had never quite been done before—to destroy enemy ground forces by airpower without having the benefit of friendly observers on the ground.

In my commands, I had always used the concept of "negative priorities." In this case, two factors would really undercut our efforts: civilian casualties, which would put political leaders under pressure to halt or pause the campaign; and aircraft losses, which would create a public perception of NATO weakness and thus of predictable eventual failure. Both had to be avoided. These were my negative priorities, and we worked hard to avoid both.

But despite our best efforts, mistakes happened. A missile hit a bridge as a train was passing over it, a pilot bombed a convoy of tractors mistakenly believing they were carrying Serb soldiers, a missile nicked a corner of a hospital, and a bomb malfunctioned and killed several schoolchildren. And finally, some of our pilots struck a farmhouse thinking it was occupied by Serb police, when in fact the Serbs had locked up eighty Albanians inside. All were killed.

Our pilots were risking their lives, double- and triple-checking their targets, and still mistakes happened. I prayed every night that we wouldn't kill innocent people. We reviewed our procedures again and again, and I fought off private questions and criticism from some of the ambassadors. Overall, we were achieving a remarkable safety record. But I knew it wasn't about procedures and statistics—it was about people's lives. A few days after the bomb malfunctioned over the schoolyard at Nis, Serbia, a letter to me arrived, in English, from Nis. "General Clerk," it began, "you and your bombs killed our granddaughter on the schoolyard. I hate you for this. I will never forgive you and I will kill you." My security detachment treated it as a threat, of course, but it was the anguish of grieving parents and grandparents I understood. It was why I prayed every night that we wouldn't have any more accidents. And it was why war must always be a last, last, last resort. However simple and direct it looks, it is complex and terrifying, it inevitably kills the innocent, and it usually brings unintended but horrible consequences.

We did a fine job handling the Serb defenses. Other than the Stealth fighter on the fourth night, only one other friendly aircraft was downed by enemy fire when we "pushed the envelope," and in both cases our air rescue helicopters were able to recover our pilots.

In seeking other ways to pressure Milošević, I asked for and received more aircraft, including strikes from U.S., British, French, and Italian aircraft carriers. We gained permission to use Bulgarian and Romanian airspace, which complicated the Serb's air defense efforts. And I asked for, and eventually deployed, a U.S. Apache helicopter task force, complete with ground combat elements, for airfield security.

The Apaches became a real saga. After I had accepted General Shelton's offer to send me Apache helicopters, I found the army was getting cold feet and balking at their deployment. I spent some capital on those helicopters, and they eventually arrived, although several weeks behind schedule. Two accidents involving these aircraft unreasonably alarmed Washington further, and despite detailed attack planning and much operational practice, the Pentagon withheld permission to use the aircraft. But at least they were in place as a rising threat against Milošević's forces.

The real problem was that, even with our best effort, the air campaign was no guarantee. We couldn't be sure the tactical strikes against Serb forces would work, and I was worried that we would run out of strategic targets or political willpower before we'd knocked out Milošević. So I asked for permission to plan for ground troops. This had been an impossible issue before the campaign began, and it was still tough. In Washington, the Republicans were expressing doubt about the military campaign and President Clinton's leadership, and the president had tried to head this off by saying he had no "intent" to use ground troops.

Fine. But that didn't mean he could change his mind.

Prime Minister Tony Blair visited in the fourth week of the campaign and asked me privately, "Will you win with airpower alone?"

When I said we couldn't guarantee it, he asked, "Will you get ground troops if you need them?"

I told him without hesitation, "For that, I'll need your help, Prime Minister!"

I wasn't going to let him down, but he would have to do his part, too. I knew Secretary Cohen was determined to resist further escalation. But it was my responsibility as the commander to advocate for what was needed to win. Then it was up to the political authorities to decide. And sure enough, in Washington a few days later, Blair persuaded the president to do "whatever is necessary," which was code for our use of ground troops. We had won that battle, at least in principle.

Day after day, the routine continued: strikes all night, planning and conferences all day. It was exhausting for the entire command. And then, as we degraded Serb defenses, we upped the tempo to include daylight strikes as well. I was working hard to supervise and coordinate the ongoing air effort, to include asking tough questions about how to gain more effectiveness from the air assets, while at the same time planning the concept for the ground action, which I saw calling for six divisions, perhaps 200,000 troops total. I would take a stand here on a variant of the Powell Doctrine, one that I had helped to formulate: Never commit American troops without going in to win.

Gert was getting a real initiation into warfare with all this. For years she had complained about my occasional need to work on a Saturday or Sunday.

"It would be different if we were at war," she would say.

"Honey, now we *are* at war!".

She didn't think it was very funny, but she proved to be a great partner in battle. I was working seven days a week, usually not getting to bed before one or two in the morning, and then up at six to start the next day with a quick intel summary, followed by a workout and a full workday at my NATO headquarters, or in Brussels, or while I was visiting air bases around Europe. She helped host visitors at the headquarters, managed the liaison officers who were stacked up waiting to coordinate with me at night in my study at home, and continually looking into ways she could support me and the battle staff at night in the study.

War is a difficult and ugly environment, even from 22,000 feet or in a command center hundreds of miles away. The life-or-death stakes and the pressure for results make minor disagreements seem unsolvable; compromises are more difficult to fashion; fatigue dulls subtle details and easily arouses emotions, so that complex issues often awaken strong reactions; and disagreements over tactics, strategy, and policies quickly become personal. I could see all this in my close colleagues and also felt them working on me. We all knew this could happen and tried our best to avoid such destructive behavior while staying calm and keeping our focus, as best we could, on the important tasks before us. At the strategic level we were working the immediate daily issues, including the press and media, as well as next week, and next month, and even considering options for the spring of 2000. We were looking at each target, but also at the highest political impacts of the campaign.

For me, strategic leadership had become a three-part drama. First, gain authority, real authority, and retain it by a steady record of success. Second, develop, refine, and re-refine a strategy that worked from desired goals backwards to the ways and means required to achieve them. And third, execute, execute, execute. It took hard work, attention to detail, and bruising personal discussions.

There was no glory in working these critical processes or in the decisions that might mean life or death to innocent people hundreds of miles away. But I would look down at my hands occasionally, remember Frank King and his tragic death at NTC, and go back in and work the issues more diligently.

When Eisenhower established the dual command function filled by those in the position I then held, he had done so at least in part to attain unity of command between allied and U.S. forces, an important part of any successful military venture. And that put individuals such as myself at the highest level of command. All orders on this NATO operation necessarily either originated in or passed through the office I held, and, at the same time, that post was the political interface, representing the official military view to all political leaders. I found myself at the pivot point, the fulcrum of the war. It was a very great responsibility. And I was determined to succeed.

A few days into the campaign, I realized I was implementing many of the principles I had articulated in my thesis at Fort Leavenworth two decades earlier. Escalation dominance. And another principle: recognizing the inherent limitations of air campaigns. In the second week of the war, Secretary Albright visited Brussels and asked to meet with me.

"It's up to you now," she said. "I've done all I can. Now it's just up to the bombing." She was thinking out loud, working through alternatives, trying to find a strategy for success.

No, it isn't, Madeleine, I explained. Bombing alone won't do it. You have to give Milošević a way out through negotiations. I worked my way through the logic and options. The secretary of state and her staff followed through on our discussion, and eventually opened a channel for negotiations: Russian deputy prime minister Viktor Chernomyrdin and Finnish president Martti Ahtisaari worked on Milošević's mindset and offered him a way out, even as we kept the military pressure high. I worked this diplomatic channel carefully to avoid the kinds of concessions that would have made the postconflict mission in Kosovo unworkable.

There was another centrally important issue for us: Russia. The Russians were threatening to sally forth their Black Sea fleet and interpose it between our Sixth Fleet vessels and the Serbs. As a minimum, this would have created a command-and-control mess, with our ships dodging theirs. But the greatest risk, I believed, was diplomatic: Such a Russian move could have broken NATO's consensus, as some nations might have feared a potential confrontation and used that as a justification to back down.

I met with U.S. deputy secretary of state Strobe Talbott, who was trying to maintain communications with Moscow, and pleaded with him,

"Tell them to stay out. If they come in, they'll be in trouble."

I also went repeatedly to the NATO political levels with my warnings. And the Russians kept their fleet at home.

In early May a U.S. bomb hit the Chinese embassy in Belgrade, and there was an outcry at home and abroad. But it was no nefarious plot—just a mistake by a CIA target analyst. CIA director George Tenet and Defense Secretary Cohen explained the mistake and took responsibility, though of course the error occurred far down inside their organizations. The alliance shuddered, but held together.

With the authority from the NATO summit we also intensified planning and preparing for a NATO ground invasion, and Ahtisaari and Chernomyrdin were able to use that planning to put more pressure on Milošević.

In late May, two new factors emerged: The Kosovar Albanians had organized a ground combat force that was actually fighting its way into Kosovo. This move forced the Serbs to deploy their hidden soldiers, and thus gave us better targets to attack.

And Milošević was indicted by the International Criminal Tribunal on Yugoslavia as a war criminal. This sealed his fate, really, because it critically reduced his legitimacy and leverage in the diplomatic negotiations.

Sure enough, within a few days, Milošević accepted the terms offered by Chernomyrdin and Ahtisaari. My on-the-scene commander in Macedonia, British three-star general Mike Jackson, led the detailed discussions with Milošević's staff. I was careful to backstop and work the actual terms from my headquarters, as had become my practice.

In seven days, the agreement was done. The United Nations accepted the work and, on a Thursday afternoon, June 10, 1999, passed a resolution authorizing the NATO-led forces to enter Kosovo. We would at last implement the very agreement that Milošević had rejected three months earlier. He had lost.

It was a long and lovely evening in early summer in Belgium when Solana called: "Wes, you have done it. You have won. They said it couldn't be done, but you did it. You will be my friend for life."

The last time I was that happy, I think, was when I was in Vietnam and got a call from the Red Cross telling me my son was born! I said many prayers that night.

The next morning, I stayed with my schedule and arrived at the office after swimming, only to hear some disturbing news: The Russian battalion in Bosnia was redeploying into Yugoslavia. They could only be headed into Kosovo, I reckoned, in some kind of Russian game to double-cross our plans. I sounded the alarm to Solana and to Washington.

What followed was a crazy seventy-two hours of zigzags, lies, high-level confusion and confrontation. On that Friday, the Russians denied they were headed to the airfield. On Solana's instructions, I ordered the preparation of a heliborne airfield occupation just to be able to keep them out, but it was never executed, at the instructions of Washington. Then late Friday night, the Russians did occupy the airfield, contrary to their government's assurances. The second day, I ordered Mike Jackson to get our forces to the airfield as rapidly as possible and co-occupy or surround them; he assured me he could be there by noon. But the force was slow and ultimately it was only Mike Jackson himself who made it to the airfield, and that at around 7:00 P.M., where he was personally harassed by the Russians and left. Washington then suggested we fly in helicopters to block the runways and prevent reinforcements. But the weather closed in. Next morning, responding to an exhausted and overwrought Jackson, the British opposed the plan, and Washington backed down.

This left me with the problem of the Russian presence and the threat that they would fly in reinforcements, seize the northern half of Kosovo, and disrupt NATO's plans. This was a threat I had no military means to prevent, so I went to the Hungarians, Romanians, and Bulgarians, and with help from the State Department, we closed their airspace, thus preventing Russian reinforcements. A few days later, Albright and Cohen flew to Finland to complete the discussions with the Russians, with me urging them from the background: "Hang tough! Stand firm!"

They did, and the Russians' apparent aim to split Kosovo was defeated. The Russian force ended up being assigned a small sector in one corner of the land, plus part of the airfield, from which they did little harm, and eventually departed.

And here's how we won: We had steadily ratcheted up the military pressure with the air campaign, added the threat of a ground intervention, and isolated Yugoslavia from Russian military assistance. And we maintained NATO's legitimacy by emphasizing our humanitarian and defensive aims, by using force only as a last resort, by using minimal force initially, by working carefully to hold down civilian casualties, by admitting our mistakes, by adhering to international law, and by branding Milošević a war criminal and his actions as genocidal. Then we gave Milošević a rational way out, which also met our objectives. Had we used some of these principles in Iraq, the results might have been different.

Along the way there were doubts, arguments, and controversies. Not one allied leader gloried in the fight, however, or thought he could gain much domestic political advantage from it. The leaders went along because it was the right thing to do, and they knew that. They also knew there were severe political penalties for failure. And, ultimately, we broke Milošević's will.

Two Brookings scholars, Ivo Daalder and Michael O'Hanlon, wrote a book entitled *Winning Ugly.* But they'd never been to a war in which political leaders' futures were at risk, where a nineteen-member alliance was under threat, and when a million and a half people were fleeing ethnic cleansing. War is always ugly, and especially this kind of war, where democratic allies need support. But the key word in that title, I think, is the first: "Winning".

In the end, Milošević lost—his Presidency, his control of Serbia, his freedom, and ultimately his life.

There were many other losers in this war, too, including all those who lost lives and families in the struggles along the way. The Serbian people themselves lost. They were increasingly isolated, impoverished, and exploited by Milošević and his group of nationalist thugs. But the way NATO and the United States won that war shows a lot about the post–Cold War world, the Europeans, and U.S. leadership. From this victory emerges some key lessons that could have averted tragedy in Iraq, and are needed today as we move forward.

The conflict exposed all the fault lines of the Atlantic alliance: United States versus Europe; military versus diplomats; the larger allied countries versus the smaller; and air versus ground. No one was altogether happy. Such is the nature of alliance warfare. But so long as we worked to resolve the complaints and stayed together, we were not going to fail. Allied consensus was everything, and for that we needed a strong foundation built on knowing that we had done everything possible to avert the use of force, and that we were fully in compliance with international law.

This was everything I had prepared for since the day I entered West Point. I was really tired, but also really proud of our whole team. Through the use of force and diplomacy, international law, and effective public diplomacy we'd saved Europe from another wave of refugees and long-term conflict, protected our mission in Bosnia, and saved the lives of a million and a half Albanians. And we hadn't lost the life of a single allied or American service member in combat. Not one.

∾

After Milošević's surrender, NATO forces quickly and smoothly occupied their assigned sectors and began their duties. The Albanians poured back in to Kosovo, abandoning the refugee camps in Albania and Macedonia with a speed that shocked the United Nations. NATO worked hard to prevent the Albanians' taking revenge on their Serbian neighbors, many of whom had participated in the ethnic cleansing against them. We understood that we had to prevent it, though it proved to be a very difficult problem with which we did not have as much success as we needed.

A few weeks later I was called by the Pentagon and told I would be retired three months early. The Pentagon had leaked this news to the press, just to be sure it stuck. The Europeans were mystified, and they asked why a victorious general would be ordered into early retirement. But I knew. I had pushed hard to do what was right in Europe, and I had apparently pushed too hard in particular against those who, from almost the beginning of my command tour in Europe, seemed to have held back and resisted virtually every step along the way to succeeding in the Balkans.

But for me, my army service had always been about doing what was right rather than what was easy. That's what I tried to do in the Balkans. Duty. Sometimes leadership means taking the hit.

President Clinton later apologized personally and profusely for the premature ending of my assignment and my military service. He had approved my early departure without understanding its significance.

As I made the round of farewell calls, the Europeans knew what had been done, and they were grateful.

Gert and I were grateful, too. We'd had an incredible three years in Europe, finding good friends and making a difference in the lives of many people. It was time to move on. I retired in a parade at Fort Myer, Virginia, on June 23, 2000. The next day was our thirty-third wedding anniversary, and we flew to Puerto Rico, back to Dorado Beach, where we had honeymooned.

Shortly after we had returned to the States, National Security Advisor Sandy Berger called from the White House. "I want to be the first to tell you," he said. "The president has decided to award you the Medal of Freedom." It's the highest award that can be given by the president.

In his remarks on August 10, 2000, President Clinton said:

"In March of 1999 as Slobodan Milošević unleashed his army and police on the people of Kosovo, Gen. Wesley Clark, NATO's supreme commander, was given the first military mission of its kind, directing the forces of a nineteen-nation alliance to end a brutal campaign of ethnic cleansing," the president said. "The stakes were monumental.

Almost a million people had been driven from their homes solely because of their ethnic and religious background. Success would save lives, strengthen NATO, advance the cause of freedom, democracy and unity in Europe. Failure would leave much of the continent awash in a sea of refugees and end the 20th century on a note of helpless indignation in the face of evil.

Wes Clark well understood the perils of the Balkans for he had already played a vital role in ending the war in Bosnia and beginning the long process of building a stable, multi-ethnic democracy in that country. He summoned every ounce of his experience and expertise as a strategist, soldier and a statesman to wage our campaign in Kosovo. He prevailed miraculously without the loss of a single combat casualty.

At the apex of a long and distinguished military career that goes back to his outstanding performance as a cadet at West Point over thirty years ago, he was assigned a challenge many experts thought was mission impossible. Instead, thanks to Gen. Clark, we now can declare it mission accomplished."

THIRTEEN

COMING HOME

I'd been waiting a long time to come home. The best we'd been able to do were occasional visits, and after my parents retired to Hot Springs in the 1970s, we seldom visited Little Rock. But in my mind I could see and sense every detail: the playgrounds at Pulaski Heights Elementary School, the particular smells of hot popcorn and chlorine at the Boys Club, and all the hamburger joints we used to go to.

Dad had called one night in 1981 and said, "Kid, we just want you to come home, even if you end up pumping gas at Ben Segalla's Exxon station." But I couldn't give up the call of duty. Six years flew by, and Mom and Dad were both gone. My cousin Mary Etzbach Campbell, who as a young girl had taught me both how to swim and how to ride a bike, was there, and she and her husband, Jim, had been good to us when Dad was dying in the hospital. And there were dozens of high school friends still there. Little Rock was the kind of place people could come home to.

A good friend of mine in Belgium was the U.S. ambassador to the European Union, Vernon Weaver. He had worked in Little Rock for years, and he made a suggestion to me: "Why don't you just go back home to Little Rock and work at Stephens?" he asked. "It's a first-class investment bank, and they could use someone like you."

And so, after spending the first few months of civilian life in Washington writing my first book, Gert and I moved to Little Rock. We were warmly welcomed by new business associates, community friends, and high school classmates. In fact, one elderly Arkansas businessman and philanthropist, Roland R. Remmel, and his family virtually adopted us. In his eighties, Rollie was over at the house almost every day, delivering doughnuts or cotton plants, along with lots of helpful ideas and insights into our community. Together, we went fishing and duck hunting, attended football games, and talked business. He was like a father to me as he told me stories I"d never heard about Little Rock and Arkansas, and he seemed to be everywhere and know everyone.

For the Clarks, the pace never slowed. Between learning investment banking and traveling around the country to give speeches or promote my book, it seemed I was on an airplane three or four days each week.

Gert was enjoying Little Rock, too. She quickly joined the Boys and Girls Club board of directors, helped the Children"s Museum of Discovery, and served on the board of the Arkansas Cancer Research Center. Together, we made a lot of new friends and connected with some of my old high school buddies.

I often drove by my old house, which Mom had sold in 1974, remembering friends and baseball games in the streets, reconnecting with my roots. I would drive downtown, thinking how many years ago Mom and Dad had driven the same streets every day, and I visited the cemetery outside town where all my family was buried. It was incredibly satisfying to be home. I"d been away thirty-nine years. And I would get a chill every time the plane in which I was flying would swoop in over the rice fields, river, and quarries to land at the airport.

"Do you have a church home?"

It was a question we were often asked. We were Catholic, and we attended mass, but in the army we had begun to attend Protestant services. After visiting a number of churches, including Pulaski Heights Baptist, where I"d grown up, I found I could have been comfortable in any of the congregations, including the Catholic. But we eventually settled on the Second Presbyterian Church, close by our neighborhood and with a wonderful congregation, pastor and choir. We were home. It was our thirty-first move.

~

Gert and I were both nonpartisan in the political world. We"d never
been members of a party, and had never given any money to candidates.
And from our experiences, we both knew how vicious partisan politics
can become. But as our move to Arkansas approached, I was constantly
receiving calls from the Arkansas Republicans. I already knew the Democrats from the Clinton administration, so I thought, "Let"s meet the
Republicans." I called Condoleeza Rice, then assisting Texas governor
George W. Bush in his presidential campaign.

"I"d like to talk with you," she said, and came over to my office in
Washington, D.C., soon after I retired. It was a brittle conversation as I
related my experiences and assessments and she passed judgment on
eight years of Clinton foreign policy. We seemed to be diametrically opposed: I was proud of our efforts in the Balkans, while she said we had
no interests there; I spoke of the need to work closely with the Europeans, while she wanted to work more closely with the Russians; I spoke
of the need to use our military to reinforce diplomacy, while she said our
troops should only do war fighting; I said we needed troops in Europe to
reinforce our interests there, while she said that our troops should be redeployed to where they would fight. We parted on a friendly promise to
talk again—and we never did.

Mark Warner, an investment banker in Washington, D.C., was an
acquaintance, and I asked him how to think about politics. He was candid. "You have to be willing to lose, and in politics, you can lose a lot. So
if you can live without it, then don"t do it!" That had the ring of hard-
earned advice. He had lost his first race, a 1996 bid for the U.S. Senate.
But he also seemed to retain an interest in high political office, and went
on to become a fine governor of Virginia.

~

The leaders at the Stephens Group were liberal in allowing me to take
time from business for a number of ancillary activities, including writing
a book, going on a book tour, and appearing occasionally on TV inter-
views. I had even signed a contract to be a military analyst in the summer of 2001, though for weeks I just wasn"t called.

On the night of September 10, 2001, as I was packing for a trip to New York, Gert asked, "You know you"re supposed to be on the *O"Reilly Factor* tomorrow night? Have you ever seen it? Do you even know who he is?" No, I didn"t.

Next morning, as I was driving to work, I tried to telephone a friend in New York, but my cell phone wouldn"t work. Terror had struck the United States, and the world had changed. Within two hours I was on CNN, speculating that this was likely to have been the work of Osama Bin Laden. I had studied him and his efforts closely, following every intelligence report I received on him. Soon CNN asked me to come to their Atlanta studios to facilitate the crisis coverage.

On the thirteenth, as Gert and I drove to Atlanta, a local Republican friend called me on the phone. "General, let me ask you a question," he said. "Which way do you think American politics will shift as a result of the terrorist attacks?"

I resisted the implication of the question, for I didn"t want to accept the politics of national security.

"Oh, I doubt that it will shift at all. I think Democrats are Democrats and Republicans are Republicans," I said.

He set me straight: "General, with all due respect, that"s a limp answer. This country is shifting to the right, and if you ever want to be elected to office, you better become one of us, because we"re going to be in charge for a very long time."

To me, using national security for partisan purposes was totally repulsive, especially after 9/11. Coming as it did amid all the appeals for unity, nothing could have made me more determined not to be a Republican than his boastful, veiled threat. All my years in uniform, all the teaching about civilian control of the military, about respect for elected authority, and about the military"s obligation to protect the country, came to the fore: Was government really just partisan politics? I perceived a political arrogance in all that Republican posturing, an arrogance I never would have believed before. Where was our country headed?

When airline service resumed, I flew to Washington to check with my Pentagon friends. To that end, I dropped in on the Joint Staff. There a senior general relayed some disturbing news: "We"re going to attack Iraq. The decision has basically been made."

"But why?" I asked.

I had already caught indications that the Bush administration and some persons associated with the Israeli political right wing were seeking to pin the blame for the 9/11 attacks on Iraqi president Saddam Hussein. Based on everything I knew—and I"d followed the intelligence very closely while in uniform—this didn"t seem likely. Saddam was a secular leader, and to the Islamic Al Qaeda, he was a sworn enemy.

"Did they discover a linkage?" I asked.

"No, nothing like that. It"s just that they don"t know what else to do. If the only tool you have is a hammer, then every problem has to be a nail, and we"re no good against terrorists, but what we can do is attack governments."

Certainly this was part of the explanation, but it wasn"t all. When I returned to the Pentagon six weeks later, as we were striking Afghanistan and chasing off the Taliban, I asked the same general if there was still a plan to go after Iraq.

"Oh, it"s worse than that," he said, and held up a memo on his desk. "Here"s the paper from the Office of the Secretary of Defense outlining the strategy. We"re going to take out seven countries in five years!" And he named them, starting with Iraq and Syria and ending with Iran. It was straight out of Paul Wolfowitz"s 1991 playbook, dressed up as the search for weapons of mass destruction and the global war on terror.

Over the next nine months, I toiled away in the business world, gave a few speeches, and appeared often on CNN, commenting on national security issues. As I traveled around the world, I would run into old colleagues from my military days and I was kept abreast of the unsuccessful efforts to seize Bin Laden during the Afghanistan campaign, the inadequate commitment of U.S. resources and premature withdrawal of U.S. capabilities, and above all, the extraordinary effort to prepare for war with Iraq. I visited friends and members of Congress like senators Bob Graham and John Kerry to discuss my concerns, because the partisan politics behind all this—the idea that going to war would give a political advantage to President Bush and the Republicans, and the indications that they were determined to find a rationale to do this regardless of the real necessity for war—were deeply disturbing.

"They"ll likely attack in March 2003," I warned John Kerry.

I briefed businesses, too, warning one group of investment bankers in April 2002 that there was a 30 percent chance of war with Iraq before the 2002 elections, and it was a certainty afterward. The war would last no more than three weeks, I told them, because Iraq"s military was decrepit, meaning we would be in Baghdad by then.

Meanwhile, the Democrats had invited me to be their candidate for Governor of Arkansas, and some were even suggesting I should give up business and devote myself to a presidential run.

Gert was more practical. First, she said, it"s ugly. Second, you know nothing about it. And third, what"s going to happen to this house we"re living in:- Who"s going to pay the mortgage? I certainly hadn"t made enough to quit worrying about house payments. I stuck with business, though I was deeply troubled by what I saw as the administration"s determination to take us to war in Iraq without good reason.

At the time, I felt the entire focus on Iraq was going to be a strategic blunder, a distraction from the real fight against Al Qaeda. As a result of TV commentary, an op-ed piece in the *Times* of London and *USA Today*, and other remarks, I was invited to testify before the House and Senate Armed Services Committees in the autumn of 2002. I laid out the risks and warned of the pitfalls and spoke out against a White House draft resolution that would have authorized the president to use force "anywhere in the region," not just against Iraq. I warned in February 2002 about the dangers of "chaos and slaughter" in Baghdad after Saddam was overthrown, and by August 2002 I was warning about the greater threat of Al Qaeda and the risk that invading Iraq was going to "feed the recruitment efforts of Al Qaeda," and called the effort against Iraq "at best a diversion, and at worst risking the possibility of strengthening Al Qaeda and undercutting our coalition at a critical time." By September 2002 I was warning the Congress not to give the president a blank-check authorization to go to war.

But the administration had wedged the Democrats into a pre-election trap—the Democrats didn"t want to campaign against the president on the issues of national security, so, in order to dispense with that discussion, they gave him exactly the resolution against which I had warned. While I couldn"t have reasonably objected to a strategy that would have referred the problem to the United Nations, I had the strong sense that the whole U.N. detour was insincere and that the administration was hell-bent on invading. Had I had a vote, I would never have supported that resolution unless there were some other assurances that the whole matter would be brought back again to Congress for another vote before going off to war.

Meanwhile, the administration"s focus looked even more bizarre after a new North Korean nuclear effort was disclosed in October 2002. If the administration was really concerned about weapons of mass destruction, I said to a reporter, then their priorities were upside down.

In February 2003 someone from the White House called CNN to complain that I was an unannounced presidential candidate. According to a friend on the inside, they told CNN to fire me—or else. CNN was concerned, but I simply wasn"t running for anything. At that point, I wasn"t even a member of a political party. I was still working as a businessman had no political staff or money. The White House charge was, at best, premature, and CNN kept me on.

Right on schedule, in March 2003, the war began in Iraq. I traveled to Atlanta where I appeared on CNN with Aaron Brown for an average of about four hours each night. By day, I wrote a column commenting on the war effort for the *Times* of London. The shortage of troops was clear to me from the outset, as was the failure to plan and prepare for what would happen next; I warned of both problems in my commentary. But after our troops reached Baghdad, the fighting died off, and my nightly appearances on CNN quickly dried up. I went back home to Little Rock.

∽

In May 2003 my son, Wes, met me on a street corner in Manhattan. He was living near Wall Street and working as a screenwriter. He"d had four good years as an armor officer at Fort Carson, but, as he told me, it wasn"t his dream. He wanted something of his own, and so he struck out for Hollywood. He had spent a couple of years in Los Angeles learning the movie business, including a dip into screenwriting, followed by a few misadventures, then advertising in New York, and now back to screenwriting. He was earning a living, too, and we remained very close.

"Dad, I"m going to get married. We"re probably going to elope, so don"t tell Mom!"

Oh, sure! One of the most important events of our lives, and . . .

Two minutes later he was on the phone with Gert. We spent much of the next two months thinking about his wedding and the reception in Little Rock.

He and Maria Astrid Oviedo were married on a boat near the Statue of Liberty. She is a brilliant art history graduate of Georgetown, and they made a beautiful and radiant couple that day. When we had commissioned Wes at Georgetown in 1992, Gert cried. Now she was crying again. We were all incredibly happy.

"Your mother would have been very proud," Gert told me.

Meanwhile, I had decided to start my own business: Wesley K. Clark and Associates. My friend Rollie Remmel, a retired Arkansas businessman, had invited me to share his office space.

I gained clients, wrote a second book, and gave some speeches. I brought Mark Nichols, a young Little Rock friend, on board, and we operated a small nonpolitical foundation called Leadership for America to help take my message of better national leadership across the country.

Meanwhile, a political rumble was building. My opinions and commentary had attracted a following, but politics is about relationships, money, experience, and trained and loyal political staff, of which I had none. But by July, tens of thousands of people were on the Internet clamoring for me to announce my presidential candidacy. I wasn"t causing the ruckus, though neither did I tell them to back off. I finally asked Gert, "Honey, is this a real draft for me to run for president?"

"Nope," she said. "It won"t be a draft until party leaders call you."

A few days later I was in Pennsylvania when I received a call from New York congressman Charlie Rangel.

"General Clark, this is Sergeant Rangel," he began in his trademark raspy voice, and he urged me to get into the race. Then a call encouraging my candidacy came from President Jimmy Carter, then another from party leaders, as well as from several other congressmen, including Arkansas raconteur Marion Berry. Meanwhile, I was pushing to finish my second book and develop my business. At the time, I still had no intention of entering the presidential race.

But over the next two weeks, the balance tilted. Predictably, my son urged me to jump in, as did my brother-in-law, Gene Caulfield. The issues continued to weigh on me personally, particularly the mess in Iraq that was developing as the insurgency began and larger numbers of American soldiers began to die. I knew what needed to be done, I believed, and as president I could get it done. We were failing in the so-called global war on terror and our country had already lost so many friends abroad. All the risks I had warned against were coming to pass; all the lessons we"d learned during the Kosovo campaign were being ignored. It was incredibly difficult for me to stay on the sidelines, as I felt a strong obligation to speak out on behalf of the men and women in uniform who couldn"t, and to use my personal experiences to head off what I saw as a deepening crisis.

At home in Little Rock, I had witnessed the growing disparity in incomes and wealth—a new form of segregation—and the struggles that brought to ordinary people, and especially single moms like my mother had been. People were holding down two, sometimes three jobs, and family life was suffering from it; yet overall family incomes were just barely holding steady. Manufacturing jobs were disappearing, and as I traveled the country, I could see us losing ground both in public education and in accessibility to affordable health care for the working people. Sure, some folks were doing just fine, but I couldn"t help but think about the country from my own leadership perspective: Be all you can be. We were falling behind.

I talked to everyone from house painters and repairmen to waiters, flight attendants, school kids, and high school friends. And so many people didn"t even understand this. As a young woman seated next to me on a plane explained, "We have to give tax cuts to wealthy people because they make jobs for the rest of us." Then she proceeded to tell me how she was working as a salesperson and struggling financially. She was seeking another job. She had bought into trickle-down economic theory, but what I was seeing on the banking side was how little of those tax refunds was going into job creation and how much was going offshore, into real estate and other investments.

I slowly realized that it was all about leadership. Not politics, but leadership, my very lifeblood. How could I not want to take on that challenge, to have a chance to help lift the American people back up where we belong?

On the morning of September 15, Gert went out for her usual morning walk.

"Please make a decision," she pleaded. "It"s up to you, but you should decide by the time I return."

There were daunting uncertainties. I had no experience in running for office, no political funds, no political staff, and certainly no strategy to win the Democratic primary. I would have to give up all of my income from the business world, and if I didn"t win, I"d have to start over again. But something Senator Joseph Biden said resonated with me, "You probably have no more than a 30 percent chance to win the primary," he said. "But if you"re the nominee, you"ll beat Bush."

I read my favorite Psalms, put my head down and prayed.

At tough times in my life, when I pray I"ve felt a connection, a calmness, an inspiration. Sometimes, I"ve felt it even when there were heavy thoughts weighing on me. But this morning there was nothing. Not a stir. I lifted my head. Blank. Then the phone rang, and a deep male voice ordered, "Wes, you must run."

"Who is this?" I asked.

"Did you hear me? I said, you need to run! This is Tom Johnson." Tom was an old friend who had retired a few years earlier as president of CNN.

Then, as if to underscore that call, an e-mail arrived: "Don"t do what others have done and back away; go for it!"

A minute later the front door opened and Gert walked upstairs and into the study. "Wes, have you made a decision?"

"Yes," I answered quietly.

It had been a busy three years for me personally. But I realized that my game plan for retirement had been wrong. It was something that Col. Larry Word, one of our observer/controllers at NTC had said years ago when he was at last promoted to full colonel: "The race isn"t over until you quit running."

But it wasn"t a spiritual calling that made me run; it wasn"t the voice of God or anything like that. Rather, it was the call of duty I felt; it was a need I saw to try to fulfill the hopes and prayers of the American people. I still had public service in my heart.

～

By noon on September 16, 2003, the small office that I was sharing with Rollie Remmel in Little Rock had standing room only. Early that morning, I had met with Eli Segal, a prominent Bostonian who"d been central to Bill Clinton"s 1992 campaign. "Eli, I need a campaign manager," I said. "Can you do that for me?"

We talked and talked about political realities. It was about judgment and control, he said, and I needed to learn to be a candidate. Mark Fabiani, another experienced political player, agreed to be the communications director. "You need to spend some time with *Newsweek*," he said. "We"ll try to get a cover story out of this."

There was a lot of motion and activity that day, and people continued to pour in. The following day, I announced my candidacy, flew to Florida, and then on to Iowa for a previously scheduled speech at a university. I was extraordinarily well received everywhere, and we did get the cover of *Newsweek*.

For me, the campaign was about my message—my values, my expertise, and my experience. I wanted to reorient our national security policy, end the neoconservative vision of smashing regimes in the Middle East, and strengthen our security at home. I emphasized working with allies, using international law ands law enforcement, and deemphasizing military action to defeat the threat of terrorism. I wanted to pursue a more fair and effective strategy for rebuilding America"s economic strength and to promote a more respectful tone in public discourse. I had plans to draw in hundreds of thousands of qualified volunteers to work in civilian public service, plans to mend our schools, ideas to improve our health-care system, thoughts on how to emphasize science and technology, and policies on how to meet environmental challenges. It was exhilarating to describe and present my ideas at town hall meetings and discussions across the country.

Immediately, though, details bogged down the campaign. No money: We borrowed a plane, but it was for a political campaign, and that created legal problems. No staff: That meant no effective scheduling. No message plan. No strategy. I bobbled a question from a top reporter, and some supporters panicked. I answered a question about my candidacy after the university speech, and suddenly there was a complaint filed with the Federal Election Commission. The volunteers were feuding with the new professionals. This was the NFL, and I hadn"t even done Pop Warner! Ideas, enthusiasm, and leadership experience just aren"t enough.

Over the next few weeks, we slowly built a staff, raised money, met with Democrats across the country, and even participated in debates.

"They tell me the first thing you lose in politics is your voice," I joked. But I did in fact lose it, and was completely without speech for several days.

By the end of November, we had bottomed out and started up in the polls. We had raised close to $20 million, and the staff had stabilized. I loved the campaigning, especially the town hall settings and meeting people afterward. In New Hampshire, New York, Illinois, Colorado, Michigan, California, and North Dakota, in New Mexico, Arizona, Oklahoma, and Texas, we had drawn big crowds everywhere. At an event in Michigan, several hundred Albanian Americans had tried to pack themselves into a suburban home to meet me, explaining to the surprised hostess: "We don"t just like General Clark, we love him!"

We were bringing in people who"d never been involved in politics before, and lots of independents and moderate Republicans as well. And President Clinton told Eli that I was the quickest study he"d seen in politics. However, we made many mistakes, too, and one proved fatal: We skipped Iowa.

Some of my advisors had been spooked by Bill Bradley"s Iowa experience in 2000: He had devoted so much of his effort there that he couldn"t build an effective effort in other states. It was a caucus state, and it soaked up time and money. But even then, there were no guarantees, and Iowa had a way of delivering surprises. By mid-October the advisers were talking to folks in Iowa, trying to determine whether to compete there or to skip it. One political leader reportedly told them to skip it; it was too late, he said. Senator Tom Harken felt otherwise, but admitted it would take twenty days and $3 million to compete effectively in his state.

Our strategy had become to focus on Howard Dean. We would let him take Iowa, make sure we finished in the top four in New Hampshire, and then take him out across the South and West in the third set of primaries.

I saw the logic, but looked at it differently. I had a very strong volunteer organization in Iowa, had been well received, and felt very much at home there. Senator Harken remarked how well I"d done at his town hall meeting, which was encouraging. The union folks that liked me wanted to deploy their teams there, where they were strong, rather than in New Hampshire, where they weren"t. And I"m a fighter. My instinct is always to go in. Against my instinct, the campaign strategists leaked a report that we wouldn"t compete there. It may have seemed logical at the time, but in retrospect, it was clearly a mistake.

After three months of nonstop effort, Gert and I took three days off and flew to Los Angeles to be with Wes and Astrid for the holidays. Our first grandchild, Wesley Pablo, was born that Christmas Day, and I saw him within the first hour, and even held him. I watched my son with his son. He had something I never had, for I"d been in Vietnam when he was born, and I hadn"t seen him until he was four months old. He would do better as a father than I had, I hoped.

I had never understood grandparents before. They flash pictures, coo about the kids, and get dewy-eyed. But it"s like a spark that jumps between you and the baby—and you"re never quite the same again. Of course, there"s also an extraordinary sense of fulfillment in seeing your own child parenting, but it"s more than that; it"s a deep, true joy that springs from the inside, from seeing life and all the potential that each new life brings.

We left the following afternoon, hopeful for what January 2004 would bring. We had a fine swing through Mississippi, Louisiana, Alabama, and Georgia. A scheduled event in South Carolina on December 30 was slow for some reason, but then we were back to New Hampshire. New Year"s Eve was magical in Portsmouth, and the next day we packed a church with an overflow crowd. I traveled through the state, speaking, meeting, walking through the snow. You could feel the momentum build. In mid-January, Eli remarked, "There are just two people between you and the White House. Not many people get to say that."

We had met so many people who loved this country and gave so much to help those they considered the right people to win office. Some people had given up jobs to campaign for me in New Hampshire; others had taken second jobs in order to send me money. Some gave up a year of school; other forfeited their businesses. Dozens of folks from Arkansas, Michigan, Alabama, Minnesota, and many other states traveled to New Hampshire to stump for me. Countless volunteers knocked on doors, hosted telephone parties, pasted signs and bumper stickers, or just stood in the snow holding signs. Their effort was amazing, and it was often totally spontaneous. We pulled in several million dollars from the Internet, and many traditional big donors broke with their party favorites to help launch my campaign and host fund-raisers for me across the country. I was humbled, grateful, and in awe.

In the military, we always prided ourselves on our service. I had no idea just how much ordinary Americans gave in every election cycle to protect our democracy. Participating in the process—working firsthand in the vineyards of democracy—justified every sacrifice we ever made in uniform

Then something unexpected happened in Iowa: Howard Dean's campaign stumbled, and John Kerry, thought in early December to be down and almost out, scored a powerful come-from-behind victory. His win undercut the strategic rationale that had been formulated for my candidacy, because Kerry was both acceptable inside the Beltway and a Vietnam veteran. Unless we could recast the campaign, it was over.

Those were busy days inside the Clark campaign. We probably should have formulated the rationale (or, in the political parlance, created a "brand") to emphasize that I was a Southerner and not just that I was a combat veteran, but a real national security professional with a war-winning record to prove it. For whatever reason, that just wasn't done. And now that Kerry had captured that almost magical momentum, it appeared too late to even hope I might make such a recovery.

We played out the campaign, picking up third in New Hampshire, and then winning Oklahoma, and finishing second in three other states where we competed: New Mexico, Arizona, and North Dakota. But the money had dried up, the press seemed to have made up its mind, and the Democratic Party establishment closed ranks. The very evening after I won in Oklahoma, my advisors were being advised to throw in the towel. We had just enough money for one more week, which included Tennessee, where we had picked up a number of endorsements, and Virginia, where we hadn"t done enough.

Then it was over. It was sad that what began with such high hopes in September ended with disappointment. I spoke to the staff in Little Rock and, amid all the tears, thanked them for having worked their hearts out. We"d basically started out on a transatlantic voyage and tried to build the ship after we pushed off from the dock. It was simple: We had started too late. All things considered, I thought the success of the campaign in getting my name on the ballots, raising the money, and building an organization were minor miracles. Gert and I were both exhausted, but when we got out of the military, we never expected I would be running to be President of the United States only three years later. We were extremely lucky people.

I went back into the business community and slowly reassembled some work in the investment banking and consulting field. A board here, a partnership there, a consulting agreement, a speaking fee. I met new people, renewed old friendships, and became thoroughly engrossed in business. And I just loved both the negotiations and the leadership and strategy aspects of the commercial world.

But I also asked a few people from the campaign to stay with me. Together we built a Political Action Committee to respond to the hundreds of Democratic candidates who were asking me to help during the election cycle, to help strengthen Democrats in the South, and to help the national party strengthen its positions on national security. During the last few weeks of the 2004 campaign I was asked to become one of John Kerry"s principal surrogates, jumping from stop to stop in New Mexico and Nevada, and a few other places, in an effort to scrape out just one more state"s electoral votes. In the end, John Kerry pulled more popular votes for the presidency than any Democrat in history.

The 2004 election was dominated by the savage personal attacks, rank partisanship, and big money—features that have become the hallmark of modern American politics. But the American people themselves cast the deciding vote. It was a vote interpreted by some to reflect increased influence of moral issues in the electorate, a factor enhanced by the presence of pro-life and antigay marriage legislation on the ballots in several states. But I found the outcome in elections to be more like a cake with a dozen layers—factors which help or hurt a candidate. Party affiliation, organization, money, speaking style, personal attacks, an effective ad, a gaffe or miscue, even the weather on election day—everything counts. In this election, Osama Bin Laden weighed in on the last few days, with a threatening message to America. Ultimately, I believed, it was the perception of threat, and the relative lack of confidence in the Democrats on the national security issue, that probably tipped the balance. Despite the growing evidence of American failure in Iraq, much of the American public still sensed a general

connection between the fighting in Iraq and safety at home and stayed
with the leader and party that had taken us into one of greatest strategic blunders in American history.

~

After the Presidential election, I continued to express concern about the
policies the administration was pursuing in Iraq. In November 2004,
writing in the *Washington Post,* I warned that we had become
"distracted . . . from marshalling the diplomatic and political support
our troops need to win," that the success of our military efforts was "directly connected to the skill of U.S. diplomacy in the region," and that
we needed to "undertake diplomatic efforts in the region and political efforts inside Iraq that are worthy of the risks and burdens borne by our
men and women in uniform." Over a year later, little had been done.
Writing in the *New York Times* on December 6, 2005, I warned that
"Iran is emerging as the big winner of the American invasion," and again
urged that we use our diplomatic strength with Syria and Iran. During
the three years after the 2004 race, I talked to top military leaders and
privates, sheikhs and businessmen, academics, journalists, and diplomats
throughout the Middle East. It was a region in turmoil and confusion.
There were many ideas but no answers. I saw U.S. efforts spiraling
downward into failure, each successive trip yielding ever more pes-
simistic findings.

Meanwhile, I was on television and giving speeches across the nation, campaigning for Democratic candidates for the 2006 election
cycle, raising funds, working in the House and Senate to help shape U.S.
policies toward Iraq and the Middle East. Looking back over some three
years, I found the magnitude of the effort surprising through the November 2006 elections. I had made twenty-three trips abroad, visited
twenty-five countries, campaigned for eighty-six congressional and sena-
torial candidates, visited twenty-six states, raised well over a million dollars for others, appeared 149 times on TV and radio, published
twenty-one articles and opinion pieces, given nineteen formal speeches,
and had several sessions with Members of the House or Senate leadership. All this was in addition to my business efforts.

Traveling in the United States, I visited dozens of businesses, met with mayors and governors and was stopped on the street, in airports, and restaurants by ordinary Americans who were looking for answers and for hope in their country"s future. Perhaps there are many Americans who are apathetic, take no interest in public affairs, and have never voted. But I met the others, by the tens, hundreds, and thousands. They were of all faiths, of all political persuasions, and of every conceivable profession; some were veterans and had even served under my command; others were antiwar protesters. Meeting and speaking with them, spontaneously and informally, was perhaps the greatest personal gift from the political campaign, for their interests and convictions gave faith to me, too. These were the Americans I knew, whom I had served with and worked with, all my life. This was the real America, and it began to speak when it turned over control of both Houses of Congress to the Democratic Party in 2006.

FOURTEEN

THE PROMISE

few months after the 2004 election I was in New York for
business. As I rode across the Queensboro Bridge into Manhattan, the Pakistani-born taxi driver interrupted my
thoughts with his story and reminded me of what this country has always been about. "We came as three brothers," he said. "We came nine
years ago . . . only I am still driving a cab . . . We own a store now, and a
restaurant, and soon I will join the others full time in the restaurant . . .
When we came we had nothing, but today . . ." He paused. "Only in
America," he said, "could we do this. Only in America."

His story was my story, and it is the story of hundreds of millions of
us and our forefathers, who came here from somewhere else, who
dreamed, dared, planned, and struggled to forge new lives, raise strong
families. Together, generation after generation, we have built a great nation. It's a connection I have felt ever more strongly over the years, as I
continued to reflect on my grandfather Jacob Kanne and my grandmother Ida Gold. They came to a new country and made it their own.
And I, too, had made that kind of journey, from North to South, from
civilian to military, to build my own family and make my way in a new
world. Just like that Pakistani-born taxi driver. We were brothers in this
New World.

I learned to love this nation as a youngster growing up without a father, at a time when all our institutions and values were under attack by Communism. I loved this nation enough to serve as a soldier, to come home from war on a stretcher, enough to stay in uniform for another thirty years. My family and I lived in Germany, Belgium, and Panama, in Kansas and Kentucky, in Colorado, Virginia, and California, in Texas and New York. Over time, we were given increasing responsibilities for others, commanding units, teaching courses, providing staff advice and assistance. We were at various times responsible for the work they did, the lessons they learned, the health care they received, the homes they lived in, the schools their children attended, the lives they led. I learned about our country and our people, and how we are perceived in the world. My greatest honor was to represent America in uniform. We were not only the most powerful nation in the world; we were, most of the time, the most admired and respected. But today, almost six years after the vicious terrorist strikes of 9/11, opinion polls show the American people believe the political and military venture in Iraq has failed, and the majority of Americans believe our country is headed in the wrong direction. Similar polls abroad show us in an even less favorable light. Billions of people in other countries believe that America's time of world leadership is passing.

However mistaken some of our policies may have been, America's fundamental strengths—the appeal of our values, the power of our institutions, and the energy and adaptability of the American people—remain intact. We need only understand these strengths and then apply them wisely.

In some ways, we are not so different from anybody else. Everywhere there is love, courage, and ambition, pride and insecurity. Americans in uniform have shown enormous courage and character—but so have our enemies. Americans have shown ingenious talents in business and engineering—but so have our competitors. Americans love their families—but so do others around the world. Americans honor their forefathers and speak with pride of their heritage—as do others around the world. In the press and media, foreigners seem different and apart, but when these very same people come as visitors to America, many of us discover that we have much in common with them.

Still, we have become a different society than we were. Over the course of American history, through slavery, and the Civil War, through desegregation and the civil rights movement, we have transformed our laws to accord with our founding principles and gradually transformed our culture to reflect our laws and vice versa. We really do believe that all men—and women—are created equal. In countless families just like mine, young men and women struggled against the preconceptions and prejudices of their elders. Increasingly, in America, we treat each other with more respect, whatever the apparent diversity of our backgrounds or circumstances.

As a people, we have struggled with our own role in the course of human destiny. Some among us have subscribed to the notion of predestination or believed in a God-driven manifest destiny for America. Others have felt that God "helps those who help themselves." We've been through successive waves of religious revival and dedication. We have struggled to "separate the sinner from the sin" and to practice the Christian message of forgiveness even while also punishing transgressors. Today we are unique among most in Western civilization for not only professing our belief in a greater power but for practicing our faiths; Americans attend their houses of worship far more diligently than most other peoples in the world.

And, by international and historical standards, we Americans have a strong sense of patriotism. Our national anthem has inspired countless other nations to seek their own. Our Fourth of July is echoed across the globe. Indeed, we have exemplified the spirit of nationalism, using it to forge a nation from diverse peoples. Yet we still have pride in our different ethnic heritages and can enjoy our native foods, languages, dress, and customs without being seen as threatening the unity of our nation.

These are American values, reflected in the way we live, and protected by the Constitution itself. As I discovered in the Balkans and in Africa, every society has its rules and laws; the question is, who benefits? What we have achieved in the United States is a limitation of the government's powers through a system of checks and balances that has kept open avenues of opportunity for almost everyone. It is an active, ongoing balancing act, now cutting taxes, now levying restrictions, now intruding, then withdrawing. It is the ebb and flow of representative government built around the Constitution. American voters may not be experts on every issue, but somehow the "voice of the people" has usually provided for common-sense, reasonable governance.

The executive agencies have provided remarkably loyal and honest service to the public. Whether it be in the armed forces, or the highway departments, most public servants in America have delivered by working hard for the public interest——as opposed to their personal interest. Policemen don't normally ask for bribes, contractors don't normally give kickbacks, and the military doesn't routinely sell its weapons for profit, though all of these are common occurrences in some other lands.

Within these institutions we have both a restless energy and a creativity that have shone brightly. The same spirit that settled a continent established worldwide commerce and then multinational corporations, and now it engineers powerful new financial strategies that have unlocked human productivity to meet mankind's needs. I see the energy and creativity almost every day in my business efforts. We Americans push at established practices, challenge existing authorities, seek new avenues for achievement, and explore new frontiers of thought. We are not conformists but achievers. We seem to shake trees and create anxieties—then kiss and make up—more often, work harder, and play less than most of the rest of the world.

Together, these values, institutions, and national character bind us together as a nation. For the truth is that most of us aren't just Republicans or Democrats or Libertarians, nor are we just Catholics, Methodists, or Jews, or Yankees or Southerners, Hispanics, or African Americans, gay or straight, or whatever shorthand is available. We have much more in common than labels would suggest, no matter what the outcome of a particular election, or the attendance at a church, or manner of dress, or lifestyle. And what we have in common provides all the foundation we ever need to secure our safety and prosperity into the future.

But we cannot allow pride in our achievements to blind us to the challenges that lie ahead. We are now in a different time. The twentieth century was truly the American Century. We entered it as the world's largest producer of iron and steel, and we ended as the lone superpower, with the world's most powerful economy and armed forces. Today, much of what we hoped and worked for in the world beyond our borders is coming to pass, and this poses profound challenges for us. We worked to end Marxist-Leninist domination in the East, and today the Iron Curtain is fading from memory. But we are faced with determined economic competition from China, a nation whose domestic market scale is potentially four times our own. In the middle of the last century we pushed hard for worldwide economic growth and development, and today sustainable economic growth is under way, not only in the post–World War II economies of Japan and Europe but throughout much of the third world. These economies are not only providing outlets for American goods and products, but also displacing our own industries and competing with America's own workers. We argued for free trade, and today global trade is expanding rapidly, and the movement of capital and ideas is freer than at any time in human history. But we find many U.S. ideas and much capital flowing offshore, seeking higher rates of return from investments abroad. We wanted to open up the world, and we have. Today technological advances have reduced the effective size of the globe and provided near instantaneous communications and next-day travel to any destination. But we find that this exposes us to new risks of terrorism and diseases, to the passions ignited by fear and ignorance as well as to the loss of good jobs and economic security.

The international environment in which we live has certainly changed. Not since the American Revolution have ordinary Americans been so affected by events abroad. There is the threat of terrorism, to be sure, but also the impact of the ongoing conflicts in Iraq and Afghanistan, the dangers of nuclear proliferation in North Korea and Iran, the volatile price of oil imported from abroad, the seemingly ceaseless flow of immigrants, struggling to come live among us, the threats of job loss and impoverishment as others develop their economies; the steady accumulation of U.S. debt abroad, the spread of new diseases, environmental degradation, and climate change. In the twenty-first century we Americans can no longer hide behind our oceans.

Instead, we need an approach—a strategy—that will build our strengths and take us to our goals. We faced a similar challenge in the aftermath of World War II. Then the fruits of victory were marred by the emerging ideological struggle with the Soviet Union and its proxy states. It was a struggle for the heart and soul of mankind, waged on every continent using every conceivable means. Led by successive

American Presidents and Members of Congress, America came together to craft a bipartisan strategy to contain the spread of Communist ideology, deter the Soviet use of force, and support those who shared our values.

Over a period of forty years we persevered—through diplomacy, alliances, ideological struggle, and armed conflict in Korea and Vietnam. We built our economy, developed international law and agreements, encouraged visitors from abroad to learn our values, used American companies as surrogate ambassadors around the world, enhanced the American public school system to focus on science and technology; encouraged American industry to deepen its investments in research and development, and promoted physical fitness as a form of national competition. And in the end, we won. The Berlin Wall came down, the Soviet empire collapsed, and the Soviet Union disintegrated into eleven separate states. That collapse was the triumph of American ideals—of the nobility of the human spirit, the priceless significance of freedom and human rights, and the incredible creative force of a free-market economy.

But when we defeated our old adversary, we not only lost our opponent, we also lost our strategy, the animating principles of our government that provided much of the cohesion that held our world together. We did well economically in the 1990s by creating and taking advantage of a global opening, but we never really replaced the cold war strategy with a new vision, despite our efforts in the Clinton administration, nor did we take all the actions necessary to mitigate new risks.

After the 9/11 terrorist attacks, we have been able to strike back at Al Qaeda. We have also strengthened cooperation between our intelligence agencies as well as with our friends abroad, efforts that seem to have disrupted terrorist leadership and have enabled us to avoid any further terrorist attacks inside the United States. The critical mistakes of the Bush administration, however, have caused us incalculable harm. The Preventive War doctrine has been an arrogant insult to the rest of the world, while refusals to talk to potential adversaries like North Korea and Iran have generated new nuclear proliferation and deepened other foreign policy problems we face. But the most damage has been caused by our invasion of Iraq, one of the greatest blunders in American history: billions of dollars wasted, tens of thousands of lives lost, and perhaps worst of all, the widespread impression in the world of a vengeful, angry, isolated and militaristic America, a perception that has badly damaged our good reputation, our "legitimacy," and our influence.

Our "legitimacy" has been further undercut by a stream of shameful official orders and policies, which include: our mistreatment of prisoners by ordering their physical and emotional abuse; our disregard of international treaties and conventions; our indefinite detention of uncharged prisoners in secret prisons; and our "outsourcing" torture by acts of "rendition," under which our prisoners are secretly sent to other countries where torture is a standard police tactic. These practices have evidently been approved at the highest levels, as a 2002 White House memo redefining "torture" demonstrates. While the abuses at Abu Ghraib may well have been the result of poorly trained people, the world believes—and I fear subsequent investigation will reveal—that a coordinated and systematic effort to extract information by illegal practices, which include acts that are considered torture by most reasonable men and women, was implemented by direction of our top national leadership and remains operational. If so, this is shocking and repulsive, and it dangerously compromises the legitimacy of America as a moral, law-abiding and just nation. In addition, it also reduces our influence in the world and greatly compounds the problems we face in coping with the threat of terrorism.

Today, we must create a new strategy to cope with new realities. Most important, we must first deal with the terrorist threat and the interrelated problems and crises that permeate the Middle East. But we must also meet the far more profound challenge posed by nations like China and India in the global economic competition. And we must do whatever we can to restore America's legitimacy in the world.

The Middle East is ripped by tension and conflict. U.S. troops are battling in Iraq, but this conflict is being fed by outside sources—Syria, Iran, and other states. Emotional fuel is drawn from the Israeli-Palestinian conflict, and from thirteen centuries of struggle between Sunni and Shia Islam. Iran is seeking to break out of three decades of isolation by claiming a larger role in the region, and by using its nuclear program as additional leverage to strengthen its advocacy for Shia Islam and to restore Persia's historic grandeur.

This struggle, in turn, is being played out in Lebanon, Pakistan, and Afghanistan as well. Our real enemy, Al Qaeda, is drawing resources and recruits from these struggles, too, and is using Iraq as a training ground to prepare its forces for later battles. The government in Afghanistan is vulnerable to subversion and insurgency supported from Pakistan, of course, but Iran is reentering the struggle there, too.

Our interests in the region are economic, legal, humanitarian and military. The region is the world's energy hub, and energy market disruptions would ripple immediately through our own economy. And we also have legal understandings and humanitarian concerns in the region. Meanwhile, we have over 250,000 U.S. service members deployed there, most engaged in active combat operations in either Iraq or Afghanistan. We want most of them safely redeployed, out of harm's way, and with those conflicts at least stabilized.

Resolving the interrelated conflicts and crises will require a new tone and diplomatic outreach by the United States. This entails setting aside the neoconservative dreams of regime change and instead opening unconditional dialogue with states like Iran and Syria, and commencing a more intensive effort to lead negotiations aimed at achieving a two-state solution for Israel and the Palestinians. Only a direct dialogue with the United States is likely to persuade Iran to give up its nuclear weapons program. Similarly, we are going to have to reach understandings with Pakistan and Iran and strengthen relations on the subcontinent between India and Pakistan in order to preserve the Afghan government and help end the conflict there. NATO's military endeavors alone won't be sufficient.

There is no purely military solution to the war in Iraq. Instead, through a combination of political, diplomatic and economic actions, as well as some military measures, we have to induce the tough political compromises among the Iraqi factions and end the conflict there. We are now far enough along to insist on a series of steps and the timelines to go with them, and to also publish a schedule for US troop redeployments. Together, all of these measures should cause the conflict to wind down.

Ending the conflict in Iraq and removing our troops from active combat will do much to help restore American legitimacy in the region, but it will not be sufficient. We will have to end the abusive detention and systematic human rights violations which characterized the Bush administration's approach. Just as a start, some restitution should certainly be made to those wrongly imprisoned. And at home, the policies and secret understandings of the Bush administration need to be investigated, and corrected.

If we act appropriately, the rising tide of global development and the hard-to-suppress ideas of justice and opportunity will reach even into places like Pakistan, Bangladesh, and Indonesia, there to overwhelm any appeal of Islamist-inspired terrorism.

The war against terrorists will continue, as it must. It should be conducted with a new resolve to work with local authorities, and use international cooperation among law enforcement and intelligence agencies, reserving military forces for use only as a last resort. Ultimately, we will prevail in this war not by killing terrorists—though that may need to be done—but by winning the battle for greater tolerance, understanding, and respect among peoples of differing political and religious convictions, which will dry up their recruiting. This is first and foremost a battle of ideas and ideologies. We need to bring terrorists to trial in open court, not hide them away somewhere. And we must carefully guard our own values and principles, for in this struggle moral leadership is far more valuable than pittances of information gained by compromising our beliefs. Torture and other abusive treatment should have no place in our efforts, for it is our own strict adherence to human rights that has consistently set us apart from other societies. And in the battle of ideas, strict adherence to our own proven principles is perhaps our greatest strength.

At the same time that America's attention is being absorbed by the conflicts in Iraq and Afghanistan, China has burst on to the global scene—with a population of 1.3 billion, and its economy growing at 10 percent per year. It is now the world's largest steel producer and it will, in a few years, become the world's largest consumer market, greatest source of wealth and it may, perhaps, resume its centuries-old place as the source of most new technology and innovation. With its scale and economic power, its low wages and human potential, China's economic development could imperil our own economic security by drawing off American jobs, diverting the flow of capital and technology, and inducing a steady deflation of America's living standards. China's economic growth will doubtless be accompanied by its growth in prestige, influence, and financial and military power, which could constrain America's freedom of action in the world. And the cumulative impact of these rapid changes in power, influence, and relative wealth could adversely affect our very character as a nation.

In other words, our most pressing challenge over the long term is not that others will attack us, but that they will emulate us economically, compete with us, and threaten the economic power that has been our real source of strength, security, and prosperity.

Responding to this challenge means putting our own house in order and reempowering the American people through initiatives in education, health care, research and development, energy independence, business climate, unions, infrastructure, and the environment. Here are just some of the many efforts we must undertake:

- In education, we should be offering public preschool across America, encouraging renewed study of mathematics, sciences, and engineering and creating the community programs needed to ensure that every American child graduates from high school. We must remember that the most important resources are not financial. They are the commitment of community leaders to create public schools emphasizing learning and character and the commitment of parents to work with their children, to assure they are fully engaged in the classroom and at home in preparing for their own productive future. We need to reward teachers for their skills and commitments, but the best form of teacher accountability is not found in standardized testing but in the dialogue between teachers and parents centered on the love and respect for each child in the class. No student who seeks to go to college should be denied that opportunity because he or she can't pay, and family investments in education should be entitled to the same preferences in law as any other investment.

- In health care, we need to practice evidence-based medicine, in which treatments and practices are based on statistically proven results—not commercial advertising—and doctors and hospitals need to be held accountable for their performance, not just by the threat of malpractice but by the day-today quality of their results. We need to harness the innovation of our biotech, pharmaceutical, and health insurance industries better to serve the public good, not just the private gain of shareholders. No child in America should grow up without regular medical checkups and care—or regular exercise and physical fitness—and every adult should be provided access to the kinds of diagnostic testing and preventive treatments that can slow the onset of aging diseases like diabetes, atherosclerosis, and Alzheimer's. Additional insurance coverage should be directed to catastrophic illness and injuries, the kind that wreck families and shatter productive lives. And inevitably this will mean transitioning over time from a workplace-centered, private payer system toward greater reliance on some form of single-payer system to ease administrative burdens, reduce costs, and remove from American business the burden of health care.

- In the business community, we must spur research, development, and innovation and the growth of the small companies that provide the majority of U.S. employment. This will mean more private-public partnerships in developing new technology and in linking our universities to business enterprises, as well as an expanded arsenal of economic and tax incentives aimed primarily at small businesses. We must assure investments in the technology infrastructure—the broadband and wireless access, improved and modernized highway, air, and rail transportation systems, and access to affordable, reliable, sustainable energy that is essential to continuing economic development.

- We must invest urgently to achieve energy independence and "de-carbonize" energy production, for this is more than an economic issue; it is a true national security problem. We need greater insulation from the Mideast and world energy markets. And we need to reduce the levels of greenhouse gases that we are dumping into the atmosphere. In fact, sustainable energy and so-called green engineering provide major growth opportunities for American ingenuity, and we must move in that direction.

- We must chart a new path for labor in America and for the
  union movement itself. While workers still need help in re-
  dressing grievances against management, perhaps the old di-
  viding lines make less sense in an age of high technology,
  social and geographic mobility, and global competition. Is it
  possible that unions could become the development agencies
  for workers, protecting their rights, but also promoting their
  training, education and career development throughout a
  lifetime of many different skills and jobs? For we know that
  in today's economy, every American in the workplace must
  take increasing responsibility for his or her own development
  of skills, pursuit of opportunities, and creation of financial
  security for the family.

While all of these efforts will reenergize our country and restore our
competitiveness, we must also work to transform the international system. This is the network of interlocking institutions—U.N., G–8,
WTO, APEC, NATO, OSCE, OAS, WHO, NAFTA, and others that
have been created to resolve crises, prevent conflict, promote trade and
development, and address global problems, such as the urgent problem
of global warming. We must rebuild the system of international laws and
institutions that two generations of American leaders fashioned and ex-
tolled. We should set the example in shaping and obeying international
law. Likewise, we should lead in the reform of the United Nations, seeking its full potential as a place for dialogue and the expression of values,
and as the source for international law and humanitarian assistance in
emerging crises. Now, while the United States is the preeminent power
in the world, we must act to ensure that these institutions protect our interests and values and prevent a backslide into the familiar patterns of rivalry and warfare that marked the twentieth century.

We will need to redirect the main thrusts of American efforts abroad.
We need to rebuild our ties with Europe, with NATO as the foundation,
and with a new Atlantic Charter as the means. Europe is our closest partner, more than 400 million people with whom we are the most closely
aligned in terms of values and interests, economics and power. And we
need to work more closely with Latin America, too. Together we can
move the international system to build a new consensus on humanitar-

ian intervention and human rights, the use of force, and adoption of an up-dated, far more stringent Kyoto Protocol. Isolated, alone in a multipolar world, we simply won't fare as well. And we should strengthen ties with India, the world's largest democracy and itself a rapidly developing superpower.

Articulating what to do is the easy part of the strategy; the challenge is putting it into practice for it is the human dimensions of the strategy that are the most difficult. It will be about leadership, reassurance, and positive direction. Restoring America's legitimacy in the eyes of the world will truly require transformational leadership. Every measure from education through labor reform will need a new American consensus. Reorienting to win the war against terrorism reconstituting the armed forces after the ordeals in the Middle East, and redirecting our nation for global competitiveness will be demanding, long-term efforts.

In political life, we will have to bridge the gulf of bad feeling and partisanship which has ripped at our society over the past two decades? Disagreements and differences in perspective are normal and necessary; unbounded personal attacks and character assassination should have no place in our system of government.

In our dealing with countries beyond our borders, we must reach out with respect, airing differences and disagreements without invoking the belief that we are somehow better than everyone else. We will have to listen to others and build coalitions around common interests that will allow us to address the enormous international problems we face.

America is at a historic turning point. We have talent, character, and resources. We have the experience and the strong institutions necessary to effect our changes. Americans come together in a crisis, and they rise to meet a challenge. I saw it as a child when Sputnik was launched; I saw it in Vietnam when the troops came forward when I was hit; and we have all seen it after 9/11. We certainly are faced with crises and challenges today. All we need to do is commit ourselves to the tasks ahead. And commit ourselves to an America in which our motto and our aim must be to BE ALL THAT WE CAN BE.

I believe that with the right leadership, we can protect the incredible promise and wondrous opportunity of America for our children and grandchildren—just as it was protected for us. All we need is the wisdom to see the course and the courage to make the change. Now is the time.